Practical Approach to Learn and Practice
PYTHON PROGRAMMING
Basics to Machine Learning

LALITA KUMARI
Associate Professor
Computer Science and Engineering
Amity School of Engineering and Technology
Amity University, Patna

RADHEY SHYAM
Scientist
National Informatics Centre
Ministry of Electronics and Information Technology
NIC Bihar State Centre, Patna

PHI Learning Private Limited

Delhi-110092
2025

*In fond memory of **Shri Asoke K. Ghosh** (October 1942–February 2024), Founder Chairman and Managing Director of PHI Learning, whose vision endlessly inspires.*

The Legacy Continues... .

Published by Pushpita Ghosh, PHI Learning Private Limited, Rimjhim House, 111, Patparganj Industrial Estate, Delhi-110092 and Printed by Syndicate Binders, A-20, Hosiery Complex, Noida, Phase-II Extension, Noida-201305 (N.C.R. Delhi).

₹595.00

PYTHON PROGRAMMING: Basics to Machine Learning
Lalita Kumari and Radhey Shyam

ISBN-978-93-5443-767-0 (Print Book)
ISBN-978-93-5443-971-1 (e-Book)

The export rights of the book are vested solely with the publisher.

To

Our Beloved Parents

Whose unwavering dedication
in valuing higher enducation have been the guiding force behind our journey.
Their love, sacrifices, and encouragement laid the foundation for every achievement.

Contents

Preface .... *xiii*

Part I — BASICS OF PYTHON

1. Introduction **3**

- 1.1 Why Python 3
- 1.2 Where Python 4
- 1.3 History of Python 5
- 1.4 Python Programming Language Features 5
- 1.5 How Useful is the Python 6
- 1.6 Starting and Terminating a Python Session 6
  - 1.6.1 MS Window Environment 6
  - 1.6.2 Linux Environment 6
- 1.7 Python IDEs 7

2. Literals and Data Types **8**

- 2.1 Literal vs Data Type 8
- 2.2 Special Literal—None 9
- 2.3 Data Type 10

2.4 Basics Data Types 10
2.4.1 Boolean 10
2.4.2 Numeric 12
2.4.3 String 13
2.4.4 String Variable Declaration 16
2.5 Compound Data Type 18
2.5.1 List [ ] 18
2.5.2 Tuples () 18
2.5.3 Set {} 18
2.5.4 Frozen Set 19
2.5.5 Dictionary 19

3. Variables and Operators 21
3.1 Variables 21
3.1.1 Scope of Variables 21
3.2 Python Enhancement Proposal 23
3.3 Operator 24
3.3.1 Arithmetic Operator 24
3.3.2 Comparison Operator 29
3.3.3 Assignment Operator 29
3.3.4 Logical Operator 31
3.3.5 Bitwise Operator 31
3.3.6 String Operator 34
3.4 Built-in String Methods 35
3.5 Regular Expression 37
3.5.1 Literals 37
3.5.2 Metacharacters 37
3.5.3 Character Classes 38
3.5.4 Quantifiers 38
3.5.5 Grouping 38
3.5.6 Escape Character 38
3.5.7 Anchors 38
3.5.8 Wildcard 38
3.5.9 Modifiers 39
3.6 Regular Expression Function 41

4. Interactive Input-Output 43
4.1 Command-Line Input 43
4.1.1 input() Function 43
4.1.2 Command-line Arguments 45
4.2 Formatted String Output 50
4.2.1 f-strings 51
4.2.2 str.format() 51
4.2.3 string.Template 52

Part II CORE PYTHON CONCEPTS

5. Control Flow 55

5.1 Code Blocks and Indentation 55
5.2 if Statement 56
5.2.1 if Syntax 56
5.2.2 if .... else 58
5.2.3 elif 59
5.3 For Loop 60
5.3.1 Iteration Over a Sequence 60
5.3.2 Using Range Function 61
5.3.3 Iterating Over Dictionary Keys 62
5.3.4 Iterating Over Dictionary Items 63
5.3.5 Iterating Over Enumerating Elements 65
5.4 FOR...ELSE Loop 66
5.5 While Loop 67
5.6 Loop Control Statements 69
5.6.1 break 69
5.6.2 continue 70
5.6.3 pass 70

6. Functions 73

6.1 Introduction to Functions 73
6.1.1 What are Functions? 73
6.1.2 Why are Functions Important in Python Programming? 74
6.1.3 Advantages of Using Functions 74
6.2 Defining Functions 74
6.2.1 Structure of a Function 74
6.2.2 Calling a Function 75
6.2.3 Docstring 76
6.3 Function Arguments 77
6.3.1 Positional Parameters 77
6.3.2 Keyword Parameters 78
6.3.3 Default Parameters 80
6.3.4 Variable-Length Parameters 81
6.3.5 Keyword-Only Parameters 83
6.4 Lambda Function 83
6.5 Filter Function 86
6.6 Map Function 87
6.7 Sorted Function 88

7. File Handling 91

7.1 Introduction to File Handling 91
7.1.1 Mode of File Handling 92

7.2 CSV File 92
7.3 Excel File 94
7.3.1 openpyxl 95
7.3.2 XLRD 97
7.3.3 Pandas 98
7.4 Image File 98
7.4.1 Pillow 98
7.4.2 Open CV 102
7.5 PDF File 103
7.5.1 ReportLab 103
7.5.2 PyPDF2 108
7.5.3 pdf2image 109

8. Object-Oriented Programming (OOP) 112

8.1 Introduction 112
8.1.1 Procedural Programming 113
8.1.2 Object-Oriented Programming 113
8.2 Class Definition 114
8.2.1 Class Declaration 115
8.2.2 Self Parameter 116
8.2.3 Class Attributes 117
8.2.4 Instance Attributes 119
8.2.5 Private Variables 121
8.3 Understanding Attributes in Python Classes 122
8.4 Name Mangling 122
8.5 Key Concepts of OOP 124
8.5.1 Encapsulation 124
8.5.2 Inheritance 126
8.5.3 Abstraction 129
8.5.4 Polymorphism 133

9. Modules and Packages 135

9.1 Python Modules 135
9.1.1 Creating a Module 136
9.1.2 Using a Module 136
9.2 Python Packages 137
9.2.1 Structure of a Package 137
9.2.2 Creating a Package 138
9.3 Module vs Package 139
9.4 Special Variable in Module 140
9.4.1 __main__ 140
9.4.2 __name__ 140
9.4.3 __doc__ 140

9.4.4 __file__ 140
9.4.5 __package__ 140
9.4.6 __dict__ 141
9.4.7 __all__ 141
9.4.8 __cached__ 141
9.5 __init__.py 142
9.6 Benefits of Modular Programming 143
9.6.1 Advantages of Using Modules 143
9.6.2 Encapsulation and Abstraction 144
9.6.3 Code Organization and Readability 144
9.7 Overview of the Python Standard Library 144
9.8 Utilizing Third-Party Packages with `pip` 144
9.9 Advance Concept in Module/Package 145
9.9.1 Namespaces and Scope 145
9.9.2 Module-Level Variables and Functions 145
9.9.3 Handling Circular Imports 145

10. Graph Plotting 147

10.1 Matplotlib 147
10.1.1 Matplotlib.pyplot: A Versatile Tool for Python Plotting 148
10.2 Plotly 159
10.2.1 Package Structure 160
10.2.2 Graph Plotting Using `plotly.express` 160
10.3 Seaborn 166
10.3.1 Pairplot 166
10.3.2 Swarm Plot 169
10.4 Graph Plotting from Excel File 170

Part III MACHINE LEARNING THROUGH PYTHON

11. Introduction to Machine Learning 177

11.1 Understanding Fundamentals 178
11.1.1 What is Machine Learning 178
11.1.2 Importance and Applications 178
11.1.3 Key Terminology 179
11.2 Types of Machine Learning 180
11.2.1 Based on Learning Style 180
11.2.2 Based on Application 180
11.3 Supervised Learning 180
11.3.1 Application of Supervised Learning 181
11.4 Unsupervised Learning 182
11.4.1 Application of Unsupervised Learning 183

11.5 Reinforcement Learning 184
11.5.1 Key Concepts of Reinforcement Learning 186
11.5.2 Components of Reinforcement Learning 186
11.5.3 Learning Algorithms 186
11.6 Building Blocks of Machine Learning 187
11.6.1 Algorithms and Models 187
11.6.2 Optimization Techniques 187
11.6.3 Tools and Frameworks 188
11.7 Future Trends and Challenges 188
11.7.1 Advancements in Research 188
11.7.2 Emerging Applications 188
11.7.3 Addressing Limitations and Risks 190
11.8 Steps of Machine Learning Implementation 190

12. Data Preprocessing 191

12.1 Introduction 191
12.1.1 Common Challenges in Raw Data 191
12.1.2 Data Preprocessing Steps 192
12.2 Data Cleaning 194
12.2.1 Imputation Techniques 194
12.2.2 Deletion Strategies 195
12.2.3 Outlier Detection and Treatment 197
12.3 Data Transformation 199
12.3.1 Normalization and Scaling 199
12.3.2 Encoding Categorical Variables 202
12.4 Feature Engineering 204
12.4.1 Creating New Features 205
12.5 Data Splitting 207
12.5.1 Importance of Data Splitting 207
12.5.2 Data Splitting Techniques 207

13. Supervised Learning 211

13.1 K-Nearest Neighbors (KNN) 211
13.1.1 KNN Algorithm : Illustration of Classification 212
13.1.2 KNN Algorithm : Illustration of Regression 215
13.2 Decision Tree 219
13.2.1 Decision Tree : Illustration of Classification 220
13.2.2 Information Gain 221
13.2.3 Gini Impurity 223
13.3 Linear Regression 229
13.4 Syntax of Supervised Learning Code 230

14. Unsupervised Learning **233**
14.1 K-Means Clustering 233
14.1.1 Working of K-Means Algorithm 234
14.1.2 Illustration of K-Means Algorithm 234
14.2 Principal Component Analysis (PCA) 240
14.2.1 Working of PCA 241
14.3 Syntax of Unsupervised Learning Code 244
14.3.1 `.fit(X)` 245
14.3.2 `.fit_predict(X)` 245

Index **247**

Preface

This book on *Python programming* is aimed at undergraduate and postgraduate students in the fields of Computer Science and Information Technology who wish to learn, practice, and excel as Python programmers. Starting from scratch, it is intended to the readers with little or no programming knowledge and progresses through core concepts of system, supplemented with numerous examples to elucidate each aspect of programming discussed in every chapter. As the readers advance through the book, they will gradually master Python programming and eventually delve into Machine learning programming and implementation. By the final chapter, the readers will be able to write their own machine learning algorithms tailored to the chosen dataset.

Divided into three parts, the book covers (1) Basics of Python, (2) Core Python Concepts, and (3) Machine Learning through Python. The First part introduces and explains the basic knowledge required to start Python programming, covering topics such as Introduction, Literals and Data Types, Variables and Operators, and Interactive Input-Output. By the end of this section, the readers will be proficient in writing simple Python code with interactive user input and formatted string output display, as well as mastering variables, data types, and understanding regular expressions.

The Second part delves into Python's core concepts across six chapters on Control Flow, Functions, File Handling, Object-Oriented Programming, Modules and Packages, and Graph Plotting. By the end of this section, readers will be equipped to write complex

Python programs with intricate logic, create their own packages, handle input from various files, process data, and generate different types of graphs.

The Third part of the book navigates readers into the realm of Machine learning using Python programming, encompassing chapters such as Introduction to Machine Learning, Data Preprocessing, Supervised Learning, Unsupervised Learning. This section elaborates on various machine learning algorithms and their implementation in Python, providing examples for importing data, preprocessing data, utilizing machine learning algorithms with different parameters, and computing results.

We welcome readers' suggestions for improvement of the book in the next edition at phi@phindia.com or er.radheyshyam@gmail.com.

Lalita Kumari
Radhey Shyam

PART

I

BASICS OF PYTHON

1. Introduction

Python is a high-level, interpreted programming language known for its simplicity and versatility. Created by **Guido van Rossum** and first released in 1991, Python has gained immense popularity in the software development world. Its easy-to-read syntax, extensive standard library, and a vast community of developers make it an ideal choice for a wide range of applications. From web development and scientific computing to machine learning and automation, Python's adaptability and beginner-friendly nature have made it one of the most beloved and widely used programming languages. Whether you're just starting your coding journey or a seasoned developer, Python is a powerful and accessible tool for bringing your ideas to life in the digital realm. Major usage of python is in data science, AI, ML, Data Analytics, Data Visuvalization, Web Development, Game Development, etc.

1.1 Why Python

Python is easy-to-learn high-level scripting language. It is designed to be highly readable and it has fewer syntactical constructions. One of its standout features is its simplicity and readability, making it an ideal language for those just embarking on their coding journey.

Python also comes equipped with an extensive standard library, offering a plethora of pre-built modules and functions. This built-in functionality not only saves time but also encourages developers to be more productive, as they can leverage existing tools to solve complex problems more efficiently.

The language's versatility is another key factor in its popularity. Python can be applied across a wide spectrum of domains, from web development and data analysis to scientific research and machine learning. Its ability to seamlessly integrate with other programming languages and technologies makes it a natural choice for creating complex, interconnected systems.

Python's vibrant and collaborative community is a crucial aspect of its appeal. It is known for its inclusivity and active engagement, which fosters knowledge sharing and ensures that developers have access to a wealth of resources and support.

In sum, Python's perfect balance between simplicity and power, its broad applicability, and the thriving community of enthusiasts have collectively solidified its place as one of the most popular and cherished programming languages globally. It is these very characteristics that make Python the ideal choice for a wide range of projects, from simple scripts to large-scale applications, and continue to draw developers to its ranks.

1.2 Where Python

Its simplicity and readability make it an ideal choice for beginners, while its powerful libraries and frameworks make it a robust tool for professionals. Python shines in web development, where frameworks like Django and Flask are popular choices for building dynamic websites and web applications. Data science and machine learning also benefit from Python's extensive libraries, such as NumPy, pandas, and scikit-learn, as well as TensorFlow and PyTorch. Large tech companies like Google, Facebook, and Amazon rely on Python in various aspects of their operations, while Dropbox employs it for backend services.

List of project/product/services which relies on python is very long. Some of the popular example, where python is extensively used are:

- YouTube's recommendation system, which suggests videos to users, is powered by Python. They use TensorFlow, an open-source machine learning framework, to build and deploy their recommendation models.
- Instagram, a popular social media platform, relies heavily on Django, a Python web framework, to handle its backend infrastructure.
- Python is used by NASA for scientific and numerical simulations, data analysis, and various mission-critical tasks. Libraries like SciPy and Astropy are essential in these applications.
- Netflix employs Python for various purposes, including content delivery and recommendation algorithms. Many of their microservices are built using Python.
- Uber uses Python for its data analytics and machine learning tasks. Python's simplicity and the extensive libraries make it a preferred choice for crunching large datasets.
- Python is used in the film industry for visual effects and animation. Industrial Light & Magic (ILM), known for its work in the Star Wars and Marvel movies, relies on Python for automating and enhancing their visual effects pipelines.
- The European Organization for Nuclear Research (CERN) uses Python for various scientific computing tasks, including data analysis from the Large Hadron Collider (LHC).
- ChatGPT, as well as other similar AI chatbot and language model services, are often built using Python at their core, enabling them to provide natural language understanding

and generation capabilities for a wide range of applications, including virtual assistants, customer support, and content generation.

These examples demonstrate the versatility and power of Python in a wide range of advanced projects and services, from web applications and machine learning to scientific research and even space exploration.

1.3 History of Python

Python, a high-level, general-purpose programming language, was conceived by Guido van Rossum in the late 1980s and first released in 1991 as Python 0.9.0. It was created with the intent to address shortcomings of the ABC language, emphasizing code readability and developer productivity. Python 1.0 was released in 1994, introducing features like lambda, map, filter, and reduce. However, it was Python 2.0, released in 2000, that brought significant improvements, including list comprehensions and garbage collection.

In 2008, Python 3.0 was a groundbreaking release, aimed at rectifying inconsistencies and improving the language's design. It introduced print as a function, eliminated duplicate modules, and emphasized Unicode support. This shift to Python 3 was a major transition for the Python community due to its incompatibility with Python 2, but it was necessary for the language's long-term health. Python 3's adoption grew over the years, and the Python Software Foundation officially declared Python 2 end-of-life in 2020.

Today, Python continues to evolve with regular releases, bringing enhancements, optimizations, and new features. The Python community is active and thriving, with a robust ecosystem of libraries and frameworks that contribute to its widespread use in various domains, including web development, data science, machine learning, and more.

1.4 Python Programming Language Features

Features of Python Programming Language can be summarized as:

Readability: Python's clean and consistent syntax, featuring significant whitespace, makes code easy to read and write, enhancing developer productivity.

Dynamic Typing: Python uses dynamic typing, allowing developers to change variable types during runtime, providing flexibility and ease of use.

Extensive Standard Library: Python offers a comprehensive standard library with modules and packages for a wide range of tasks, reducing the need for external dependencies.

Cross-Platform Compatibility: Python code can run on various operating systems without modification, promoting code portability.

Multiparadigm: Python supports multiple programming paradigms, including object-oriented, procedural, and functional programming, enabling developers to choose the best approach for their tasks.

Community and Ecosystem: Python has a thriving community and an extensive ecosystem of third-party libraries and frameworks, facilitating development in various domains.

Open Source: Python is open-source, making it accessible to everyone and fostering a collaborative environment for continuous improvement.

Interpreted Language: Python is an interpreted language, which means code is executed line by line, allowing for quick testing and debugging.

Large Developer Community: Python has a large and active developer community, resulting in extensive documentation, tutorials, and support resources.

Integration: Python easily integrates with other languages like C, C++, and Java, making it versatile for different software development scenarios.

High-Level Language: Python provides high-level abstractions that simplify complex tasks, making it an excellent choice for rapid application development.

1.5 How Useful is the Python

Python supports object-oriented programming with classes and multiple inheritances. Its code can be grouped into modules and packages. It supports raising and catching exceptions, resulting in cleaner error handling. Python's automatic memory management frees us from having to manually allocate and free memory in our code.

Python can be used to automate tasks, perform calculations, create user interfaces, create website backend, access databases, download information from the Internet, etc. Its versatility and rich base library makes it excellent for many situations.
Major usage of Python in: data science, AI, ML, Data Analytics, Data Visualization, Web Development, and Game Development.

1.6 Starting and Terminating a Python Session

Starting and stopping Python is an essential skill for any Python programmer, and it provides a convenient way to interact with the Python programming language. Starting and stopping Python in the Windows Command Prompt or in the Linux terminal is a straightforward process.

1.6.1 MS Window Environment

- Open the Command Prompt by searching for *"cmd"* in the Windows search bar or press window + R key and type *"cmd"* and press enter key.
- Once the Command Prompt is open, type *"python"* and press Enter. This will launch the Python interpreter, allowing you to execute Python code.
- To stop Python, you can use the keyboard shortcut *Ctrl + Z* and then press Enter. This will exit the Python interpreter and return you to the Command Prompt.

1.6.2 Linux Environment

To start Python, open your terminal application and simply type *"python"* and then press Enter. This will initiate the Python interpreter, enabling you to run Python code and interact with the language.

To exit the Python interpreter and return to the terminal prompt, you can use the *"Ctrl + D"* keyboard shortcut. Alternatively, you can type *"exit()"* or *"quit()"* and then press Enter. These commands will gracefully close the Python interpreter, allowing you to continue using the Linux terminal for other tasks.

1.7 Python IDEs

An IDE (or Integrated Development Environment) is a program dedicated to software development. Writing Python using Python Shell is great for simple things, but for larger programming use of IDE is preferred. IDEs integrate several tools specifically designed for software development. These tools usually include: (i) An editor designed to handle code (with features like syntax highlighting and auto-completion), (ii) Build, execution, and debugging tools.

Python-Specific Editors and IDEs are:

- PyCharm
- Spyder
- Thonny
- Jupyter Notebook
- jupyterlab
- Visual Studio Code
- IDLE

2. Literals and Data Types

At the heart of any programming language lies the foundational concept of literals—immutable values such as numbers, strings, and booleans that serve as the bedrock of Python code. Delving into the manipulation and comprehension of these essential entities is a crucial step for those aspiring to become proficient Python developers. Just as words form the basis of a language, literals are the elemental components of Python, representing fixed values like numbers, strings, and booleans. Understanding how to manipulate and work with these literals is crucial for any aspiring Python developer. This chapter delves into the concept of data types, exploring the various categories that Python uses to classify and organize data. Ranging from integers to strings, and from lists to dictionaries, a comprehensive understanding of these data types is not merely advantageous but essential for harnessing the full potential of Python's versatile data structures.

2.1 Literal vs Data Type

Literals and data types are closely related concepts, but they refer to different aspects of the language. The difference between literals and data type is summarized in Table 2.1.

Literals are the explicit, raw representations of values in the source code. They are the fundamental, unchanging data elements used to express information directly. Literals are a notation for representing a fixed value in source code. They can also be defined as raw values or data given in variables or constants. Literal values can take various forms, such as numeric literals (e.g., 42, 3.14), string literals (e.g., "hello"), boolean literals (True or False), and more complex structures like list literals ([1, 2, 3]) or dictionary literals ('key': 'value'). Literals are constants that provide actual data to be used in computations, comparisons, or assignments within the code. They serve as the essential building blocks from which variables are initialized and computations are performed.

Data types categorize values and variables based on their nature and define the set of operations that can be applied to them. Each data type specifies how the values are stored in memory, what operations are allowed on them, and how these operations are carried out. Python includes various built-in data types, such as integers (int), floating-point numbers (float), strings (str), booleans (bool), lists (list), dictionaries (dict), and more. Data types play a crucial role in ensuring the correctness and efficiency of operations, as they provide a blueprint for the behavior of variables and values during program execution.

Table 2.1: Difference between Literals and Data Types

Aspect	Literals	Data Types
Definition	Raw, explicit values in the source code.	Categories that classify and organize values.
Role	Fundamental building blocks of data.	Provide a structure for organizing and managing data.
Examples	Numeric literals, string literals, boolean literals.	Integers, floats, strings, booleans, lists, etc.
Representation	Direct representation of specific values.	High-level abstraction defining a category of values.
Initialization	Used to initialize variables with specific values.	Variables are assigned a specific data type.
Variability	Fixed values representing data directly.	Categories can include multiple values of the same type.
Mutability	Immutable; values are fixed in the source code.	Immutable or mutable, depending on the data type.
In Code	Explicitly written in the code.	Implied by the variable or context in which values are used.
Purpose	Provide concrete data for computations and assignments.	Organize and manage data, dictate permissible operations.
Flexibility	Limited flexibility; values are explicit and unchanging.	Offers flexibility by allowing dynamic typing.

2.2 Special Literal—None

The literal "**None**" is a special constant representing the absence of a value or a null value. It serves as a placeholder when a variable or an object does not have a meaningful value or when the absence of a value needs to be explicitly conveyed. None is a singleton object, meaning there is only one instance of it in the Python interpreter.

- **None** is used to define a **null** value.
- If **None** is compared with anything else other than a **None**, it will return **false**.
- **None** is not the same as **0**, **False**, or an **empty string**.
- **None** is a data type of its own *NoneType* and **only None can be None**.

2.3 Data Type

Understanding data types is essential for any programmer, as they define how data is stored, manipulated, and interacted with in your programs. Since everything is an object in Python programming, data types are actually classes and variables are instance (object) of these classes.

The classification of data types in Python can be broadly categorized into two main groups: **primitive** or built-in data types and **user-defined** data types. Primitive data types include numeric, floats, booleans, strings, and complex numbers. These types are fundamental and directly supported by the language. Python's dynamic typing allows variables to change their type during runtime, adding to the language's flexibility. On the other hand, user-defined data types are created by the programmer to address specific needs. Common examples of user-defined data types are lists, tuples, sets, and dictionaries. These composite data types enable the organization and manipulation of more complex structures. Understanding the classification of data types is crucial for efficient programming, as it dictates how data is stored, processed, and interacted with throughout the execution of a Python program

2.4 Basics Data Types

The basic or primitive data types in Python encompass a diverse set of elements designed to represent different kinds of information. Python, being a dynamically typed language, allows us to create variables without explicitly specifying their data types. However, behind the scenes, each variable has a data type associated with it. We'll begin by unraveling the basics—integers, floating-point numbers, strings, and booleans. Learn how to declare variables, perform basic operations, and grasp the nuances of working with these fundamental data types.

2.4.1 Boolean

- Objects of Boolean type may have one of two values: **True** or **False**.
- It is denoted by the class **bool**.
- Non-Boolean objects can be evaluated in Boolean context as well and determined to be true or false.
  - Any string is **True**, except empty strings.
  - Any number is **True**, except 0.

Examples

Ex.1

```
bool("Hello")
```

Output: True

Explanation:
bool() returns *True* for All the String having length 1 character or more than one characters. Here in function bool(), the string "Hello" is passed which has length 5 characters.

Ex.2

```
bool("   ")
```

Output: True

Explanation:
Here in function bool(), the parameter provided is "   " which is a string of length more than zero. The provided string has blank spaces only but it is a string of length more than zero.

Ex.3
```
bool('    ')
```

Output: True

Explanation:
Here in function bool(), the parameter provided is '   ' which is a string of length more than zero. The provided string has blank spaces only but it is a string of length more than zero.

Ex.4
```
bool("False")
```

Output: True

Explanation:-
Here in function bool(), the parameter provided is *"False"* which is a String of length 5 characters.

Ex.5
```
bool(False)
```

Output: False

Explanation:
Here in function bool(), the parameter provided is *False* which is not a String.

Ex.6
```
bool('')
```

Output: False

Explanation:
Here in function bool(), the parameter provided is an empty String.

Ex.7
```
bool('-10')
```

Output: True

Explanation:
Here in function bool(), any number returns true, except zero.

Ex.8
```
bool('0')
```

Output: False

Explanation: Here in function bool(), any number returns true, except zero.

2.4.2 Numeric

Python supports various numeric data types that cater to different needs in programming.

int

- Integers represent whole numbers without decimals
- Integers can also be represented in Octal & Hexadecimal
- Hexadeciml starts with "$0X$" (Number Zero and then Alphabet X in small or capital)
- Octal number starts with "0o" (Number Zero and then Alphabet o in small or capital)
- Binary number starts with "0b" (Number Zero and then Alphabet b in small or capital)
- There is no limit on how long an integer value can be, it depends on system memory.

Float

- Floating-point numbers ($float$), handle numbers with decimal points.
- To indicate the power of 10, "e" or "E" can be used.

Complex

- Python also provides support for complex numbers, allowing representation of numbers with both real and imaginary components.
- Imaginary part is represented by alphabet j
- Real part is accessed through **.real** and imaginary part is accessed through **.imag**.

Fraction

- Fraction type enables exact representation of rational numbers, making it useful for precise fractional arithmetic.
- The $fractions$ module required for this feature.
- The $fractions$ module provides support for rational number arithmetic.

A *integer* data x can be converted to floating point or complex type by command $float(x)$ or $complex(x)$ command respectively. Similarly A floating point data x can be converted to integer or complex type by command $int(x)$ or $complex(x)$ command respectively.

Ex.9
```
x=5.2
x=3
type(x)
```

Output: <class 'int'>

Explanation:
type() function gives data type of a variable. Python is dynamically typed language. When we set x=5.2 its data type is taken as <class 'float'> but in next line when we set x=3, its data type is converted to <class 'int'>.

Ex.10
```
x=0x10
y=0o10
z=0b10
print(x*y*z)
```

Output: 256

Explanation:
value of x start with OX which means it is '10' in Hexadecimal whose value is 16. Similarly value of y start with Oo which means it is '10' in Octal whose value is 8 and the value of z start with Ob which means it is '10' in Binary whose value is 2. Therefore actually value of x, y, and z are 16, 8, and 2 respectfully.

Ex.11
```
x=5-4j
print(type(x.real))
```

Output: <class 'float'>

Explanation:
In a complex type numeric, both real and imaginary part are always of type *float*.

Ex.12
```
x=5-4j
print(printx.imag)
```

Output: –4

Explanation:
Data set on x is $5-4j$ which is complex data type. Real part of data is accessed through command *x.real* and imaginary part of data is accessed through command *x.imag*. So x.real will give number 5 and *x.imag* will give number –4.

2.4.3 String

- String is a collection of one or more characters.
- It is arrays of bytes representing Unicode characters.
- String can be enclosed using **single quotes** or **double quotes**.
- **Triple quoted** string is for multiple line strings, and all associated whitespace will be included in the string.
- There is no character data type, a character is a string of length one.
- Strings are a sequence of characters, one can access it through slicing and indexing

- index no. starts from **0 for the direction left to right**.
- index no. also starts from **−1 for the direction right to left**.

Ex.13.

```
x='Hello World'
print(x[1])
```

Output: e

Explanation:
First character of a string can be accessed by index 0, so the second character is accessed by index 1.

Ex.14

```
x='ABCD EFGH IJKL'
print(x[-2])
```

Output: K

Explanation:
Last character of a string can also be accessed by index -1, so the second last character is accessed by index –2.

Range slicing

Range slicing in python is used to slice out a sub string from a given string. Format of range slicing is [**Start index (included): Stop index (excluded)**]

- If start index is left blank, it is considered as 0, i.e. range slicing starts from beginning.
- If end index is left blank, range slicing continue from beginning.
- String can be enclosed using **single quotes** or **double quotes**.
- **Triple quoted** string is for multiple line strings, and all associated whitespace will be included in the string.
- There is no character data type, a character is a string of length one.
- Strings are a sequence of characters. As shown in Figure 2.1 one can access it through slicing and indexing.
  - index no starts from **0 for the direction left to right**.
  - index no also starts from **−1 for the direction right to left**.

0	1	2	3	4	5	6	7	8	9	10	11	12	13	14	15
L	E	A	R	N		P	Y	T	H	O	N		N	O	W
-16	-15	-14	-13	-12	-11	-10	-9	-8	-7	-6	-5	-4	-3	-2	-1

Figure 2.1: Index of string to locate a character. Either of top index or bottom index can be used for accessing its characters.

Ex.15

```
x='Learn Python Now'
print(x[1:12])
```

Output:
earn Python

Explanation:
In this range slicing, start index is 1 and stop index is 12 (see Figure 2.1). So the output will be from 2nd character to less than 12th characters, i.e. 2nd character to 11th character of the given string.

Ex.16
```
x='LEARN PYTHON NOW'
print(x[4:-4])
```

Output:
N PYTHON

Explanation:
As shown in Figure 2.1, start index is 4 which has letter N. The excluded stop index is -4 or 12 so the sliced data will be from array index 4,5,6,7,8,9,10,11.

Ex.17
```
x='Practice Python'
print(x[:-4])
```

Output:
Practice Py

Explanation:
In this range slicing, start index is not provided which means from first characters and stop index is –4 which means it has to leave last 4 characters. So the output will be from first character to 11th character of the given string.

Ex.18
```
name = "DESSERTS"
new_name = name[::-1]
print(new_name)
```

Output:
STRESSED

Explanation:
Here -1 is the step size. It means next character will be -1 character forward, i.e it will progress in reverse direction forming reverse string.

Ex.19
```
name = "DESSERTS"
new_name = name[::2]
print(new_name)
```

Output:
DSET

Explanation:
Here step size is +2 which means while taking sub-string it will always take 2nd character leaving one character. It means it result string will contain string with once character omitted between two characters.

Ex.20
```
name = "DESSERTS"
new_name = name[::-2]
print(new_name)
```

Output:
SRSE

Explanation:
Here step size is 22 which means while taking sub-string it will always take 2nd character in reverse direction leaving one character. It means it result string will contain string with once character omitted between two characters but in reverse direction.

2.4.4 String Variable Declaration

In Python, you can declare a string variable in several ways:

Single Quotes (')

When you declare a string variable using single quotes ('), you're creating a string with a specific value.

Ex.21
```
my_string = 'Hello, world!'
```

Explanation:
Here `Hello, world!` is a string literal, meaning it's a fixed value that represents the string itself. It's enclosed within single quotes to denote that it's a string.

Double Quotes (")

When you declare a string variable using double quotes ("), you're creating a string with a specific value.

Ex.22
```
my_string = "Hello, world!"
```

Explanation:
Here `Hello, world!` is a string literal, meaning it's a fixed value that represents the string itself. It's enclosed within double quotes to denote that it's a string.

Triple Single Quotes (''')

When you use three single quotes (''') to declare a string variable, you're creating a multi-line string.

Ex.23
```
multi_line_string = '''
This is a
multi-line
string.
'''
```

Explanation:
When you use three single quotes (''') to declare a string variable, you're creating a multi-line string. In this case, '''This is a multi-line string.''' is a string literal, but it spans multiple lines. It allows you to include line breaks within the string without needing to use escape characters like \n.

Triple Double Quotes (" " ")

When you use three double quotes (" " ") to declare a string variable, you're creating a multi-line string.

Ex.24
```
multi_line_string = """
This is a
multi-line
string.
"""
```

Explanation:
When you use three double quotes (" " ") to declare a string variable, you're creating a multi-line string. In this case, " " "This is a multi-line string." " " is a string literal, but it spans multiple lines. It allows you to include line breaks within the string without needing to use escape characters like \n.

str() constructor

This `str()` constructor Convert other data types to strings.

Ex.25
```
my_string = str(123)  # Converts integer to string
```

Explanation:
Here *str()* constructor converted integer into string.

2.5 Compound Data Type

A compound data type or *user-defined data type* refers to a type that can store multiple elements or values within a single variable. These data types are essential for organizing and managing complex data structures efficiently. The primary compound data types in Python include lists, tuples, sets, and dictionaries. Python's versatility in handling compound data types makes it a powerful language for tasks ranging from simple data storage to complex data manipulation and analysis.

2.5.1 List `[ ]`

Lists in Python are ordered collections of elements, meaning the sequence of items is maintained, and each element has a specific position.

- `List[]` is a collection which is **ordered** and **mutable**.
- It is written as a list of comma-separated values (items) between square brackets [].
- Since lists are indexed, duplicate items can occur, i.e. lists can have items with the same value.
- Items are indexed starting from 0 for the direction left to right.
- Items are indexed starting from –1 for the direction right to left.
- A list can contain elements of **different data types**, providing flexibility in storing *various types of data within a single list.*
- Lists can dynamically grow or shrink in size as elements are added or removed.
- Python provides a rich set of built-in methods for lists, including **append()**, **extend()**, **pop()**, **remove()**, and more, facilitating efficient.
- Lists support common operations like **concatenation**, **repetition**, and **iteration**.
- The `list()` function can be used to construct list.

2.5.2 Tuples `()`

Tuple is an ordered and immutable collection of elements, denoted by parentheses. Tuples are used to write-protect data and are usually faster than lists as they cannot change dynamically. *Unlike lists, tuples cannot be modified after creation*, making them a suitable choice for situations where data integrity and immutability are essential.

- Tuple is a collection which is **ordered** and **immutable**.
- It is written as a list of comma-separated values (items) between small parenthesis `()`.
- The main difference between List and Tuple is that tuples are immutable, meaning their *elements cannot be changed or modified after the tuple is created.*
- Tuples are defined using parentheses `()`.

2.5.3 Set `{}`

A Python set is an unordered collection of unique elements, defined by curly braces `{}`. Unlike lists or tuples, sets do not have a specific order, and their primary feature is the absence of duplicate values.

- Set is an **unordered** and **unindexed** collection of items with **no duplicate** elements.

- Sets are **mutable**, allowing the addition and removal of elements, making them dynamic data structures.
- Sets can grow or shrink in size as elements are added or removed, adapting to changing data requirements.
- Set can be written as a list of comma-separated values (items) between Curly braces `{}`.
- Set objects also support mathematical operations such as union, intersection, difference, and symmetric difference, etc.

2.5.4 Frozen Set

Frozen set is an **immutable** counterpart to the mutable set data type. While sets are dynamic and allow modifications, frozen sets, once created, cannot be altered—neither by adding, removing, nor modifying elements. Despite their inability to be modified, frozen sets share common set operations with their mutable counterparts, including union, intersection, and difference.

- Frozen sets are immutable.
- Similar to sets, frozen sets are **unordered** and **unindexed**.
- Frozen sets support common set operations such as union, intersection, and difference.
- Frozen set support hash() function to compute hash of a frozen set. This hash value can be used as key to compare.
- Frozen sets are created using the syntax `frozenset()`.

2.5.5 Dictionary

A dictionary is unordered collection of key-value pairs. *Keys within a dictionary are immutable*, such as strings or numbers, while the corresponding values can be of any data type, including lists, sets, or even other dictionaries. Dictionaries offer fast and direct access to values through key-based indexing, making them highly efficient for tasks that involve data lookup and retrieval.

- Dictionaries in Python consist of key-value pairs.
- Its keys are unique and does not allow duplicates.
- Dictionaries are *mutable*, meaning their content can be modified but, *Keys* within a dictionary are *immutable.*
- It is Unordered Collection, dictionaries are designed for efficient key-based retrieval rather than sequential access.
- Values in a dictionary can be of any data type,
- It support dynamic operations, allowing the addition, modification, or deletion of key-value pairs to accommodate changing data requirements.

Ex.26
```
x={1,'Hello',0,False,5.36}
print(type(x))
```

Output: <class ‘set’>

Explanation:
Set are defined in curly bracket `{ }`

Ex.27

```
x=[1,'Hello',0,False,5.36]
print(type(x))
```

Output: <class ‘list’>

Explanation:
List are defined in Square bracket `[]`

Ex.28

```
x=(1,'Hello',0,False,5.36)
print(type(x))
```

Output: <class ‘tuple’>

Explanation:
Tuple are defined in small bracket `()`

Ex.29

```
x=(1,'Hello',0,False,5.36)
y=list(x)
z=set(x)
print(y)
print(z)
```

Output:
[1, ‘Hello’, 0, False, 5.36]
{ 1, ‘Hello’, 0, False, 5.36 }

Explanation:
A *tuple* can be converted into list or set through function **list()** or **set()** respectively. **list()**, **set()**, **tuple()** or **frozenset()** functions are used to convert datatyape from one to another among list, set, tuple, and frozenset respectively.

3. Variables and Operators

3.1 Variables

As Python is dynamically typed language, there is no need to declare variables before using them or to declare their type. A variable is created the moment we first assign a value to it. The value stored in a variable can be changed during program execution.
A variable is only a name given to a memory location, all the operations done on the variable effects that memory location. Rules for creating variable/identifier names are:

- It must **start with a letter** or the **underscore** character.
- It cannot start with a number.
- It can only contain alphabet of lower-case(**a-z**), upper-case (**A-Z**), **underscore**, or digit (**0–9**).
- It is case-sensitive (**Apple**, **apple**, and **appLe** are three different variables).
- The reserved words (**keywords**) cannot be used for naming a variable.

3.1.1 Scope of Variables

A variable's scope defines the regions of code where the variable can be referenced or modified. Python follows a **hierarchical structure** for variable scope. The **LEGB** rule (Local, Enclosing, Global, Built-in) governs the order in which Python searches for variable references, allowing for a clear resolution of variable names in different scopes. This rule dictates the sequence in which Python searches for a variable, starting from the innermost local scope and progressively moving outward to encompass enclosing functions or classes, the global scope, and finally, the built-in scope, which includes Python's predefined names. There are two main types of variable scopes: *global* and *local.*

Local Variable

A local variable in Python is a variable defined within a specific block of code, such as a *function* or a *loop.* It is accessible only within that block and has a limited lifespan, existing only for the duration of the block's execution. In Python, if a variable is assigned within a function, it is automatically considered local unless explicitly declared as *global* using the `global` keyword, which allows it to be accessed outside the function.

Global Variable

A global variable in Python is a variable defined outside any function or block, making it accessible throughout the entire program. Unlike local variables, a global variable retains its value across different scopes, allowing it to be referenced and modified from any part of the code.

- Global variables are the ones that are defined and declared outside any function and are not specified to any function.
- They can be used by any part of the program.
- To define a variable as global scope, or to access/manipulate a global variable inside a function, '**global**' keyword is used.

Ex.1

```
x='Hello World'
def f1():
    x="You are Learning Python"
    print(x)

f1()
print(x)
```

Output:
You are Learning Python
Hello World

Explanation:
Variable x is set outside of all the block but while defining function $f1()$, it is *not declared about x that, it is global variable* so inside function $f1()$ variable x is different local variable and is different from variable used on top of the code. Scope of variable x used inside function $f1()$, is inside $f1()$ only. Therefore inside function $f1()$, the value of x is "*You are Learning Python*" and outside function $f1()$ the value of x is "*Hello World*", and therein no effect of value set inside function $f1()$, outside the function.

Ex.2

```
x='Hello World'
def f1():
    global x
    x="You are Learning Python"
    print(x)

f1()
print(x)
```

Output:
You are Learning Python
You are Learning Python

Explanation:
Variable x is set outside of all the block and while defining function $f1()$, it is *declared that x is global variable* so inside function $f1()$ variable x is same variable as the one variable used on top of the code. Therefore inside function $f1()$ the value of x is set as "*You are Learning Python*" and once the function $f1()$ is called, the value of x is changed globally.

3.2 Python Enhancement Proposal

The Python naming convention, as outlined in PEP 8 (Python Enhancement Proposal 8), provides guidelines for naming various identifiers such as variables, functions, classes, and modules. Adhering to these conventions helps promote consistency and readability across Python codebases. Here are some key points:

- **Variable Names**: Use lowercase letters with words separated by underscores. For example: `my_variable`, `count_of_students`.
- **Function Names**: Follow the same convention as variable names, using lowercase letters with words separated by underscores. For example: `calculate_average`, `generate_report`.
- **Class Names**: Use *CamelCase*, also known as PascalCase, where each word in the name is capitalized without underscores. For example: `MyClass`, `EmployeeDetails`.
- **Module Names**: Use lowercase letters with underscores to separate words (snake_case). Module names should be descriptive and concise, reflecting the functionality they provide. For example: `utils.py`, `data_processing.py`.
- **Constants**: Constants, which are variables whose values are not intended to be changed, should be named using all uppercase letters with underscores separating words. For example: `MAX_SIZE`, `PI`.
- **Private Variables and Functions**: Prefix variable and function names with a single underscore (_) to indicate that they are intended for internal use only. For example: `_internal_variable`, `_helper_function`.

- **Protected Variables and Functions**: Prefix variable and function names with a double underscore (___) to indicate that they are intended for internal use, but are also subclasses of the class where they are defined. For example: `__protected_variable`, `__helper_function` Python uses special method names, often referred to as magic methods, for operator overloading, customization, and other purposes. These names are surrounded by double underscores (___). For example: `__init__` for constructor initialization, ___str___ for string representation.
- **Magic Method Names**: Python uses special method names, often referred to as magic methods, for operator overloading, customization, and other purposes. These names are surrounded by double underscores (___). For example: `__init__` for constructor initialization, ___str___ for string representation.

3.3 Operator

An operator is a symbol or function that performs a specific operation on one or more operands. Operators are fundamental elements in programming languages and mathematical expressions, allowing for the manipulation and transformation of data. They are used to carry out various tasks, such as arithmetic computations, logical operations, and relational comparisons. The type of operator and the number of operands it acts upon determine the nature of the operation being performed. Operators play a crucial role in expressing algorithms, making computations, and creating meaningful interactions within a program.

3.3.1 Arithmetic Operator

Arithmetic operators are fundamental components that enable the manipulation of numerical values through various mathematical operations. These operators include addition (+), subtraction (–), multiplication (*), division (/), and modulus (%), among others.

Addition

Addition (+) combines two values to produce their sum. When applied to numeric operands, the addition operator calculates the sum of the values on either side. Beyond its primary role in basic arithmetic, the addition operator in Python also exhibits versatility by concatenating strings and combining other data types, providing a concise and intuitive means to join and unify different elements. Whether employed for straightforward numerical calculations or for merging strings and sequences, the addition operator in Python stands as a versatile tool for creating expressive and dynamic code.

Ex.3

```
a=5
b=3
result = a + b
print(result)
```

Output:
8

Explanation:
5+3 =8.

Ex.4
```
string1 = "Hello"
string2 = " World!"
string3 = string1 + string2
print(string3)
```

Output:
Hello World!

Explanation:
String get concatenated on using + operator.

Ex.5
```
x1 = [1, 2, 3]
x2 = [4, 5, 6]
x= x1 + x2
print(x)
```

Output:
[1, 2, 3, 4, 5, 6]

Explanation:
List get concatenated on using + operator.

Subtraction

The subtraction operator (−) serves as a fundamental arithmetic tool for computing the difference between two numeric values. When applied to variables or constants, the subtraction operator calculates the result of subtracting the right operand from the left operand.

In addition to calculating numerical differences, the subtraction operator in Python has alternative uses across different data types, providing versatility in various programming context such as Set Difference, Datetime Operations, etc.

Ex.6
```
set1 = {1, 2, 3, 4, 5}
set2 = {3, 4, 5, 6, 7}
set3 = set1 - set2
print(set3)
```

Output:
1, 2

Explanation:
The subtraction operator can be used to find the set difference, i.e., elements that are present in the first set (set1) but not in the second set (set2).

Ex.7

```
from datetime import datetime, timedelta
current_date = datetime(2023, 12, 29, 12, 45, 00, 00)
days_to_subtract = 7
new_date = current_date - timedelta(days=days_to_subtract)
print(new_date)
```

Output:
2023-12-22 12:45:00

Explanation: The *datetime* class is part of the standard library, and the datetime module needs to be imported before using it. You can set a custom date and time using the datetime module. The datetime module provides the datetime class, which allows you to create objects representing specific dates and times
The $datetime(2023, 12, 29, 12, 45, 00, 00)$ sets a datetime type object with year = 2023, month = 12, day = 29, hour = 12, minute = 45, second = 0, microsecond=0. The subtraction operator can be applied to datetime objects to calculate a new date by subtracting a specific duration, represented by a **timedelta** object.

Multiplication

Multiplication operator ($*$) is a fundamental arithmetic operator used to calculate the product of two numerical values. It is a versatile operator that extends beyond numeric multiplication to *concatenate strings and replicate elements* within a list.

Ex.8

```
x = "Python"
y = x * 5
print(y)
```

Output:
PythonPythonPythonPythonPython

Explanation:
On multiplying a string with a number, The string is replicated. In this case the String "Python" got replicated 5 times.

Ex.9

```
x = "5"
y = x * 5
print(y)
```

Output:
55555

Explanation:
The String '5' got replicated 5 times forming a string '55555'.

Division

Division operator (/) is used to divide one number by another, producing a quotient that may or may not have a remainder. For integers, the division operator returns a floating-point result, even if the division yields a whole number.

Ex.10

```
result = 10 / 2
print(result)
```

Output:
5.0

Explanation:
Division Operator always returns <class ‘float’>.

Integer Division

Floor division or Integer division is performed using the double forward slash operator (//). Unlike regular division, which returns a floating-point result, floor division yields the largest integer that is less than or equal to the division result. This operation is particularly useful when the result needs to be an integer without any decimal points.

Ex.11

```
result = 10 // 3
print(result)
type(result)
```

Output:
3
<class ‘int’>

Explanation:
Floor Division Operator always returns floor value. Here in this case floor of 3.33 is 3. Operand and operator, both are integer so data type of result will be <class ‘int’>.

Ex.12

```
result = 2.5 // 3
print(result)
type(result)
```

Output:
0.0
<class ‘float’>

Explanation:
Floor Division Operator always returns floor value. Here in this case floor of 0.833 is 0. As one operand, i.e., 2.5 is of type <class ‘float’>, so data type of result will be <class ‘float’>.

Modulus

The modulus operator, represented by the percent sign (%), is an arithmetic operator that calculates the remainder when one number is divided by another. It is particularly useful for extracting periodic information or checking divisibility. Modulus operator may be applied on *integer* or *float* data type.

Ex.13

```
result = 15 % 2
print(result)
```

Output:
1

Explanation:
when 15 is divided by 2, one is the remainder.

Ex.14

```
result = 10 % 3.2
print(result)
```

Output:
0.4

Explanation:
In some case the output may be 0.39999999999999947, and this is because of the inherent limitations of floating-point representation in computers. Floating-point numbers in Python, and many other programming languages, are represented using binary, which can lead to precision issues when dealing with certain decimal values.

Exponent

The exponentiation operator is represented by two asterisks (**). This operator is used to raise a base number to the power of an exponent, providing a concise and intuitive way to perform exponentiation operations. The exponentiation operator is versatile and can handle integer, floating-point, or even complex numbers as the base or exponent.

Ex.15

```
result = 3 ** -2
print(result)
```

Output:
0.1111111111111111

Explanation:
$3^{-2} = 0.11$

Ex.16

```
base = 1+2j
result = base ** 2
print(result)
```

Output:
-3+4j

Explanation:
$(1+2j)^2 = -3+4j$

3.3.2 Comparison Operator

Comparison operators play a crucial role in facilitating the evaluation of conditions and making decisions within programs. These operators enable developers to compare values, variables, or expressions, ultimately determining the logical relationship between them. Comparison operator on evaluation gives binary result **True** or **False**. Python offers a diverse set of comparison operators, including *equality* (==), *inequality* (! =), *greater than* (>), *less than* (<), greater than or equal to (>=), and *less than or equal to* (<=).

Ex.17
```
a=10
b=10.0
print(type(a)==type(b))
```

Output:
False

Explanation:
Data type of a is *<class 'int'>* where as data type of b is *<class 'float'>* therefore their data types are not equal.

Ex.18
```
a=10
b=10.0
print(a==b)
```

Output:
True

Explanation:
In Python, the comparison operator == checks for equality between values, not necessarily their data types. When comparing $a == b$, Python performs an automatic type conversion or implicit type casting. In this case, the integer 10 is automatically cast to a float before the comparison takes place.

3.3.3 Assignment Operator

The assignment operator (=) is the primary mechanism through which values are assigned to variables, allowing developers to store and update data dynamically. It is fundamental tools for manipulating and managing variables within a program.

Basic Assignment Operator

The basic assignment operator (=) is the foundation of variable assignment in Python. It is used to assign a value to a variable. For example, **a = 10** assigns the value **10** to the variable **a**. This operator does not perform any arithmetic or logical operations; it simply assigns the right-hand value to the variable on the left-hand side.

Complex Assignment Operator

Python offers several complex assignment operators that combine an operation with assignment in a concise manner. These operators are particularly useful for performing operations on a variable and updating it in a single step. The most common complex assignment operators are shown in Table 3.1.

Table 3.1: The most common complex assignment operators

Assignment Name	Symbol	Example	Equivalent to
Addition Assignment	+=	a += 5	a = a + 5
Subtraction Assignment	-=	a -= 5	a = a - 5
Multiplication Assignment	*=	a *= 5	a = a * 5
Division Assignment	/=	a /= b	a = a / b
Modulus Assignment	%=	a %= 3	a = a % 3
Exponentiation Assignment	**=	a **= 2	a = a^2
Floor Division Assignment	//=	a //= 3	a = a // 3

Comma-Separated Assignment Operator

Python allows multiple assignments in a single line using the comma-separated assignment. This feature enables developers to assign values to multiple variables in a single statement.

Ex.19

```
x, y, z = 1, 2, 3
print(y)
```

Output:
2

Explanation:
In this comma-separated assignment system, value of x, y, and z has been assigned as 1, 2, and 3 respectively in one go.

Ex.20

```
a = 10
b = 5
a, b = b, a
print(b)
```

Output:
10

Explanation:
It is particularly useful in swapping values between variables without using a temporary variable.

3.3.4 Logical Operator

Python supports only three basic logical operators **and**, **or**, **not**. The **and** operator returns **True** if both operands are true, otherwise, it evaluates to **False**. The **or** operator returns **True** if at least one of its operands is true, and it evaluates to **False** only if both operands are false. The **not** operator, on the other hand, **negates** the boolean value of its operand, transforming True to False and vice versa.

Ex.21

```
x, y = True, Flase
print(x and y)
```

Output:
False

Explanation:
and operator gives result True only when both the operands are True.

3.3.5 Bitwise Operator

Bitwise operators in Python perform operations at the bit level, manipulating individual bits of integers. These operators are particularly useful when dealing with low-level programming, optimization, and certain algorithmic tasks.

Bitwise AND (&):

The bitwise AND operator (&) performs a bitwise *AND* operation on each pair of corresponding bits of two integers. The result of the operation is a new integer where each bit is set to 1 only if the corresponding bits of both operands are 1. Otherwise, the bit is set to 0.

Ex.22

```
x = 6
y = 5
z = x & y
print(z)
```

Output:
4

Explanation:
Number 6 in binary is 0110 and number 5 in binary is represented as 0101. On performing bitwise **AND** operation on x and y, it gives result as 0100 which is 4 in decimal representation.

Bitwise OR (|):

The bitwise OR operator (|) performs a bitwise *OR* operation on each pair of corresponding bits of two integers. The result of the operation is a new integer where each bit is set to 1 if at least one of the corresponding bits of the operands is 1.

Ex.23

```
x = 5
y = 3
z = x | y
print(z)
```

Output:
7

Explanation:
Number 5 in binary is 0101 and number 3 in binary is represented as 0011. On performing bitwise **OR** operation on x and y, it gives result as 0111 which is 7 in decimal representation.

Bitwise XOR (^):

The bitwise XOR operator (^) performs an exclusive OR operation on each pair of bits. If the bits are different, the result is 1; if they are the same, the result is 0.

Ex.24

```
x = 5
y = 3
z = x ^ y
print(z)
```

Output:
6

Explanation:
Number 5 in binary is 0101 and number 3 in binary is represented as 0011. On performing bitwise **XOR** operation on x and y, it gives result as 0110 which is 6 in decimal representation.

Bitwise NOT (~):

The bitwise NOT operator (~) inverts each bit of the operand. It changes 1s to 0s and 0s to 1s. This operator is useful for creating the complement of a binary number

Ex.25

```
x = 5
z = ~x
print(z)
```

Output:
-6

Explanation:
Number 5 in binary is 0101. On performing bitwise **NOT** operation on x, it inverse the bit 0 to 1 and vice versa, producing result as 1010 which is -6 in decimal representation.
Note: Any integer in python is represented in memory by 28 bytes. So 5 will be represented by 28*8-1=223 numbers of 0 or 1. One bit is fixed for sign: 0 for (+) and 1 for (–). Therefore in actual representation of -6 is 219 no of 1 followed by 1010.
Number ......11111010 in 2's complete representation is ....00000101 + 1 = ...00000110.
Therefore ......11111010 is representation of -6.

Left Shift ($<<$):

The Left Shift operator shifts the bits of data towards the left. In a one-bit left shift, the entire data is shifted to the left, and a 0 bit is inserted in the rightmost position, effectively doubling the data. Its syntax is $x << n$, where x is the data to be left-shifted, and n is the number indicating how many shifts are to be performed.

Ex.26

```
x = 5
z = x<<2
print(z)
```

Output:
20

Explanation:
Number 5 in binary is 0101. On performing left shift 2 times, the data will be 010100, which is 20 in decimal representation.

Right Shift ($>>$):

The Right Shift operator in Python shifts the bits of data towards the right. During a one-bit right shift, for positive numbers, the entire data is shifted to the right, and a 0 bit is inserted in the leftmost position, effectively halving the data. However, for negative numbers, a 1 bit is inserted in the leftmost position during the right shift. Its syntax is $x >> n$, where x represents the data to be right-shifted, and n denotes the number of right shifts to be performed.

Ex.27

```
x = 13
z = x>>2
print(z)
```

Output:
3

Explanation:
Number 15 in binary is 01101. On performing right shift 2 times, the data will be 00011, which is 3 in decimal representation.

3.3.6 String Operator

String operators play a crucial role in manipulating and working with textual data. The primary string operators in Python include:

Concatenation Operator (+)

This operator is used for combining two or more strings into a single string.

Repetition Operator (*)

This operator duplicates a string a specified number of times.

Membership Operators ((*in* and *not in*))

These operators are used to check if a substring is present in a given string.

Identity Operator (*is* and *is not*)

The **is** operator returns **True** if the two variables *reference the exact same object*, and False otherwise.
The **is not** operator returns **True** if the two variables do not reference the same object, and False otherwise.
It's important to note that the *is* and *is not* operators are different from the == (equality) operator, which checks if the values of two objects are equal, not whether they refer to the same object in memory. When dealing with strings, the == operator is generally used for comparing their contents, while *is* and *is not* are used for identity comparison.

Slice ([ ])

Slicing is not specifically referred to as a "slice operator", but it is a powerful technique for manipulating strings. Slicing involves the use of colons (:) within square brackets to extract a portion of a string. The general syntax for slicing is **start _index:end_index**, where the **start_index** is inclusive, and the **end_index** is exclusive.

Ex.28

```
main_string = "Hello, World!"
x = "World" in main_string
print(x)
```

Output:
True

Explanation:
Here variables b refers to the same list as a whereas variable a and c are different objects with the same content.

Ex.29

```
a = [1, 2, 3]
b = a
c = [1, 2, 3]
```

```
print(a is b)
print(a is c)
```

Output:
True
False

Explanation:
"World" is present in the main string.

3.4 Built-in String Methods

Python's rich set of built-in string methods provides a powerful toolkit for efficient string manipulation and processing. These methods offer diverse functionalities, enhancing the versatility of string handling in Python. Table 3.2 shows some common built-in string operator with there uses. These built methods are used through dot operator after the string variable.

Table 3.2: The most common built-in string methods

Method	Uses
len()	Returns the length of a string.
lower()	Convert strings to lowercase.
upper()	Convert strings to uppercase.
capitalize()	Capitalizes the first letter of a string.
title()	Capitalizes the first letter of each word.
find()	Search for substring, and returning the lowest index of a substring. If substring not found then returns -1.
index()	Search for substring, and returning the lowest index of a substring. If substring not found then raise a *ValueError*.
count()	It counts frequency of a specified substring found in the given main string.
replace()	It substitutes all occurrences of a specified substring with another.
split()	Perform tokenization by breaking a string into a list of substrings based on a specified delimiter.
join()	Concatenate a list of strings into a single string.
startswith()	Check if a string begins with a specified substring.
endswith()	Check if a string ends with a specified substring.

Ex.30

```
main_string = "Hello, World! Say Hello to every one."
x = main_string.find("Hello")
print(x)
```

Output:
0

Explanation:
First occurrence of word "Hello" is at index 0.

Ex.31

```
main_string = ``Hello, World! Say Hello to every one.''
x = main_string.count("Hello")
print(x)
```

Output:
2

Explanation:
Word "Hello" is repeated twice in the given main string.

Ex.32

```
main_string = "Hello, World! Say Hello to every one."
x = main_string.replace("Hello", "Hi")
print(x)
```

Output:
Hi, World! Say Hi to every one.

Explanation:
All the occurrence of word "Hello" is replaced with word "Hi" twice in the given main string.

Ex.33

```
csv_data = "Mohan Das,1869,Gujarat,India"
csv_list = csv_data.split()
print(csv_list)
```

Output:
['Mohan', 'Das,1869,Gujarat,India ']

Explanation:
If nothing is specified, the split function splits the words from *blank space*, resulting *list of two items.*

Ex.34

```
csv_data = "Mohan Das,1869,Gujarat,India"
csv_list2 = csv_data.split(",")
print(x)
```

Output:
['Mohan Das', '1869', 'Gujarat', 'India']

Explanation:
Here comma (,) is specified as split delimiter. So, the split function splits the words from *comma (,)*, resulting *list of four items.*

Ex.35

```
words = ['This', 'is', 'a', 'sample', 'sentence.']
subtext = " "
sentence = subtext.join(words)
print(sentence)
```

Output:
This is a sample sentence.

Explanation:
String method *join()*, joins all the items of list with putting contents of variable *subtext* between two items of the list. Here value of subtext is a blank space, so all the list items has been joined by potting blank space between tow list items.

3.5 Regular Expression

A regular expression, often abbreviated as *regex* or *regexp*, is a powerful sequence of characters that defines a search pattern. It's a versatile tool for text processing, allowing us to *match*, *search*, and *manipulate* strings based on **specific patterns**. Regular Expression enable the identification of specific character combinations, sequences, or structures, allowing for tasks such as data validation, text parsing, and information extraction. The expressive power of **regex** is exemplified through a combination of metacharacters, quantifiers, and character classes, allowing developers to construct intricate patterns that match precisely defined criteria. The syntax and rules for writing regular expressions follow a set of conventions. Here are some key components and rules for creating regular expressions:

3.5.1 Literals

Regular expressions can include literal characters that match themselves. For example, the regular expression **abc** will match the string "abc" in the input.

3.5.2 Metacharacters

Certain characters have special meanings and are called metacharacters. Common metacharacters include:

- .
  matches any character except a newline
- *
  matches 0 or more occurrences of the preceding character
- \+
  matches 1 or more occurrences of the preceding character

- **?**
  matches 0 or 1 occurrence of the preceding character
- ⌢
  matches the start of a string
- **$**
  matches the end of a string

3.5.3 Character Classes

Square brackets [] are used to define character classes. For example, **[aeiou]** matches any vowel. A hyphen - inside a character class denotes a range, such as **[0-9]** for any digit.

3.5.4 Quantifiers

Quantifiers specify the number of occurrences of the preceding character or group. Common quantifiers include:

- *
  0 or more
- +
  1 or more
- ?
  0 or 1
- **n**
  exactly n occurrences
- **{n,m}**
  between n and m occurrences

3.5.5 Grouping

Parentheses ( ) are used for grouping characters or expressions. They also capture matched substrings for later use.

3.5.6 Escape Character

The **backslash** \ is used to escape a metacharacter, making it match the literal character. For example, \. matches a literal dot.

3.5.7 Anchors

⌢ is used to specify the start of a line or string
$ is used to specify the end of a line or string

3.5.8 Wildcard

The dot **.** is a wildcard that matches any single character except a newline.

3.5.9 Modifiers

Flags or modifiers can be used with the regular expression to change its behavior. Common modifiers include **re.IGNORECASE** (case-insensitive matching) and **re.MULTILINE** (multiline matching)

Ex.36
```
import re

pattern = r'\d+
text = "The price is $25.99, and we have $50."
search_output = re.findall(pattern, text)

print(search_output)
```

Output:
['25', '99', '50']

Explanation:
The \d+ pattern matches one or more digits. *re.findall()* returns a list of all occurrences of one or more digits in the text.

Ex.37
```
import re

pattern = r'\b[0-9]+\.?[0-9]*+\b'
text = "5 computers are connected for last 1.5 hour.
        IP address is 101.188.67.134"
search_output = re.findall(pattern, text)

print(search_output)
```

Output:
['5', '1.5', '101.188', '67.134']

Explanation:
This regular expression is searching for one or more continuous digits (**[0-9]+**) then one time or zero time a decimal (**\.?**) and then one or more time digits (**[0-9]+**).

Ex.38
```
import re

pattern = re.compile(r'\b[a-z0-9._-]+@[a-z0-9.-]+\.[a-z]{2,}\b')
text = "For more information, contact me at
        kumaril2003@yahoo.co.in or er.radheyshyam@gmail.com"
search_output = re.findall(pattern, text)

print(search_output)
```

Output:
['kumaril2003@yahoo.co.in', 'er.radheyshyam@gmail.com']

Explanation:
This regular expression is for email matching. It searches for pattern: one or more occurrence of lowercase letters (a-z), digits (0-9), and certain special characters like period (.), underscore (_), and hyphen (-) (**[a-z0-9._-]**+) then one character @ (@), which is compulsory. Then after again one or more occurrence of lowercase letters (a-z), digits (0-9), and certain special characters like period (.), underscore (_), and hyphen (-) (**[a-z0-9._-]**+) and at the end one dot (\.) followed by at least 2 alphabet (**[a-z]{2,}** +).

Ex.39

```
import re

pattern = r'<.*?>'

text = "<p>This is <strong>important</strong>.</p>"
search_output = re.findall(pattern, text)

print(search_output)
```

Output:
['<p>', '<strong>', '</strong>', '</p>']

Explanation:
This regular expression is to search html tag. It searches for string starting with < and then **.*?** which means any character except for a newline character **(explained by dot)**, repeated zero or more times (**explained by star**), match as little text as possible (**explained by question mark**), and end with >.

Ex.40

```
import re

pattern = r'<.*?>'

text = "<p>This is <strong>important</strong>.</p>"
replaced_output = re.sub(pattern, '', text)

print(replaced_output)
```

Output:
This is important.

Explanation:
re.sub(pattern, '', text) will replace all the occurrence of *pattern* (parameter-1) by *blank space* (parameter-2) from string *text* (parameter-3).

3.6 Regular Expression Function

Python's **re** module provide a robust set of functions for working with regular expressions, facilitating powerful string manipulation and pattern matching. Some of the available functions are:

- `re.search(pattern, string, flags=0)` It searches for the first occurrence of a pattern within a string and returns a match object.
- `re.match(pattern, string, flags=0)` It specifically checks if the pattern matches at the beginning of the string.
- `re.findall(pattern, string, flags=0)` This function is instrumental in finding all occurrences of a pattern in a string and returning them as a list of substrings.
- `re.finditer(pattern, string, flags=0)` It produces an iterator of match objects, allowing iteration over individual matches.
- `re.sub(pattern, replacement, string, count=0, flags=0)` This function facilitates substitution, replacing occurrences of a pattern with a specified replacement in the string.
- `re.split(pattern, string, maxsplit=0, flags=0)` It splits a string based on occurrences of the pattern, producing a list of substrings

Ex.41

```
# Validate PAN Card
import re
pattern = r'[A-Z]{5}[0-9]{4}[A-Z]{1}'

text = "ABCDE1234K1"

result = re.fullmatch(pattern, text)
print(result)
```

Output:
None

Explanation:
The above regular expression is for: 5 Alphabets, then 4 digits, then 1 alphabet. Matching is `fullmatch()` which will give result only if it matched exactly ones and the text does not contains any additional character other than the provided pattern, any addition character after one match. In this case one addition digit is available in *text* after one match, Resulting no match. If no match found, it will give `None`.

Ex.42

```
# Validate Postal PIN Code
import re
pattern = r'[1-9]{1}[0-9]{5}'

text = "800001"
```

```
result = re.fullmatch(pattern, text)

print(result)
```

Output:
<re.Match object; span=(0, 6), match='800001'>

Explanation:
The above regular expression is for: 1st character as number (other than 0).
Next 5 character as any digit (between 0 to 9).
In this case, match found so the result obtained is other than None.

4. Interactive Input-Output

In this chapter, we dive into the fundamental aspects of interacting with users through command-line input and output in Python. As developers, the ability to seamlessly gather information from users and present results in a clear and concise manner is crucial. Additionally, we'll delve into the art of formatting output strings, ensuring that the information presented to users is not only informative but also visually appealing. By mastering these essential skills, you'll be equipped to create Python programs that are not only functional but also user-friendly and professional in their presentation.

4.1 Command-Line Input

Command-Line Input allows a Python program to receive data from the user at runtime. It is entered by the user through the Command-Line Interface (CLI), which serves as a direct channel for input and output between users and computer programs (e.g., Command Prompt, Linux Bash, or macOS Terminal). In Python, there are primarily two ways to gather command-line input: *using the input() function* and by *parsing command-line arguments*.

4.1.1 input() Function

The command-line input can be gathered using `input()` Function. The input() function is a simple and straightforward way to collect user input from the command line. It prompts the user for input, waits for them to enter a value, and returns the entered *value as a string*.

Ex.1

```
x = input("Enter a Number")
print(x)
```

Output:
Enter a Number *<Will wait for user to type through keyboard.>*
<When Enter key is Pressed, It will print the data You have just entered.>

Explanation:
On execution of first line, it will display a message *"Enter a Number"* and will wait for user to type through keyboard. Whatever data will you type will be stored in variable x as a string. Second line will print the data stored in variable x (The data you have typed).

Ex.2

```
        # Suppose you will type number 5, when prompted for input
x = input("Enter a Number")
type(x)
```

Output:
<class 'str'>

Explanation:
What ever data you typed will be stored as string. So The number you have typed (say 5) will be stored as string '5'.

Ex.3

```
        # Suppose you will type number 5, when prompted for input
x = input("Enter a Number")
x = x + 1
print(x)
```

Output:
TypeError

Explanation:
Whatever data you typed will be stored as string. So The number you have typed (say 5) will be stored as string '5'. Now on execution of next line (`x = x + 1`), it will give error as integer (1) can not be added to a string variable x.

Ex.4

```
        # Suppose you will type number 5, when prompted for input
x = input("Enter a Number")
x = x + x
print(x)
```

Output:
55

Explanation:
Data type of x is *string* and its value is 5 which is stored as string. Now string can be concatenated using + operator. therefore (x+x) will concatenate the same string two times.

Ex.5

```
# Suppose you will type number 5, when prompted for input
x = input("Enter a Number")
x = x * 4
print(x)
```

Output:
5555

Explanation:
Data type of x is *string* and its value is 5 which is stored as string. Now string can be concatenated using * operator. therefore (x*4) will concatenate the same string two times.

4.1.2 Command-line Arguments

Command-line arguments allow users to pass parameters directly to Python scripts when executing them from the command line. These arguments are accessed using the *`sys.argv`* module or by using the *`argparse`* module for more complex argument parsing.

sys.argv

`sys.argv` is a list in Python that contains the command-line arguments passed to the script. It's a part of the `sys` module and is available by default. It allows access to command-line arguments as a list of strings. The first element (`sys.argv[0]`) is always the name of the script itself, and subsequent elements contain the arguments provided by the user.

Basic Steps of writing python code with Command-line Arguments and executing it is as follow:

- Write complete python program in a file and save it with .py extension (say *mycodefile.py*).
- Open Command prompt or a terminal and change the directory to the location where your python code file (*mycodefile.py*) has been stored.
- type syntax **`python filename.py «arguments»`** and press enter. In our case `python mycodefile.py «arguments»`. Here multiple arguments are required to be separated from each other by space.

Ex.6

```
#--------- Contents of mycodefile.py -------------
import sys
mydata1 = sys.argv[1]
```

```
mydata2 = sys.argv[2]

print(mydata1)
#--------------End of file mycodefile.py--------------------

# -----Below is the Command entered on command prompt
python mycodefile.py  Hello Dear
```

Output:
Hello

Explanation:
All the data entered after python file name are stored in array of `sys.argv`. The Word "Hello" is stored in `sys.argv[1]` and Word "Dear" is stored in `sys.argv[2]`. Now in variable my On execution of first line, it will display a message *"Enter a Number"* and will wait for user to type through keyboard. Whatever data will you type will be stored in variable x as a string. Second line will print the data stored in variable x (The data you have typed).

Ex.7

```
#--------- Contents of mycodefile.py -------------
import sys
x= sys.argv[0]
print(x)
#--------------End of file mycodefile.py--------------------

# -----Below is the Command entered on command prompt
python mycodefile.py  Hello Dear
```

Output:
mycodefile.py

Explanation:
While executing a python code file through command line, first argument of `sys.argv` is the text entered just after the keyword `python`, which is always the name of the python code file.

Ex.8

```
#--------- Contents of mycodefile.py -------------
import sys
x= sys.argv[1]
print(x)
#--------------End of file mycodefile.py--------------------
```

```
# -----Below is the Command entered on command prompt
python mycodefile.py  Hello Dear
```

Output:
IndexError: list index out of range

Explanation:
Length of `sys.argv` is 1 as no additional parameter as argument has been provided. Therefore we only have data `sys.argv [0]` and we are trying to access `sys.argv [1]` which gives *list index out of range.*

Ex.9

```
#--------- Contents of mycodefile.py -------------
import sys
x= len(sys.argv)
print(x)
#--------------End of file mycodefile.py--------------------

# -----Below is the Command entered on command prompt
python mycodefile.py  Hello Dear
```

Output:
3

Explanation:
1st argument provided is "**mycodefile.py**", 2nd argument is "**Hello**", and 3rd argument is "**Dear**".

argparse

`argparse` is a comprehensive module in Python for parsing command-line arguments. It provides a more sophisticated and user-friendly way to handle command-line input compared to `sys.argv`. `argparse` allows defining command-line arguments with different types, specifying optional arguments, providing help messages, and performing argument validation. Feature of `argparse` is summarized as:

- Supports positional arguments, optional arguments, and flags.
- Automatically generates help messages and usage information based on argument definitions.
- Handles data type conversion and validation of input arguments.
- Offers a structured and organized way to define and parse command-line arguments.

Ex.10
```
#--------- Contents of mycodefile.py -------------
import argparse

parser  = argparse.ArgumentParser(description='My sample description')

parser.add_argument('myarg1', type=int, help='A Compulsory')
parser.add_argument('myarg2', type=str, help='Compulsory Argument -2')

args = parser.parse_args()

print([args.myarg1, args.myarg2])

#--------------End of file mycodefile.py--------------------

# -----Below is the Command entered on command prompt
python mycodefile.py  5 Hello
```

Output:
[5, 'Hello']

Explanation:
First argument passed after python file name will be matched with integer type variable myarg1 and 2nd argument passed after python file name will be matched with string type variable myarg2.

Ex.11
```
#--------- Contents of mycodefile.py -------------
--Same as mentioned in  |Ex.10|
#--------------End of file mycodefile.py--------------------

# -----Below is the Command entered on command prompt
python mycodefile.py  --help
```

Output:
```
usage:  scratch.py [-h] myarg1 myarg2

My sample description

positional arguments:
myarg1              A Compulsory
myarg2              Compulsory Argument -2

options:
-h, -help show this help message and exit
```

Explanation:
–h or –help argument if provided then help information about the script is displayed. This help information provide description text about the code file which has been set by command argparse.ArgumentParser(). It also gives details about the arguments.

Ex.12
```
#--------- Contents of mycodefile.py -------------
--Same as mentioned in  |Ex.10|
#--------------End of file mycodefile.py--------------------

# -----Below is the Command entered on command prompt
python mycodefile.py  Hello Word
```

Output:
```
usage:  scratch.py [-h] myarg1 myarg2

scratch.py:  error:  argument myarg1:  invalid int value:  'Hello'
```

Explanation:
Arguments are always matched (in `argparse` environment) with the data type, declared in the python code. In our case it is `parser.add_argument('myarg1', type=int, help='A Compulsory')`. Here *myarg1* is the name of positional argument. As per the code, 1st argument is declared as *integer* and 2nd argument is declared as *string*, but data provided at the time of calling is both of string type.

Optional Arguments in argparse

One of its key features of `argparse` module is the ability to define optional arguments, which are parameters that may or may not be provided when running a script. These optional arguments can add flexibility and customization to your scripts, allowing users to adjust the behavior of the program based on their specific needs. When using `argparse` to define optional arguments, you typically create instances of the `ArgumentParser` class and then use methods like `add_argument()` to specify the arguments your script accepts. For optional arguments, you use the `-` prefix followed by a unique identifier to distinguish them from positional arguments.

Ex.13
```
#--------- Contents of mycodefile.py -------------
import argparse

parser  = argparse.ArgumentParser(description='My sample description')
parser.add_argument('myarg1', type=int, help='Text about Argument-1')
parser.add_argument('myarg2', type=str, help='Text about Argument-2')
parser.add_argument('--my_oparg1', type=str, default='myDefaultData',
                                    help='About optional argument-1')
```

```
parser.add_argument('--my_oparg2', type=int, default=0,
                                        help='About optional argument-2')

args = parser.parse_args()


print([args.myarg1, args.myarg2,args.my_oparg1,args.my_oparg2])

#--------------End of file mycodefile.py--------------------

# -----Below is the Command entered on command prompt
python mycodefile.py   5 Hello
```

Output:
[5, 'Hello', 'myDefaultData', 0]

Explanation:
Only two arguments are compulsory here. If optional arguments are not provided, its default value are taken automatically.

Ex.14
```
#--------- Contents of mycodefile.py ------------
--Same as mentioned in  |Ex.13|
#--------------End of file mycodefile.py--------------------

# -----Below is the Command entered on command prompt
python mycodefile.py  --my_oparg1=Welcome 5 Hello
```

Output:
[5, 'Hello', 'Welcome', 0]

Explanation:
Compulsory arguments are positional but optional arguments are not positional. Optional arguments can be provide in any order by putting its name with double hyphen (--).

4.2 Formatted String Output

Formatted string output in Python refers to the practice of generating strings that include dynamic content, such as variables or expressions, formatted in a specific way. Python provides several methods for creating formatted strings, which include:

4.2.1 f-strings

Method *f-strings* has been introduced in Python 3.6. It provide easy interpolation of variables and expressions within a string literal by prefixing the string with '*f*' or '*F*' and enclosing the expressions in curly braces { }. This concise and readable syntax makes it simple to embed variables directly into strings without the need for complex concatenation or formatting functions.

Ex.15
```
name = "Rishabh"
age = 13

message = f"Hello, {name}. You are {age} years old."

print(message)
```

Output:
Hello, Rishabh. You are 13 years old.

Explanation:
data of variable *{name}* and *{age}* are concatenated in `f-string` to form the message.

4.2.2 str.format()

This method allows you to insert values into a string by specifying placeholders { } and then passing the values as arguments to the format() method. **.format()** method is applied on a string variable like `string_variable.format()` and all the {} in *string_variable* is replaced by the data passed in *.format()*.

Ex.16
```
name = "Rishabh"
age = 13

message = "Hello, {}. You are {} years old.".format(name, age)

print(message)
```

Output:
Hello, Rishabh. You are 13 years old.

Explanation:
Arguments are passed in *format() method* separated by comma. These data are placed in the string at the place of {} in ordered way.

4.2.3 string.Template

The `string.Template` class provides a simple and safe way to perform string interpolation. It uses dollar sign (**$**) prefixed placeholders and a substitute() method to replace them with values.

Ex.17
```
from string import Template
name = "Rishabh"
age = 13

template = Template("Hello, $myname. You are $myage years old.")
message = template.substitute(myname=name, myage=age)
print(message)
```

Output:
Hello, Rishabh. You are 13 years old.

Explanation:
We can format string message through `string.Template` class by calling `substitute()` method.

PART II

CORE PYTHON CONCEPTS

5. Control Flow

Control flow in a computer programming language dictates the direction and execution of code, empowering developers to craft intricate algorithms and applications. Python offers a versatile array of control statements, enabling programmers to dictate the flow of execution based on conditions, loops, and function calls. At its core, control flow facilitates decision-making within a program, allowing for dynamic responses to varying inputs and circumstances. Whether it's making decisions based on specific conditions, iterating over collections of data, or defining the scope of execution within functions, Python's control statements provide the necessary tools to navigate the complexities of software development. From the foundational if-else statements to the iterative power of loops such as for and while, Python's control flow mechanisms empower developers to craft elegant, efficient, and scalable solutions to a myriad of computational challenges.

5.1 Code Blocks and Indentation

A *code block* refers to a group of statements that are logically grouped together to perform a specific task within a program. In Python, code blocks are defined by control flow structures such as loops, conditional statements, and function definitions. For example, in an **'if'** statement, the code block consists of the statements that are executed if the condition evaluates to true. Similarly, in a loop like **'for'** or **'while'**, the code block contains the statements that are executed repeatedly for each iteration of the loop. *Indentation*, on the other hand, is the practice of starting each line of code within a code block with a consistent amount of *whitespace* (usually *spaces* or *tabs*). In Python, indentation is not just a stylistic choice but a fundamental aspect of the language's syntax.

In summary, while *code blocks* represent logical groupings of statements within a program, *indentation* is the visual representation of the structure of these code blocks, indicating their hierarchical relationship and ensuring proper interpretation by the Python interpreter.

Programming Languages Like *ALGOL*, *Pascal* uses the **begin** and **end** keywords to mark the beginning and end of a code block. Programming Languages like *C*, *Java*, *JavaScript* use *curly braces { }* to denote code blocks. Unlike these programming languages, Python relies solely on indentation to define the scope and hierarchy of code. This design decision was made to promote code readability and enforce a consistent coding style across projects. The indentation level in Python typically consists of *four spaces*, although *tabs* can also be used. However, it's essential to maintain consistency within a codebase, as mixing tabs and spaces can lead to confusion and errors. Python's interpreter is designed to be strict about indentation, meaning that incorrect indentation will result in syntax errors or unexpected behavior.

5.2 if Statement

The *if statement* is a fundamental control structure used to execute a block of code conditionally. It allows a program to make decisions based on whether a specified condition evaluates to **True** or **False**.

5.2.1 if Syntax

The basic syntax of the **if statement** in Python consists of 4 parts:

1. **if**
   The keyword `if` is used to declare a if syntax.
2. **Condition**
   After `if`, a condition is written which may evaluate to **True** or **False**. Condition may be written directly of in small brackets.
3. **Colon (:)**
   After Condition, a colon is written to complete the *if statement.*
4. **Code Block**
   After writing `if` statement (**if condition :**) a new line is entered and one line or multi-line code block is written with uniform indention (1 space, 2 space, 4 spaces, 1 tab, 2 tab, etc.) as per programmer's choice. All the lines of codeblock under if statements should be given same indention as per programmer's choice. But mixing different type of indention will give *IndentationError*.

Ex.1
```
x = 5
if x>0 :
print('Hello World')
```

Output:
Syntax Error

Explanation:
Indention block is expected in line no 3 after colon (:) in line no 2. As there is no indention provided, it gives Syntax Error "**IndentationError: expected an indented block after 'if' statement on line 2**".

Ex.2
```
x = 5
if x>0 :
        print('Hello-1')
    print('Hello-2')
print('Hello-3')
```

Output:
Syntax Error

Explanation:
Line number 3 is correct as if statement expect indention in next line. But indention in line no. 4 is ambiguous, it is not clear that line no. 5 is with code block of `if` statement or is outside of `if` code block. It happens because indention is not uniform. Either indention of line no. 4 should be as of line no. 2 or it's indention should be that of line no. 1,2,5.

Ex.3
```
x = 5
if x >10 :
        print('Hello-1')
        print('Hello-2')
print('Hello-3')
```

Output:
Hello-3

Explanation:
Here condition given with `if` statement gives result *False*, so code block of line no. 3 and line no. 4 will not execute. It will execute only line no. 5.

Ex.4
```
x = 5
if x <10 :
        print('Hello-1')
        print('Hello-2')
print('Hello-3')
```

Output:
Hello-3

Explanation:
Here condition given with `if` statement gives result *True*, so code block of line no. 3 and line no. 4 will be executed followed by execution of line no. 5.

5.2.2 if .... else

To execute different blocks of code based on some condition, the `if-else` statement is used. Out of provided two code blocks, only one code block is executed. If condition is true then code block written under `if`, is executed and if condition is `False`, the code block written under `else` is executed. The basic syntax of the **if-else statement** in Python consists of 6 parts:

1. **if**
   The keyword `if` is used to declare a if syntax.
2. **Condition**
   After `if`, a condition is written which may evaluate to **True** or **False**. Condition may be written directly of in small brackets.
3. **Colon (:)**
   After Condition, a colon is written to complete the *if statement.*
4. **Code Block-1**
   After writing `if` statement (**if condition :**) a new line is entered and one line or multi-line code block is written with uniform indention (1 space, 2 space, 4 spaces, 1 tab, 2 tab, etc.) as per programmer's choice.
5. **else :**
   The text `else :` is written in new line just after code block-1. Its indent should be matched with that of `if` statement.
6. **Code Block-2**
   After writing `else :` statement, a new line is entered and one line or multi-line code block is written with uniform indention as per programmer's choice.

Note: It is to be noted that indention of code block -1 and code block -2 to may or may not equal. The indention of `if statement` and indention of `else statement` must be equal.

Ex.5
```
x = 5
if x >10 :
        print('Hello-1')
        else:
        print('Hello-3')
```

Output:
Invalid Syntax Error

Explanation:
The `else:` statement in line no 4 is written in code block of `if` statement. In this code block else is written without any `if` statement inside this code block. Therefore due to wrong indention, it becomes *Invalid Syntax Error*.

Ex.6
```
x = 5
if x % 2 == 0 :
        print('x is Even number')
else:
        print('x is Odd number')
```

Output:
x is Odd number

Explanation:
When 5 is divided by two, its reminder is 1, so *x % 2* is 1. Now `(x % 2 == 0)` becomes **False**, so Code block of `else statement` will only be executed.

5.2.3 elif

In Python, the `elif` statement, short for `"else if"`, is used to introduce additional conditional statements following an initial *if statement*. When the condition specified in the *if statement* evaluates to *False*, the program proceeds to check the conditions specified in one or more `elif` statements. If any of these conditions evaluate to *True*, the corresponding block of code associated with that `elif` statement is executed.
The `elif` statement allows for the creation of more complex decision-making structures in Python code.

Ex.7
```
score = 85

if score >= 90:
    grade = "A1"
elif score >= 80:
    grade = "A2"
elif score >= 70:
    grade = "B1"
elif score >= 60:
    grade = "B2"
elif score >= 50:
    grade = "C"
elif score >= 40:
    grade = "D"
```

```
else:
    grade = "F"

print("Your grade is:", grade)
```

Output:
Your grade is: A2

Explanation:
The First The `elif statement` gives **True** on execution.

Ex.8
```
score = 65

if score >= 90:
    grade = "A1"
elif score >= 80:
    grade = "A2"
elif score >= 70:
    grade = "B1"

print("Your grade is:", grade)
```

Output:
NameError: name 'grade' is not defined

Explanation:
All the condition gave result *False*, so none of the code block from `if` or `else` got executed. So variable never got initialized, resulting error showing variable *grade* is not defined.

5.3 For Loop

The *for loop* is a powerful construct used to iterate over elements in a sequence. It can also be iterated through any iterable object, such as lists, tuples, strings, or dictionaries.

5.3.1 Iteration Over a Sequence

Iteration over a sequence allows us to access each element within a collection such as a list, tuple, or string, and perform operations on them sequentially. The syntax for this type of iteration is:

1. **for**
   The keyword `for` is used to mark the beginning of a for loop.
2. **loop variable**
   After `for`, a *loop variable* is written that represents each element in the sequence. It can be any valid variable name chosen by the programmer.
3. **in**
   The keyword *in* is written after *loop variable*. It indicate the sequence being iterated over.

4. **Sequence**
   After keyword `in`, the sequence variable is written, which refers to any iterable object containing multiple elements
5. **:**
   After the sequence variable, a colon (:) is written to indicate start of *Loop code block* under the *for* loop.
6. **Loop Block**
   After writing `else :` statement, a new line is entered and one line or multi-line Loop block is written with uniform indention as per programmer's choice.

Ex.9
```
fruits = ["apple", "banana", "orange"]
for fruit in fruits:
    print("I Like ",fruit)
```

Output:
I Like apple
I Like banana
I Like orange

Explanation:
One element of sequence variable *fruits*, is stored in variable *fruit* in each iteration of *for* loop. The loop is iterated for each element of the sequence variable *fruits*.

5.3.2 Using Range Function

Range Function is used to generate a sequence of numbers. The syntax of the range() function in Python is as follows:
`range(start, stop, step)`

- **start (optional):**
  Specifies the starting value of the sequence (inclusive). If omitted, it defaults to 0.
- **stop:**
  Specifies the stopping value of the sequence (exclusive). The sequence will end before reaching this value.
- **step (optional):**
  Specifies the increment (or decrement if negative) between each value in the sequence. If omitted, it defaults to 1.

Using the *range()* function in a *for loop* is a common technique in Python for iterating over a sequence of numbers. The range() function generates a sequence of numbers according to the specified parameters, allowing for flexible control over the range of values to iterate through. The syntax of for loop using range function is:

1. **for**
   The keyword `for` is used to mark the beginning of a for loop.

2. **loop variable**
   After `for`, a *loop variable* is written that represents each value generated by the range() function during iteration. It can be any valid variable name chosen by the programmer.
3. **in**
   The keyword *in* is written after *loop variable.* It indicate the sequence being iterated over.
4. **range()**
   After keyword `in`, the range function is written to generate a sequence of number.
5. **:**
   After the range function, a colon (`:`) is written to indicate start of *Loop code block* under the *for* loop.
6. **Loop Block**
   After writing `else :` statement, a new line is entered and one line or multi-line Loop block is written with uniform indention as per programmer's choice.

Ex.10
```
for i in range(6):
    print(i)
```

Output:
0
1
2
3
4
5

Explanation:
range(5) is equivalent to range(0,6,1) which will generate numbers starting from 0 with step of 1 and up to before reaching 6 (i.e. 0, 1, 2, 3, 4, 5).

Ex.11
```
for i in range(-2,1,5):
    print(i)
```

Output:
-2

Explanation:
range(-2, 1, 5) will generate numbers starting from -2 with step of 5 and up to before reaching 1 (i.e. -2).

5.3.3 Iterating Over Dictionary Keys

Iterating over dictionary keys in a for loop in Python allows programmers to access each key within a dictionary and perform operations based on those keys. The syntax of for loop using

Iterating Over Dictionary Keys is:

1. **for**
   The keyword `for` is used to mark the beginning of a for loop.
2. **loop variable**
   After `for`, a *loop variable* is written that represents each each key in the dictionary during iteration. It can be any valid variable name chosen by the programmer.
3. **in**
   The keyword *in* is written after *loop variable.* It indicate the sequence being iterated over.
4. **dictionary**
   After keyword `in`, a dictionary variable (containing key-value pairs) is written whose keys are being iterated over.
5. **:**
   After dictionary, a colon (`:`) is written to indicate start of *Loop code block* under the *for* loop.
6. **Loop Block**
   After writing `else :` statement, a new line is entered and one line or multi-line Loop block is written with uniform indention as per programmer's choice.

Ex.12
```
stateleader_age = {"Biden": 81, "Gabriel Attal": 35, "Modi": 73}

leader_name=""
leader_age=0;

for name in stateleader_age:
    if stateleader_age[name] > leader_age:
        leader_age = stateleader_age[name]
        leader_name = name

print(leader_name)
```

Output: Biden

Explanation:
Each key of the dictionary is taken at a time in iteration and its key value is checked. If it is greater than the value of variable *leader_agethat*, then its *key name* and *age* is stored in the variables `leader_name` and `leader_age` respectively. In this way oldest leader is searched from this dictionary through the for loop.

5.3.4 Iterating Over Dictionary Items

Iterating over dictionary items in Python *for* loop provides a convenient way to access both keys and values simultaneously within a dictionary. It involves using the `for` keyword followed by two loop variables separated by a comma, the `in` keyword, and the dictionary whose items are to be iterated over. During each iteration, the first loop variable represents the keys, while the second loop variable represents the corresponding values from the dictionary. This allows programmers to access both keys and values within the loop block and perform operations based on each key-value pair. The syntax of for loop, iterating over dictionary items, is:

1. **for**
   The keyword `for` is used to mark the beginning of a for loop.
2. **loop variables**
   After `for`, *Two loop variables*, (separated by comma), are written that represents each key in the dictionary during iteration.
3. **in**
   The keyword *in* is written after *loop variable.* It indicate the sequence being iterated over.
4. **dictionary**
   After keyword `in`, a dictionary variable (containing key-value pairs) is written whose key-value pairs are being iterated over.
5. **:**
   After dictionary, a colon (`:`) is written to indicate start of *Loop code block* under the *for* loop.
6. **Loop Block**
   After writing `else :` statement, a new line is entered and one line or multi-line Loop block is written with uniform indention as per programmer's choice.

Ex.13
```
stateleader_age = {"Biden": 81, "Gabriel Attal": 35, "Modi": 73}

leader_name=""
leader_age=0;
for name, age in stateleader_age.items():
    if age > leader_age:
        leader_age = age
        leader_name = name

print(leader_name)
```

Output: Biden

Explanation:
We iterate over the `stateleader_age` dictionary using the *items()* method, which returns key-value pairs as *tuples.* We then unpack each tuple into `name` and `age` variables, allowing us to access both keys and values within the loop block.

Ex.14
```
stateleader_age = {"Biden": 81, "Gabriel Attal": 35, "Modi": 73}

sum_age=0;
for age in stateleader_age.values():
    sum_age = sum_age + age
```

```
agerage = sum_age / len(stateleader_age)
print("Average Age is ",agerage)
```

Output: Average Age is 63.0

Explanation:
Here, we iterate over the `stateleader_age` dictionary using the *values()* method, which returns the values of the dictionary. We then sum up all the values to calculate the sum of ages which is latter divided by no of items in dictionary to calculate average age.

5.3.5 Iterating Over Enumerating Elements

Enumerating elements in a *for* loop in Python allows for accessing both the index and value of each element in a sequence simultaneously. This is particularly useful when you need to keep track of the index while iterating over a list or any other *iterable object.* The syntax involves using the *enumerate()* function within the for loop, which generates a tuple containing the index and the corresponding value for each element in the sequence. The syntax of for loop, iterating over enumerating elements, is:

1. **for**
   The keyword `for` is used to mark the beginning of a for loop.
2. **loop variables**
   After `for`, *Two loop variables*, (separated by comma), are written that represents each key in the dictionary during iteration.
3. **in**
   The keyword *in* is written after *loop variable.* It indicate the sequence being iterated over.
4. **enumerate()**
   After keyword `in`, a enumerate() function is written with an iterable object as argument. It is used to generate an index-value pair for each element in the sequence.
5. **:**
   After *enumerate()* function, a colon (:) is written to indicate start of *Loop code block* under the *for* loop.
6. **Loop block**
   After writing `else :` statement, a new line is entered and one line or multi-line Loop block is written with uniform indention as per programmer's choice.

Ex.15
```
fruits = ["apple", "banana", "orange"]

for index, fruit in enumerate(fruits):
    print("Index:", index, "Fruit:", fruit)
```

Output:
Index: 0 Fruit: apple
Index: 1 Fruit: banana
Index: 2 Fruit: orangeBiden

Explanation:
During each iteration, the *enumerate()* function generates a tuple containing the index of the current element and the element itself. The loop variables *index* and *fruit* represent the index and value of each element in the fruits list, respectively.
This approach allows us to iterate over the fruits list while simultaneously accessing both the index and value of each fruit, facilitating tasks such as data manipulation or processing based on the position or value of the elements in the list.

5.4 FOR...ELSE Loop

In Python, the `for...else` loop is a unique construct that combines the functionality of a for loop with an optional `else` block that executes if the loop completes normally, without encountering a `break` statement. The syntax of the `for...else` loop is similar to that of a regular `for` loop, with an additional `else` block following the loop body. Here's the general syntax:

```
for item in iterable:
    # Loop body
    # Perform some operations

else:
   # Else block
   # Execute if the loop completes without encountering a 'break' statement
```

The `for...else` loop iterates over each item in the specified iterable, executing the loop body for each iteration. If the loop completes all iterations without encountering a `break` statement, the `else` block is executed. However, if a `break` statement is encountered during the loop execution, the `else` block is skipped.

Ex.16
```
numbers = [1, 2, 3, 4, 5]

for num in numbers:
    if num == 0:
        print("Zero encountered. Exiting loop.")
        break
    print(num)
else:
    print("Loop completed without encountering zero.")
```

Output:
1
2
3
4
5
Loop completed without encountering zero.

Explanation:
While executing the *for loop*, the `break` statement never executed, resulting execution of `else` block too.

5.5 While Loop

`while` loop in python provides a powerful mechanism for executing a block of code *repeatedly until a certain condition becomes false.* As long as this condition evaluates to true, the code block within the loop will continue to execute. One must be cautious to ensure that the condition will eventually become false to avoid an infinite loop. Syntax of a while loop in Python is:

- **while**
  The keyword `while` is used to mark the beginning of a while loop.
- **condition**
  After *while* keyword a condition expression is written that determines whether to continue the loop (evaluates to either True or False).
- **:**
  After *condition*, a colon (`:`) is written to indicate start of *Loop code block* under the *while* loop.
- **Loop block**
  After writing *colon* (:), a new line is entered and one line or multi-line Loop block is written with uniform indention as per programmer's choice.

Note: Remember to update the variables or conditions within the loop to ensure the condition eventually becomes False and the loop exits, preventing an infinite loop.

Ex.17
```
count = 0
while count < 5:
    print("Count is:", count)
    count += 1

print("Loop finished!")
```

Output:
Count is: 0

Count is: 1
Count is: 2
Count is: 3
Count is: 4
Loop finished!

Explanation:
The *while* loop will run for value of variable `count` as 0, 1, 2, 3, 4. When the value of variable `count` will reach 5, the condition will return *false* and the loop will break.

Ex.18
```
# Print Prime Numbers
prime_numbers=[2]
max_number=50
current_number=3
while current_number <= max_number :
    is_prime = True
    for prime_number in prime_numbers:
        if current_number % prime_number == 0 :
            is_prime = False
            break
    if is_prime :
        prime_numbers.append(current_number)
    current_number = current_number +1
print(prime_numbers)
```

Output:
[2, 3, 5, 7, 11, 13, 17, 19, 23, 29, 31, 37, 41, 43, 47]

Explanation:
The above code will print all prime numbers less than on equal to 50.
A list of prime numbers has been created (variable name `prime_numbers` with initial value of first prime number, 2. All the numbers starting from 3, and upto 50 is being checked through `while` loop. The current number is checked by dividing through prime numbers (using `for` loop), and if it is divisible (i.e. reminder is zero) through `if` condition. If it is not divisible by any prime number less than the current number then the current number is added into list of prime numbers (`prime_numbers`) otherwise it is declared as non prime number and checked for next number. At the end of code all prime numbers is printed.

Note: This code may be optimized by checking the divisibility upto only half the value of current number.

5.6 Loop Control Statements

Loop control statements in Python provide programmers with the ability to control the flow of execution within loops. These statements include *break*, *continue*, and *pass*. Loop control statements are essential for enhancing the flexibility and efficiency of loops, enabling developers to tailor the loop's behavior based on specific requirements. They provide greater control over program flow, improve code readability, and facilitate the implementation of complex algorithms and logic within loops.

5.6.1 break

The `break` statement in Python is a control flow statement that is used to terminate the execution of a loop prematurely. When encountered within a loop (such as a `for` or `while` loop), the `break` statement causes the loop to immediately exit, regardless of the loop's remaining iterations. This is particularly useful when a certain condition is met during the execution of the loop, and further iterations are no longer necessary. By using the `break` statement, programmers can efficiently exit the loop and continue with the rest of the program's execution. This helps in improving the efficiency and readability of the code by avoiding unnecessary iterations. Additionally, the break statement can be used in nested loops to exit multiple levels of looping simultaneously.

Ex.19
```
names = ["India", "Nepal", "SriLanka", "Bangladesh", "Pak"]
search_name = "Nepal"
loop_count=0
for name in names:
    loop_count = loop_count+1
    if name == search_name:
        print("Name found:", name)
        break
print(f"Loop runs {loop_count} times")
```

Output:
Name found: Nepal
Loop runs 2 times

Explanation:
As soon as the word *Nepal* found, *Break* statement is executed and exited from the loop. So the loop count is 2.

Ex.20
```
names = ["India", "Nepal", "SriLanka", "Bangladesh", "Pak"]
search_name = "Sri Lanka"
loop_count=0
for name in names:
```

```
        loop_count = loop_count+1
        if name == search_name:
            print("Name found:", name)
            break
    print(f"Loop runs {loop_count} times")
```

Output:
Loop runs 5 times

Explanation:
Until search is not found or all the items searched out. As no search found, *break* statement is not executed. So the loop will run 5 times.

5.6.2 continue

The `continue` statement in Python is a control flow statement that is used to skip the rest of the code within a loop for the current iteration and proceed to the next iteration. When encountered within a loop (such as a `for` or `while` loop), the `continue` statement causes the loop to jump to the next iteration, bypassing any remaining code within the loop block. This is particularly useful when certain conditions are met during the execution of the loop, and you want to skip the current iteration without exiting the loop entirely. Table 5.1 explain the difference between `break` and `continue` statement with example.

Ex.21
```
for num in range(1, 11):
    if num == 6:
        continue  # Skip printing 6 and proceed to the next iteration
    if num % 2 == 0:
        print(num)
```

Output:
2
4
8
10

Explanation:
The *continue* statement escape the code below the continue statement withing the loop.

5.6.3 pass

The *pass* statement in Python is a null operation, meaning it performs no action when executed. It is primarily used as a placeholder where syntactically required but no action is needed. The *pass* statement allows the programmer to create empty code blocks or placeholder functions without causing any syntax errors. It is commonly used in situations where the programmer intends to add functionality later but wants to keep the code structure intact in the meantime. The *pass* statement does not alter the program's behavior and is effectively a no-op. It is

Table 5.1: Comparison between `break` and `continue` statements in Python

Feature	`break` **Statement**	`continue` **Statement**
Purpose	Terminates the loop prematurely.	Skips the current iteration of the loop.
Effect	Exits the loop immediately when encountered.	Jumps to the next iteration of the loop.
Usage	Typically used when a specific condition is met and further iterations are unnecessary.	Typically used to skip certain iterations based on specific conditions.
Application	Used to exit the loop when a certain condition is met, regardless of the loop's remaining iterations.	Used to skip the current iteration of the loop and proceed to the next iteration.
Control Flow	Breaks out of the loop entirely.	Skips the remaining code in the current iteration and continues with the next iteration.

Example	for i in range(10):
	    if i == 5:
	        break
	    print(i)
		for i in range(10):
		    if i == 5:
		        continue
		    print(i)

Output	0 1 2 3 4	0 1 2 3 4 6 7 8 9

particularly useful when defining classes, functions, or conditional statements where the body of the block is not yet implemented but needs to be syntactically valid.

- The pass statement is a null statement.
- The difference between a comment and a pass statement in Python is that while the interpreter ignores a comment entirely, pass is not ignored.
- The pass statement does nothing.

Ex.22
```
def placeholder_function():
    pass
```

Explanation:
It defines a function that does nothing.

Ex.23
```
class EmptyClass:
    pass
```

Explanation: It defines an empty class.

Ex.24
```
x = 10
if x < 5:
    pass  # No action is taken if x is less than 5
```

```
else:
    print("x is greater than or equal to 5")
```

Output:
x is greater than or equal to 5
Explanation:
It define a conditional statement with no action.

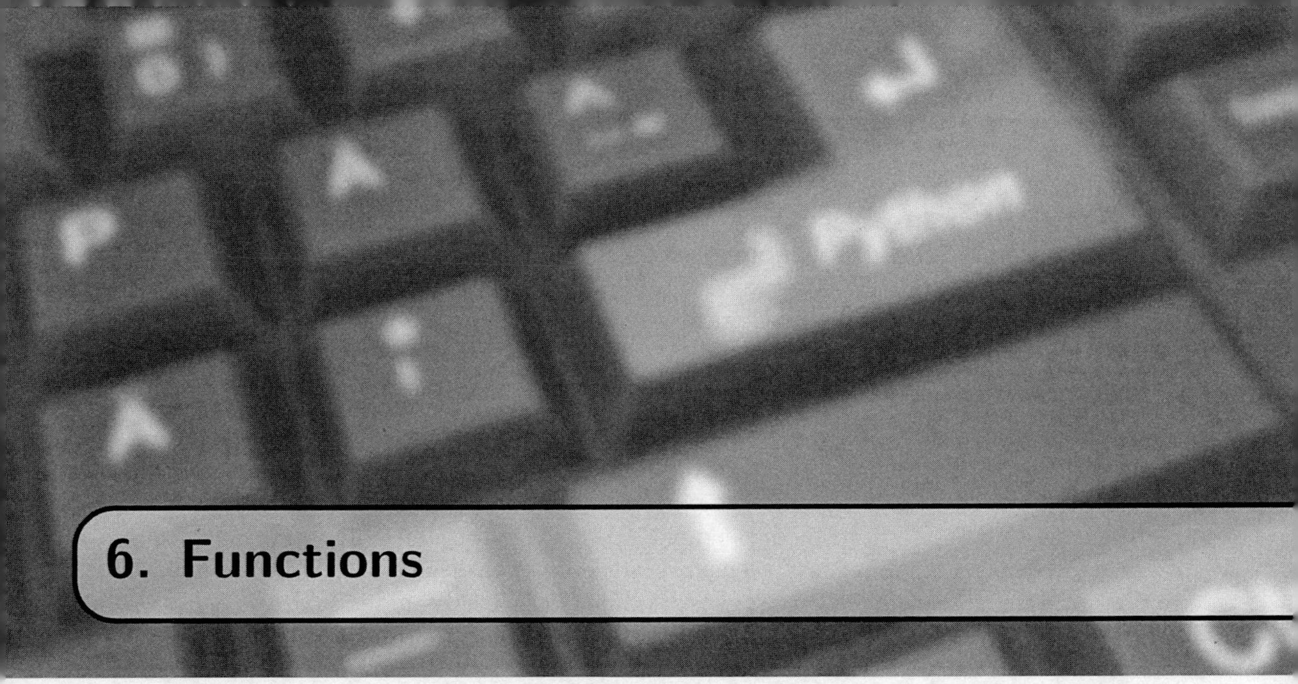

6. Functions

Functions is a fundamental aspect of programming that empowers you to write efficient, reusable, and organized code. Functions serve as building blocks, encapsulating specific tasks or operations that can be executed with a single call. Mastering functions is essential for enhancing code readability, promoting code reuse, and facilitating modular design.

6.1 Introduction to Functions

Functions stand as essential tools for organizing code and streamlining the execution of specific tasks. At their core, functions are encapsulated blocks of code designed to perform a particular operation when called upon. They serve as a means to modularize code, breaking down complex tasks into smaller, more manageable units. Functions not only enhance code readability by providing a clear structure but also promote reusability, allowing developers to leverage existing functionality across different parts of their programs. Whether it's performing arithmetic calculations, processing data, or implementing algorithms, understanding the fundamentals of functions is pivotal for any Python programmer.

6.1.1 What are Functions?

Functions in Python are self-contained blocks of code designed to perform a specific task or set of tasks. They encapsulate a series of instructions, often accepting input parameters and producing output. By defining functions, programmers can modularize their code, breaking it down into smaller, more manageable units. This modular approach enhances code organization and readability, making it easier to understand and maintain complex programs. Functions can be called multiple times throughout a program, allowing for code reuse and minimizing redundancy. In essence, functions serve as the building blocks of Python programs, enabling developers to structure their code in a logical and efficient manner.

6.1.2 Why are Functions Important in Python Programming?

Functions play a crucial role in Python programming for several reasons. Firstly, they promote code reuse, allowing developers to write a function once and call it whenever needed, rather than duplicating the same code in multiple places. This not only saves time and effort but also reduces the chances of errors and inconsistencies. Secondly, functions enhance code readability by providing a clear and concise way to encapsulate specific tasks. By giving meaningful names to functions and documenting their purpose, developers can easily understand the functionality of different parts of a program. Finally, functions facilitate modular design, enabling developers to break down complex problems into smaller, more manageable components. This modular approach promotes code organization and maintainability, making it easier to add new features or make changes to existing code without affecting other parts of the program.

6.1.3 Advantages of Using Functions

There are several advantages to using functions in Python programming. One major advantage is code reusability, as functions allow developers to encapsulate common tasks and reuse them throughout their programs. This not only saves time and effort but also promotes consistency and reduces the chances of errors. Additionally, functions enhance code readability by providing a clear structure and allowing developers to give meaningful names to different parts of their code. This makes it easier for other developers to understand and maintain the code. Furthermore, functions promote modular design, enabling developers to break down complex problems into smaller, more manageable components. This modular approach facilitates code organization and makes it easier to test and debug individual parts of the program. Overall, functions are a powerful tool in Python programming that helps developers write cleaner, more efficient, and more maintainable code.

6.2 Defining Functions

In a Python program, function is required to define ones and then it may be called one or many times, when ever required. Understanding how to define a function is crucial for any developer, as it enables the creation of reusable and modular code.

6.2.1 Structure of a Function

A function in Python is defined using the **def** keyword followed by the *function name* and *parentheses.* Within the parentheses, parameters (also known as arguments) may be specified to accept input values. The *function body*, containing the code to be executed when the function is called, *indented beneath the function definition.* Proper indentation is essential in Python to denote the scope of the function. Syntax of Function Definition is:

- **def**
  This keyword indicates the start of a function definition.
- **function_name**
  After keyword *def*, the name of function is written. The Function should follow Python naming convention as outlined in PEP 8 (see 3.2 in page no. 23).
- **parentheses**
  After *function name*, a parenthesis is essentially required. Within the parenthesis, parameter names (also known as arguments) may be specified to accept input values.
- **Colon :**
  After parenthesis, a colon is placed. The colon denotes the end of the function header and the start of the function body. It marks the end of the function header.
- **Function body**
  The function body is indented beneath the function definition. It contains the code to be executed when the function is called.
- **return**
  Optional statement used to return a value from the function back to the caller.

6.2.2 Calling a Function

Calling a Python function involves invoking the function to execute its defined code block with specified arguments, if any. Once a function is defined, it can be called from another function or directly from the Python prompt. The defined function can be called by simply typing the function name with appropriate parameters. Furthermore, Python supports the concept of default argument values, allowing functions to be called without specifying all parameters explicitly.

Ex.1
```
def myfunction(number):
    reminder = number % 2
    if(reminder==1):
        print(f"Number {number} is Odd Number")
    else:
        print(f"Number {number} is Even Number")

myfunction(15)
```

Output:
Number 15 is Odd Number

Explanation:
The syntax `myfunction(15)` call the function defined above with parameter value 15 which will become value of variable `number = 15` .

6.2.3 Docstring

Docstring is description of the function's purpose, usage, and any additional information. It is enclosed in triple quotes ("““ ”””). Writing descriptive and informative *docstrings* is essential for documenting functions effectively, enabling other developers (including future you!) to understand their functionality without inspecting the implementation details. They provide important information about how to use a function or module, including details about parameters, return values, and any exceptions that may be raised.

Accessing Docstrings

Python provides built-in functions and modules for accessing docstrings:

- **help()**: When called with the name of a function or module as an argument, `help()` prints the *docstring* associated with that function or module.
  E.g. `help(function_name)`
- **__doc__** : Every function and module in Python has a __doc__attribute that contains its *docstring.* You can access this attribute directly to retrieve the docstring programmatically. E.g. `function_name.__doc__`.

Ex.2
```
def add(x, y):
    """
    Add two numbers together.
    Args:
        x (int): The first number.
        y (int): The second number.
    Returns:
        int: The sum of x and y.
    """
    return x + y

print(add.__doc__)
```

Output:
Add two numbers together.

Args:
    x (int): The first number.
    y (int): The second number.

Returns:
    int: The sum of x and y.

Explanation:
The `__doc__` contains the *docstring* of a function.

Ex.3
```
#-------------------------------------
-- Function definition same as given in |\ref{item:docstringexample}|
#-------------------------------------

print(add.__doc__)
```

Output:
Help on function add in module ___main___:
add(x, y)
Add two numbers together.

Args:
    x (int): The first number.
    y (int): The second number.

Returns:
    int: The sum of x and y.

Explanation:
The `__doc__` contains the *docstring* of a function.

6.3 Function Arguments

Function parameters are the input values that are passed to a function when it is called. They allow functions to accept data from the caller, perform operations on that data, and optionally return results back to the caller. Python supports various types of function parameters, including positional parameters, keyword parameters, default parameters, variable-length parameters, and keyword-only parameters.

6.3.1 Positional Parameters

Positional parameters are the most basic type of parameters in Python. They are defined in the function signature and correspond to the order in which arguments are passed during a function call. When calling a function with positional parameters, the values are matched to the parameters based on their position.

- Positional arguments are arguments that need to be included in the proper position or order.
- The first positional argument always needs to be listed first when the function is called.
- The second positional argument needs to be listed second and the third positional argument listed third, etc.

Ex.4
```
def greet(name, message):
    print(f"Hello, {name}! {message}")
```

```
# Calling the function with positional arguments
greet("Rishabh", "How are you?")
```

Output:
Hello, Rishabh! How are you?

Explanation:
First argument passed during calling the function is mapped with the first parameter defined in the function, And 2nd argument passed during calling the function is mapped with the 2nd parameter defined in the function.

Ex.5
```
def cylinder_volume(radius, height):
    vol = 3.14 * radius * radius * height
    print(f"Raduis={radius}, Height={height}, and Volume = {vol}")

# Calling the function with positional arguments
cylinder_volume(5, 4)
```

Output:
Raduis=5, Height=4, and Volume = 314.0

Explanation:
First argument passed during calling the function is mapped with the first parameter defined in the function, And 2nd argument passed during calling the function is mapped with the 2nd parameter defined in the function.

6.3.2 Keyword Parameters

Keyword parameters allow specifying arguments by their parameter names during a function call, regardless of their order. This makes the function call more readable and explicit.

- Keyword argument is passed to a function by a keyword and an equals sign.
- Keyword arguments may be given in function call after one or more positional arguments.
- A positional argument after keyword arguments will result in errors.

Ex.6
```
def cylinder_volume(radius, height):
    vol = 3.14 * radius * radius * height
    print(f"Raduis={radius}, Height={height}, and Volume = {vol}")

# Calling the function with positional arguments
cylinder_volume(height=5, radius=4)
```

Output:
Raduis=4, Height=5, and Volume = 251.2

Explanation:
While calling the function, keywords are used with the argument, so irrespective of position of argument in function definition, the arguments are directly matching with the keywords in function calling and function definition.

Ex.7
```
def calculate_total_price(item_price, quantity, discount_rate):
    """
    Calculate the total price of items after applying a discount.
    Args:
    - item_price (float): The price of a single item.
    - quantity (int): The number of items purchased.
    - discount_rate (float): The discount rate to be applied (in %).
    Returns:
    - float: The total price after applying the discount.
    """

    total_price = item_price * quantity
    discount_amount = total_price * (discount_rate / 100)
    total_price_after_discount = total_price - discount_amount
    return total_price_after_discount


total_price = calculate_total_price(100, quantity=5, discount_rate=20)
print("Total price after discount:", total_price)
```

Output:
Total price after discount: 400.0

Explanation:
First argument is positional argument as no keyword has been provided. So First argument is mapped with *item_price* in the defined function. 2nd and 3rd argument is provided with keyword so it is mapped with respective argument names in the defined function.

Ex.8
```
#------------------------------------
-- Function definition same as given in |\ref{item:functioncallexample}|
#------------------------------------
```

```
total_price = calculate_total_price(item_price=100, quantity=5, 20)
print("Total price after discount:", total_price)
```

Output:
Syntax Error : Positional argument follow keyword argument

Explanation:
A positional argument after keyword arguments result in errors.

6.3.3 Default Parameters

Default parameters have predefined values that are used, when the caller does not provide a value for those parameters, during the function call. They allow functions to be called with fewer arguments, as the default values are automatically used for any unspecified parameters.

- Function arguments can have default values.
- Default value can be provided to an argument by using the assignment operator (=)

Ex.9
```
def format_message(message, sender="Anonymous"):
    return f"{sender}: {message}"

message = format_message("Hello there!")
print(message)
```

Output:
Anonymous: Hello there!

Explanation:
In the function definition, the parameter `sender` has a default value. So at the time of calling this function, argument `sender` is optional. When no argument is provided, the default value is taken for parameter `sender`.

Ex.10
```
def format_message(message, sender="Anonymous"):
    return f"{sender}: {message}"

message = format_message("Hello there!", "Professor Xavier")
print(message)
```

Output:
Professor Xavier: Hello there!

Explanation:
In the function definition, the parameter `sender` has a default value, but at the time of calling this function, explicit argument has been provided so the value of parameter `sender` in function definition has been replaced by the value provided in function call.

6.3.4 Variable-Length Parameters

Variable-length parameters allow functions to accept an arbitrary number of arguments. In Python, this is achieved using *args for positional arguments and **kwargs for keyword arguments. These parameters collect all excess arguments into tuples or dictionaries, respectively. When using *args, any number of positional arguments can be passed to the function, which are then collected into a tuple within the function body. Similarly, **kwargs collects any number of keyword arguments into a dictionary, where the keys are the argument names and the values are the corresponding values passed during the function call. These parameters are particularly useful when the number of arguments to be passed to a function is unknown or variable, allowing the function to handle a wide range of inputs dynamically.

- Variable-length parameters are indicated by using *args and **kwargs in the function signature.
- *args collects additional positional arguments into a *tuple*, while **kwargs collects additional keyword arguments into a *dictionary.*
- Variable-length parameters can be combined with other parameters, but *they must come after regular parameters* in the function signature.
- It's a best practice to use meaningful parameter names when using **kwargs to enhance code readability.
- When using variable-length parameters, ensure clear documentation to indicate their usage and expected behavior.

Ex.11
```
def print_args(*args):
    for arg in args:
        print(arg)

print_args("Hello", "World", "!")
```

Output:
Hello
World
!

Explanation:
The three positional arguments passed during function call is stored in tuple `arg`.

Ex.12
```
def myfunction(**kwargs):
    for key, value in kwargs.items():
```

```
        print(f"{key}: {value}")

myfunction(name="Alice", age=30, city="New York")
```

Output:
name: Alice
age: 30
city: New York

Explanation:
The three keyword arguments arguments passed during function call is stored in a dictionary `kwargs` which is latter printed through *for* loop.

Ex.13
```
import math
def calculate_area(shape, **kwargs):
    if shape == 'rectangle':
        width = kwargs.get('width', 0)
        height = kwargs.get('height', 0)
        return width * height
    elif shape == 'square':
        side = kwargs.get('side', 0)
        return side ** 2
    elif shape == 'circle':
        radius = kwargs.get('radius', 0)
        return math.pi * radius ** 2
    else:
        return "Invalid shape"

print("Area of rectangle:", calculate_area('rectangle', width=5, height=3))
```

Output:
Area of rectangle: 15
Explanation:
The variable length keyword arguments are captured in function based on the value of argument *shape* and are calculated accordingly.

Ex.14
```
#------------------------------------
-- Function definition same as given in |Ex.13|
#------------------------------------

print("Area of circle:", calculate_area('circle', radius=2.5))
```

Output:
Area of circle: 19.634954084936208

Explanation:
The variable length keyword arguments are captured in function based on the value of argument *shape* and are calculated accordingly.

6.3.5 Keyword-Only Parameters

Keyword-only parameters force the caller to specify arguments using keyword syntax. They are defined after a single * in the function signature, indicating that all following parameters must be passed as keywords.

Ex.15
```
# Defining a function with keyword-only parameters
def greet(*, name, message):
    print(f"Hello, {name}! {message}")

greet(name="Alice", message="How are you?")
```

Output:
Hello, Alice! How are you?

Explanation:
This function can only be called as keyword-only parameter. It is explicitly declared in function definition through giving star (*) as first parameter.

Ex.16
```
# Defining a function with keyword-only parameters
def greet(*, name, message):
    print(f"Hello, {name}! {message}")

greet("Alice", "How are you?")
```

Output:
TypeError: greet() takes 0 positional arguments but 2 were given

Explanation:
This function can only be called as keyword-only parameter as it is explicitly declared in function definition through giving star (*) as first parameter.

6.4 Lambda Function

A *lambda* function in Python is a small anonymous function defined using the lambda keyword. It's called "*anonymous*" because it doesn't have a name like a regular function defined with the *def* keyword. Lambda functions are often used when you need a simple function for a short period of time and don't want to define a full-fledged function using def. The syntax of a lambda function is:

```
lambda arguments:  expression
```

- `lambda` keyword used to define a lambda function.
- `arguments` is the Comma-separated list of input parameters (similar to the arguments in a regular function).
- expression is a Single expression that defines the return value of the *lambda* function.

Lambda functions are often used for short, simple operations where defining a full function using `def` would be overkill or unnecessary. They are particularly useful in cases where a function is required as an argument to higher-order functions such as `map()`, `filter()`, or `sorted()`, or where a function needs to be defined inline for readability.

Ex.17
```
add = lambda x, y: x + y

print(add(5, 3))
```

Output:
8

Explanation:
Python created a *lambda* function named *add* that takes two parameters x and y and returns their sum x + y. The *lambda* function defined by `lambda x, y:  x + y` can be called similarly to a regular function.

Ex.18
```
# Lambda function to check if a string is a palindrome
is_palindrome = lambda s: s == s[::-1]

# Example usage
print(is_palindrome('radar'))
```

Output:
True

Explanation:
Here in lambda function, it is declared that string is compared with its reverse (s[::-1]), and will return result as True or False. This lambda function is called using `is_palindrome(1radar')` where string *'radar'* is passed as argument. The lambda function returns *True* as it is a palindrome.

Ex.19
```
people = [('Raju', 30), ('Mohan', 25), ('Khyati', 10), ('Aman', 40)]

sorted_people = sorted(people, key=lambda x: x[1])

print(sorted_people)
```

Output:
[('Khyati', 10), ('Mohan', 25), ('Raju', 30), ('Aman', 40)]

Explanation:
We specify a lambda function lambda `x: x[1]` as the key parameter to sorted(). This lambda function takes a tuple x and returns its second element (the age). The sorted() function sorts the people list based on the ages of the individuals, in ascending order.

Ex.20
```
people = [(`Aman', 40), (`Khyati', 10), (`Mohan', 25), (`Raju', 30)]

sorted_people = sorted(people, key=lambda x: x[0])

print(sorted_people)
```

Output:
[('Aman', 40), ('Khyati', 10), ('Mohan', 25), ('Raju', 30)]

Explanation:
We specify a lambda function lambda `x: x[0]` as the key parameter to sorted(). This lambda function takes a tuple x and returns its first element (the name). The sorted() function sorts the people list based on the name of the individuals, in ascending order.

Ex.21
```
# Lambda function to convert Celsius to Fahrenheit
celsius_to_fahrenheit = lambda celsius: (celsius * 9/5) + 32

celsius_temperatures = [0, 10, 20, 30, 40]
fahrenheit_temperatures = map(celsius_to_fahrenheit, celsius_temperatures)

print(list(fahrenheit_temperatures))
```

Output:
[32.0, 50.0, 68.0, 86.0, 104.0]

Explanation:
Here lambda function is defined as the formula of converting Celsius to Fahrenheit. The *map()* function is applied to the *lambda* function on each temperature in the

celsius_temperatures list. The *map()* function returns an iterator that applies the lambda function to each element of the input *celsius_temperatures*. Map function is explained in detail in section 6.6.

6.5 Filter Function

The *filter()* function in Python is a built-in function that is used to filter elements from an *iterable* (such as a list, tuple, or set) based on a specified condition. It takes two arguments: a function (or None) and an iterable. The function provided to filter() should return **True** or **False** for each element in the iterable. If the function returns True, the element is included in the filtered result; if it returns False, the element is excluded. Syntax of Filter function is:

```
filter(function_name, sequence)
```

- function_name is the name of function that tests whether each element of a sequence is true or not.
- sequence is the iterable data, which needs to be filtered. It can be sets, lists, tuples, or containers of any iterators.
- It returns an iterator that is already filtered.

Ex.22

```
def is_even(num):
    return num % 2 == 0

numbers = [1, 2, 3, 4, 5, 6, 7, 8, 9, 10]
filtered_numbers = filter(is_even, numbers)
filtered_numbers_list = list(filtered_numbers)

print(filtered_numbers_list)
```

Output:
[2, 4, 6, 8, 10]

Explanation:
The *filter* method pass all the data to the function and keep only those data in result which returns true on passing the data to the function. The *filter()* function effectively filtered out the even numbers from the original list, demonstrating its utility for selectively extracting elements from iterables based on specific criteria.

Ex.23

```
numbers = [1, 2, 3, 4, 5, 6, 7, 8, 9, 10]

even_numbers = filter(lambda x: x % 2 == 0, numbers)
```

```
even_numbers_list = list(even_numbers)

print("Even numbers:", even_numbers_list)
```

Output:
[2, 4, 6, 8, 10]

Explanation:
`lambda x: x % 2 == 0` is the lambda function which takes one argument (x) and checks if x is even `(x % 2 == 0)`. It returns True if the condition is satisfied (i.e., x is even) and False otherwise. This lambda function is passed as the first argument to the `filter()` function, along with the numbers list. The *filter()* function applies the lambda function to each element in the numbers list and includes only those elements for which the lambda function returns True.

6.6 Map Function

The **map()** function in Python is a built-in function that applies a specified function to each item in an iterable (such as a list) and returns a new iterable containing the results. It essentially transforms the elements of an iterable using a function provided as an argument. The *map()* function takes two parameters: the first parameter is the function to apply, and the second parameter is the iterable containing the elements to be transformed. The function provided can be a built-in function, a user-defined function, or even a lambda function. The *map()* function returns an iterator, which can be converted to other iterable types like a list, tuple, or set using functions like list(), tuple(), or set(). The Synatx of *map()* function is:

```
map(function, iterable, ...)
```

- The first parameter is function which is to be applied to each element in the iterables. It can be a *built-in function*, a *user-defined function*, or a *lambda function*.
- One or more iterable(s) are provided after *function*, whose elements are required to be passed to the `map()` function.
- You can provide multiple iterables to the *map()* function, and the function will apply to corresponding elements from each iterable.
- if the iterables are of different lengths, *map()* will stop when the shortest iterable is exhausted.

Ex.24
```
def square(x):
    return x * x

numbers = [1, 2, 3, 4, 5]
result_map = map(square, numbers)
# Convert the iterator to a list for visualization
```

```
result_list = list(result_map)

print(result_list)
```

Output:
[1, 4, 9, 16, 25]

Explanation:
All elements of list `numbers` passed to function `square()` through `map()` function.

Ex.25
```
def multiply(x,y):
    return x * y

numbers1 = [1, 2, 3, 4, 5]
numbers2 = [2, 0, 5]
result_map = map(multiply, numbers1,numbers2)
# Convert the iterator to a list for visualization
result_list = list(result_map)

print(result_list)
```

Output:
[2, 0, 15]

Explanation:
One element of each iterable (`numbers1`, and `numbers2`) are passed at a time in `multiply()` function through `map()` function. This *map()* function will stop passing elements as soon as any one iterable is exhosted. In this case as soon as all the elements of `numbers2` exhausted, it stops. Therefore the result has only 3 items.

6.7 Sorted Function

The **sorted()** function in Python is a built-in function that returns a new sorted list from the elements of any iterable, including lists, tuples, and strings. It provides a convenient way to sort data without modifying the original iterable. The sorted() function takes two optional parameters: *key* and *reverse.* If the iterable contains elements of different data types, `sorted()` will attempt to sort them based on their natural order or using the custom comparison function provided via the *key parameter.* The `sorted()` function returns a new sorted list, leaving the original iterable unchanged.

```
sorted(iterable, *, key=None, reverse=False)
```

- **iterable:**
  This is the iterable (such as a list, tuple, or string) whose elements will be sorted. The *sorted()* function returns a new list containing the sorted elements of the iterable.

- **key (optional):**
  This is an optional parameter that specifies a function to be called on each element of the iterable. The return value of this function will be used to determine the order of the elements during sorting. If not provided, the elements are sorted based on their natural order (e.g., numerical or lexicographical order).
- **reverse (optional):**
  This is another optional parameter that specifies whether the sorting should be done in reverse order. If set to *True*, the elements will be sorted in *descending order*; otherwise, the default behavior is *ascending order*.

Ex.26
```
numbers = [5, 2, 8, 1, 3]

sorted_numbers = sorted(numbers)

print(sorted_numbers)
```

Output:
[1, 2, 3, 5, 8]

Explanation:
No any *key* has been provided while calling the *sorted()* function, so it is sorted by number value. *Reverse* parameter is also not provided, so the sorting is done in ascending order.

Ex.27
```
numbers = [5, 2, 8, 1, 3]

sorted_numbers = sorted(numbers, reverse=True)

print(sorted_numbers)
```

Output:
[8, 5, 3, 2, 1]

Explanation:
Reverse parameter is set as *True*, so the sorting is done in descending order.

Ex.28
```
words = ["apple", "banana", "orange", "kiwi"]

sorted_words = sorted(words, key=len, reverse=True)

print(sorted_words)
```

Output:
['banana', 'orange', 'apple', 'kiwi']

Explanation:
The *keyword* is provided as *"len"* due to which sorting is done by length of each data. *Reverse* parameter is set as *True*, so the sorting is done in descending order. Therefore the sorted result contains longest word first.

7. File Handling

File handling is a fundamental aspect of programming, allowing developers to read, write, and manipulate data stored in files. In Python, file handling is straightforward and versatile, offering various functions and methods to interact with files efficiently. Interaction with stored file while executing the python code is the essential requirement for any programmer. In this way input data can be read for data processing, and result or intermediate (semi processed) data can be stored as file for future use. File handling is very much easy in Python. Steps for file handling is: (1) Define file path and file name, (2) Open file, (3) Close file (After completion of task). File can be opened as reading mode, writing mode, appending mode as per the requirements.

7.1 Introduction to File Handling

File handling, a core aspect of programming, encompasses the ability to read, write, and manipulate data stored in external files. It constitutes a fundamental component of software development, enabling the interaction with data beyond the scope of program execution. By facilitating the storage and retrieval of information in persistent storage, file handling extends the capabilities of programs, allowing them to handle large datasets, persist user data, and interact with external resources. Understanding file handling concepts is paramount for developers as it empowers them to effectively manage data across different file formats and storage mediums.

7.1.1 Mode of File Handling

Modes of File Operations provides an overview of the various modes used for opening files in Python, each catering to specific file manipulation requirements. The open() function serves as the gateway to file operations, allowing developers to specify the desired mode for accessing files. The modes encompass a spectrum of functionalities, including reading (*'r'*), writing (*'w'*), appending (*'a'*), and more. The *'r'* mode facilitates reading data from existing files, enabling the extraction of information for processing and analysis. Conversely, the *'w'* mode enables the creation of new files or overwriting existing ones, offering the capability to write data to files. The *'a'* mode facilitates appending data to the end of existing files, allowing for incremental updates without overwriting existing content. Additionally, modes such as *'rb'* and *'wb'* are utilized for handling binary data, catering to scenarios involving non-textual file formats. Each mode presents distinct use cases and implications, empowering developers to tailor file operations to their specific requirements while ensuring data integrity and security. There are additional library required to handle different type of file, however handling a *notepad file (text file)* does not require any additional library. Table 7.1 shows the different library file required for handling different types of file.

Table 7.1: Additional library required for handling different types of file

File Type	Library/Module Requirement
Text Files (*.txt, .csv*)	No additional library required.
Word Documents (*.docx*)	`python-docx`
PDF Files (*.pdf*)	`PyPDF2`
Excel Files (*.xlsx, .xls*)	`pandas`
JSON Files (*.json*)	`json`
XML Files (*.xml*)	`xml.etree.ElementTree`
HTML Files (*.html*)	`BeautifulSoup`
SQLite Database Files (*.db*)	`sqlite3`
Image Files (*.png, .jpg, .jpeg, .gif, etc.*)	`Pillow`
Audio Files (*.mp3, .wav, etc.*)	`pydub`
Video Files (*.mp4, .avi, etc.*)	`opencv-python`
Compressed Files (*.zip, .tar, .gz, .bz2, etc.*)	`zipfile`

7.2 CSV File

CSV (Comma Separated Values) files are *plaintext* files where each line represents a row of data, and each value within the row is separated by a delimiter, often a comma (,), although other delimiters like tabs or semicolons may also be used. Python's built-in `csv` module is commonly used for reading and writing CSV files. It provides functions and classes for parsing CSV data into Python data structures like lists or dictionaries.

When working with CSV files in Python, you typically start by importing the csv module. Then, you can use its functions and classes to open a CSV file, read its contents, manipulate the data, and write back to the file if needed. The `csv` module offers various functions and classes to handle CSV files, such as `csv.reader`, `csv.writer`, and `csv.DictReader`.

Ex.1 Create a csv file and save data

```
import csv

# Example data
data = [
    ['Name', 'Age', 'City'],
    ['John', '30', 'New York'],
    ['Alice', '25', 'Los Angeles'],
    ['Bob', '35', 'Chicago']
]

# Writing data to a CSV file
with open('data.csv', 'w', newline='') as file:
    writer = csv.writer(file)
    writer.writerows(data)

print("Data written to data.csv")
```

Output: «*Create a csv file with specified data and stroe the scv file to the storage. The resulting CSV file will contain the provided data with the specified column headers.*»

Explanation:

- The `csv` module has been imported because it provides functionalities to work with CSV files.
- Command `open('data.csv', 'w', newline='')` opens a CSV file named *data.csv* in write mode (`'w'`). If the file doesn't exist, it will be created. The `newline=''`.
- Command `with open(...)` uses a context manager to ensure that the file is properly closed after writing.
- Command `writer = csv.writer(file)` creates a csv.writer object associated with the opened file.
- Command `writer.writerows(data)` writes all the rows of data from the data list to the CSV file.

Ex.2 Read a csv file

```
import csv

# Specify the path to the CSV file
csv_file_path = 'data.csv'

# Initialize an empty list to store all the data
all_data = []

# Reading data from the CSV file
with open(csv_file_path, 'r') as file:
    # Iterate over each row in the CSV file
    reader = csv.reader(file)
    for row in reader:
        all_data.append(row)


# Print the list containing all data
print(all_data)
```

Output: «*Read the specified csv file into list.*»

Explanation:

- The `csv` module has been imported because it provides functionalities to work with CSV files.
- Command `open(csv_file_path, 'r')` opens a CSV file named *data.csv* in read mode (`'r'`).
- Command `with open(...)` uses a context manager to ensure that the file is properly closed after reading.
- Command `reader = csv.reader(file)` creates a csv.reader object associated with the opened file.
- `for row in reader` Iterates over each row in the CSV file.
- Command `all_data.append(row)` appends each row of data (which is represented as a `list`) to the all_data list.

7.3 Excel File

Handling Excel files in Python involves working with spreadsheets, including reading, writing, and manipulating data stored in Excel format. Python offers several libraries for Excel file handling, such as `openpyxl`, `xlrd`, and `pandas`, each with its own set of functionalities and advantages. Table 7.2 shows the comparison between `openpyxl`, `xlrd`, and `pandas` library.

Table 7.2: Comparison table between `openpyxl`, `xlrd`, and `pandas` in terms of Excel file handling

Feature	openpyxl	xlrd	pandas
Reading Excel Files	Yes (xlsx/xlsm/xltx/xltm files)	Yes (xls files)	Yes (xlsx/xlsm/xltx/xltm/xls files)
Writing Excel Files	Yes (xlsx/xlsm/xltx/xltm files)	No	Yes (xlsx/xlsm/xltx/xltm files)
Compatibility	Excel 2010 and later	Excel 97-2003 and later	Excel 2003 and later
Data Extraction	Provides access to cell values, styles, etc.	Provides access to cell values, formatting, etc.	Provides DataFrames for data manipulation
Performance	Efficient for writing large files	Efficient for reading large files	Efficient for data manipulation tasks
Dependencies	No additional dependencies	No additional dependencies	Requires xlrd and openpyxl for Excel handling
Active Development	Actively maintained and updated	No longer actively maintained	Actively maintained and updated

7.3.1 openpyxl

Openpyxl is a powerful Python library designed for interacting with Excel files, providing developers with extensive capabilities for reading, writing, and manipulating spreadsheet data. One notable feature of `openpyxl` is its ability to work with Excel files in the *".xlsx"* format, enabling users to access and modify various elements within a spreadsheet seamlessly.

Ex.3 Read an excel file and print the names of all sheets present in it

```
from openpyxl import load_workbook

# File path of the Excel file
file_path = "myExcelFile.xlsx"

# Load the workbook
workbook = load_workbook(filename=file_path)

# Get the names of all sheets
sheet_names = workbook.sheetnames

# Print sheet names
for sheet_name in sheet_names:
    print(sheet_name)
```

Explanation:

- Function `load_workbook` from the `openpyxl` library is imported to load the Excel file.
- The `load_workbook` function is used to load the Excel file into a `Workbook` object.
- We use the `sheetnames` attribute of the `Workbook` object to get a list of all sheet names.
- Finally, we iterate over the list of sheet names and print each one.

Ex.4 Read an excel file and Mark the Cell as RED if its value is more than 100

```
from openpyxl import load_workbook
from openpyxl.styles import PatternFill

# File path of the Excel file
file_path = "myExcelFile.xlsx"

# Load the workbook
workbook = load_workbook(filename=file_path)

# Select "Sheet2"
sheet = workbook["Sheet2"]

# Define the column to check
column_to_check = 'B'

# Define red fill color
red_fill = PatternFill(start_color='FF0000', end_color='FF0000',
                                                    fill_type='solid')

# Iterate over cells in the specified column starting from the second row
for cell in sheet[column_to_check][1:]:
    if cell.value is not None and cell.value > 100:
        # Apply red fill color to the cell
        cell.fill = red_fill

# Save the workbook
workbook.save("myExcelFile_modified.xlsx")
```

Explanation:

- The `load_workbook` function is used to load the Excel workbook from the specified file path.

- Command `workbook["Sheet2"]` selects a specific sheet named "Sheet2" from the workbook.
- The variable `column_to_` check is set to `'B'`, indicating that column B (the second column) will be checked.
- A red fill color is defined using the `PatternFill` class `PatternFill(start_color = 'FF0000', end_color='FF0000', fill_type='solid')`.
- The script iterates over cells in the specified column, starting from the second row.
- For each cell in the specified column, if the cell is not empty and its value is greater than 100, the red fill color is applied.
- Finally, the modified workbook is saved to a new file using `workbook.save()`.

7.3.2 XLRD

Python library *xlrd* is designed for reading data and formatting information from Excel files. It provides developers with a convenient interface to extract data from various types of Excel files, including older formats like `.xls`. Overall, xlrd empowers Python developers with the tools needed to efficiently read and analyze Excel files, offering a versatile solution for a wide range of data extraction tasks.

Ex.5 Read a sheet of excel file and print number of rows and column

```
import xlrd

# File path of the Excel file
file_path = "myExcelFile.xls"

# Open the workbook
workbook = xlrd.open_workbook(file_path)

# Select the second sheet
sheet = workbook.sheet_by_index(1)

print("Number of Rows: ", sheet.nrows)
print("Number of Columns: ",sheet.ncols)
```

Explanation:

- The xlrd library is imported, which provides functions for reading data from Excel file.
- The `open_workbook()` function from *xlrd* is used to open the Excel file specified by `file_path`. The result is stored in the workbook variable, which represents the entire workbook.

- Second sheet in the workbook is selected through `workbook.sheet_by_index()`. Indexing starts from 0.
- Number of rows and columns from the selected sheet is extracted using the `nrows` and `ncols` attributes of the sheet object, respectively.

7.3.3 Pandas

Data analysis library *pandas* can handle Excel files efficiently, allowing you to perform data manipulation, filtering, and analysis directly on Excel data.

Ex.6 Read a sheet of excel file and print data of specific column

```
import pandas as pd

file_path = "myExcelFile.xls"
mysheet_name = "Sheet2"

# Read the excel sheet
df = pd.read_excel(file_path, sheet_name=sheet_name)

print(df['Percentage of Budget'])
print(df['Expense Category'])
```

Explanation:

- Pandas provide function `pd.read_excel()` to read the Excel file specified by `file_path` and extract the data from the sheet specified by `mysheet_name`.
- Data of excel file is stored in a pandas *DataFrame* object named `df` .
- It assumes that the Excel file has a column with name *"Percentage of Budget"*.
- Command `print(df['Percentage of Budget'])` prints the column, labeled "Percentage of Budget", from the DataFrame `df`.

7.4 Image File

Image manipulation using Python involves the process of modifying digital images to achieve desired effects or enhancements. Python offers several powerful libraries for image processing and manipulation, enabling developers to perform a wide range of tasks.

7.4.1 Pillow

One of the most commonly used libraries for image manipulation is Pillow (Python Imaging Library, PIL), which provides a comprehensive set of functionalities for opening, manipulating, and saving images in various formats. Pillow allows users to open, create, modify, and save images in various formats, including JPEG, PNG, BMP, GIF, and TIFF. Pillow allows tasks such as resizing, cropping, rotating, filtering, adding text, adjusting colors, and more. Additionally, Pillow supports more advanced operations such as image blending, masking, and alpha compositing, making it suitable for tasks ranging from basic image editing to complex computer vision and multimedia applications.

Ex.7 Resize and save a image file

```
from PIL import Image

image_path = 'input.png'
output_path = 'resized_image.png'

# Open an image file
img = Image.open(image_path)

width, height = img.size

# Set the new width and height for resized image
new_width = width // 2
new_height = height // 3

# Resize the image to the new dimensions
resized_img = img.resize((new_width, new_height))

# Save the resized image
resized_img.save(output_path)
```

Output: «*Open an image file "input.png", resize the image and save back as new image file "resize_image.png". Width of output image is half of original and height is one third of original.*»

Explanation:

- `open()` function from the `Image` module to open the image file specified by `image_path` and load it into memory.
- The new dimensions are set to half of the original width and one-third of the original height.
- Command `img.resize((new_width, new_height))` resizes the original image to the new dimensions.
- Resized image is saved to the file, specified by `output_path` using the `save()` method. The resized image will be written to the file `'resized_image.png'`.

Ex.8 Detect Edges of image and save as a image file

```
from PIL import Image, ImageFilter

# Open an image file
image_path = 'input.jpg'
img = Image.open(image_path)

# Apply various filters and effects
edge_detected_img = img.filter(ImageFilter.FIND_EDGES)

# Save the filtered images
edge_detected_img.save('edge_detected_image.jpg')
```

Output: « *This code opens an image file, applies the edge detection filter to it, and saves the resulting filtered image to a new file.* »

Explanation:

- Command `Image.open(image_path)` open input image file using the `Image.open()` function.
- Command `img.filter(ImageFilter.FIND_EDGES)` applies the edge detection filter to the input image using the *filter()* method with the `ImageFilter.FIND_EDGES` `parameter`.
- Command `edge_detected_img.save('edge_detected_image.jpg')` save the the filtered image (with the edge detection effect applied) to a new file.

Ex.9 Convert Color image to gray scale image file

```
from PIL import Image

# Open a color image file
image_path = 'input.jpg'
img = Image.open(image_path)

# Convert the image to grayscale
gray_img = img.convert('L')

# Save the grayscale image
output_path = 'gray_im.jpg'
gray_img.save(output_path)
```

Output: «*Convert the color image to grayscale and save the resulting grayscale image*»

Explanation:

- Command `Image.open(image_path)` open input image file using the `Image.open()` function.
- Command `img.convert('L')` converts the color image to grayscale. The argument **'L'** specifies that the image should be converted to grayscale mode (*luminance*).

Ex.10 Convert Color image to Binary image with threshold value

```
from PIL import Image

# Open a color image file
image_path = 'input.jpg'
im = Image.open(image_path)

# Convert the image to grayscale
gray_im = im.convert('L')

# Apply a threshold to create the binary image
threshold = 170  # Adjust threshold value as needed
binary_im = gray_im.point(lambda pixel: 0 if pixel < threshold else 255, '1')

# Save the binary image
output_path = 'binary_image.jpg'
binary_im.save(output_path)
```

Output: «*Opens a color image file, converts it to grayscale, applies a threshold to create the binary image, and saves the resulting binary image to a new file.*»

Explanation:

- Command `Image.open(image_path)` open input image file using the `Image.open()` function.
- Command `im.convert('L')` converts the color image to grayscale. The argument **'L'** specifies that the image should be converted to grayscale mode (*luminance*).
- The lambda function `lambda pixel:  0 if pixel < threshold else 255` sets pixels below the threshold to black (0) and pixels above the threshold to white (255). The **'1'** argument specifies that the resulting image should be in binary mode.
- Binary image is created using the `point()` method of the `gray_im object`.
- Binary image is saved to a file named `'binary_image.jpg'` using the `save()` method of the `binary_im` object. The `save()` method writes the image data to the specified file.

Ex.11 Decrease blue channel of a color image and save it as new image file

```
from PIL import Image

# Open an image file
image_path = 'input.jpg'
img = Image.open(image_path)

# Split the image into its RGB components
r, g, b = img.split()

# Modify the red channel (e.g., increase brightness)
b = b.point(lambda pixel: pixel * 0.5)  # Adjust the multiplier as needed

# Merge the modified channels back into a single image
modified_img = Image.merge('RGB', (r, g, b))

# Save the modified image
output_path = 'modified_image.jpg'
modified_img.save(output_path)
```

Output: «*modifies the blue channel of the input image, keeps the red and green channels unchanged, merges the modified channels back into a single image, and saves the resulting modified image to a new file. Adjustments to the blue channel are made by applying a lambda function to each pixel value.*»

Explanation:

- Command `Image.open(image_path)` open input image file using the `Image.open()` function.
- Command `img.split()` splits the image into its red (`r`), green (`g`), and blue (`b`) channels.
- The blue channel is modified (e.g., by decreasing its brightness) using the `point()` method with a `lambda` function.
- The lambda function applies the modification to each pixel value in the blue channel.
- Modified image is saved to a file named '`modified_image.jpg`' using the `save()` method.

7.4.2 Open CV

Another popular library is `OpenCV` (Open Source Computer Vision Library), which offers advanced computer vision algorithms along with image processing capabilities. `OpenCV` provides functions for tasks like object detection, image segmentation, feature extraction, and facial recognition. OpenCV is known for its efficiency, versatility, and extensive documentation, making it suitable for both research and production-level projects. With its easy-to-use Python interface, developers can quickly prototype and deploy computer vision applications. Moreover, OpenCV's support for multiple platforms, including Windows, Linux, macOS, iOS, and Android, makes it accessible for a wide range of applications across different domains, including robotics, healthcare, automotive, and surveillance. Table 7.3 shows the comperision between Pillow (PIL) and OpenCV (cv2).

Table 7.3: Comparison between Pillow (PIL) and OpenCV (cv2)

Feature	Pillow (PIL)	OpenCV (cv2)
Image Processing	Primarily focused on image processing.	Comprehensive computer vision library.
Interface	Pythonic and user-friendly API.	C/C++ core with Python bindings.
Supported Image Types	Supports various image formats (JPEG, PNG, etc.).	Wide range of image and video formats.
Image Display	Limited display capabilities.	Rich display features, including GUI windows.
Image Manipulation	Basic image manipulation functions.	Advanced image processing and analysis functions.
Performance	Generally slower, especially for complex tasks.	Highly optimized, faster performance.
Community Support	Active community, but smaller than OpenCV.	Large and active community.
Learning Curve	Easy-to-learn and use for basic tasks.	Steeper learning curve due to its complexity.
Documentation	Well-documented with examples.	Extensive documentation and tutorials.
Use Cases	Simple image editing, basic tasks.	Computer vision tasks, machine learning projects.
Dependencies	Fewer dependencies, lightweight library.	Larger, more dependencies.

7.5 PDF File

Reading PDF files in Python involves several steps, from extracting text or images to manipulating the content. To accomplish these tasks, various libraries and modules are available, each serving different purposes.

7.5.1 ReportLab

ReportLab is a powerful Python library used for generating PDF documents programmatically. It provides a wide range of functionalities for creating complex PDF files with text, images, shapes, and more.

- **reportlab.lib:** It provides tools for managing page size, fonts, colors, and other resources. Additionally, it offers support for internationalization, allowing developers to work with different languages and character sets seamlessly.

- **reportlab.pdfgen:** It is responsible for generating PDF content. It provides the canvas. Canvas class, which represents a PDF canvas onto which text, graphics, and images can be drawn.
- **reportlab.platypus:** It introduces the concept of flowable elements, such as paragraphs, tables, and images, which automatically flow from one page to another based on available space.

Ex.12 Create a pdf file with a paragraph

```
from reportlab.lib.pagesizes import letter
from reportlab.pdfgen import canvas

output_pdf_path = 'output.pdf'
paragraph = "This is a sample paragraph."

pdf_canvas = canvas.Canvas(output_pdf_path, pagesize=letter)
pdf_canvas.setFont("Helvetica", 12)

# Set the position to start drawing text
x = 100
y = 750

# Draw the String paragraph into pdf file.
pdf_canvas.drawString(x, y, paragraph.strip())

# Save the PDF canvas
pdf_canvas.save()
```

Output: «*Convert a paragraph into pdf and save into storage.*»

Explanation:

- `from reportlab.lib.pagesizes import letter` Imports the predefined page size "letter" from the *ReportLab* library, which represents the standard US letter paper size.
- `from reportlab.pdfgen import canvas`: Imports the Canvas class from the *ReportLab* library, which allows drawing on a PDF document.
- Command `canvas.Canvas(output_pdf_file, pagesize=letter)` creates a new PDF canvas object named `pdf_canvas` using the Canvas class imported from the `pdfgen` module. It sets the page size to the standard *letter* size.
- `pdf_canvas.setFont("Helvetica", 12)`: Sets the font of the text to Helvetica with a size of 12 points.

- `x = 50` and `y = 750` define the starting position (x and y coordinates) on the PDF canvas where the text will be drawn. In PDF coordinates, (0, 0) is the bottom-left corner of the page, and the units are in points (1/72 of an inch).
- `paragraph.strip()` is the actual text content that will be drawn on the canvas. The ***.strip()*** is a string method used to remove any leading or trailing whitespace characters (spaces, tabs, newlines) from the text. It ensures that there are no unwanted spaces or line breaks added to the text when it's drawn on the canvas
- Command `pdf_canvas.save()` saves the PDF canvas to the output PDF file specified by `output_pdf_file`.

Ex.13 Create a pdf file with word wrap paragraph

```
from reportlab.lib.pagesizes import letter
from reportlab.pdfgen import canvas

output_pdf_path = 'output.pdf'

long_paragraph = """This is a long paragraph that needs to be
converted into a PDF file. It should automatically wrap to multiple
lines when it reaches the end of the line. The text will continue
to wrap until it reaches the specified width of the text box."""

pdf_canvas = canvas.Canvas(output_pdf_path, pagesize=letter)
pdf_canvas.setFont("Helvetica", 12)

# Set the position to start drawing text
x = 100
y = 750

# Define the width and height of the text box
available_width = letter[0] - 2 * x
height = 600  # Adjust as needed
wrapped_para = ""
for word in long_paragraph.split():
    # Check if adding the word exceeds the available width
    if pdf_canvas.stringWidth(wrapped_para + " " + word) < available_width:
        # Add the word to the wrapped paragraph
        wrapped_para += " " + word
    else:
        # If adding the word exceeds the available width, start a new line
        pdf_canvas.drawString(x, y, wrapped_para.strip())
        wrapped_para = word  # Start a new wrapped paragraph
```

```
        y -= 15  # Move to the next line

# Draw the last part of the wrapped paragraph
pdf_canvas.drawString(x, y, wrapped_para.strip())

# Save the PDF canvas
pdf_canvas.save()
```

Output: « *Wrap a long paraggraph and convert into a pdf file. Save the pdf file into storage.* »

Explanation:

- `from reportlab.lib.pagesizes import letter`: Imports the predefined page size "letter" from the *ReportLab* library, which represents the standard US letter paper size.
- `from reportlab.pdfgen import canvas`: Imports the Canvas class from the *ReportLab* library, which allows drawing on a PDF document.
- Command `canvas.Canvas(output_pdf_file, pagesize=letter)` creates a new PDF canvas object named `pdf_canvas` using the Canvas class imported from the `pdfgen` module. It sets the page size to the standard *letter* size.
- `pdf_canvas.setFont("Helvetica", 12)`: Sets the font of the text to Helvetica with a size of 12 points.
- `x = 50 and y = 750` define the starting position (x and y coordinates) on the PDF canvas where the text will be drawn. In PDF coordinates, (0, 0) is the bottom-left corner of the page, and the units are in points (1/72 of an inch).
- `pdf_canvas.stringWidt()` gives the width of the specified paragraph as per the set font size.
- `paragraph.strip()` is the actual text content that will be drawn on the canvas. The ***.strip()*** is a string method used to remove any leading or trailing whitespace characters (spaces, tabs, newlines) from the text. It ensures that there are no unwanted spaces or line breaks added to the text when it's drawn on the canvas.
- Command `y -= 15` decrements the y coordinate by 15 points after drawing each line of text, effectively moving the drawing position to the next line.
- Command `pdf_canvas.save()` saves the PDF canvas to the output PDF file specified by `output_pdf_file`.

Ex.14 Create a pdf file with contents from a text file

```
from reportlab.lib.pagesizes import letter
from reportlab.pdfgen import canvas

def text_to_pdf(input_text_file, output_pdf_file):
```

```
    with open(input_text_file, 'r') as file:
        text_content = file.read()

    # Create a PDF canvas
    pdf_canvas = canvas.Canvas(output_pdf_file, pagesize=letter)

    # Set the font and font size
    pdf_canvas.setFont("Helvetica", 12)

    # Set the position to start drawing text
    x = 50
    y = 750

    # Split the text into lines and draw each line on the PDF canvas
    for line in text_content.split('\n'):
        pdf_canvas.drawString(x, y, line)
        y -= 15  # Move to the next line

    # Save the PDF
    pdf_canvas.save()

# Example usage
text_file_path = 'input_file.txt'  # Input file for pdf conversion
pdf_file_path = 'output_file.pdf'  # Generated pdf file
text_to_pdf(text_file_path, pdf_file_path)
```

Output: «*Convert text file into pdf file.*»

Explanation:

- Command `open(input_text_file, 'r')` opens a file in *read* mode. The `with` statement is used to ensure that the file is properly closed after reading.
- Command `canvas.Canvas(output_pdf_file, pagesize=letter)` creates a new PDF canvas object named `pdf_canvas` using the Canvas class imported from the `pdfgen` module. It sets the page size to the standard *letter* size.
- `x = 50` and `y = 750` define the starting position (x and y coordinates) on the PDF canvas where the text will be drawn. In PDF coordinates, (0, 0) is the bottom-left corner of the page, and the units are in points (1/72 of an inch).
- Command `y -= 15` decrements the y coordinate by 15 points after drawing each line of text, effectively moving the drawing position to the next line.
- Command `pdf_canvas.save()` saves the PDF canvas to the output PDF file specified by `output_pdf_file`.

7.5.2 PyPDF2

One commonly used library for working with PDF files in Python is **PyPDF2**. It allows for *reading*, *merging*, *splitting*, and *extracting information* from PDF documents.

Ex.15 Extract and print text of a PDF file

```
import PyPDF2

def extract_text_from_pdf(pdf_path):
    with open(pdf_path, 'rb') as file:
        reader = PyPDF2.PdfFileReader(file)
        text = ''
        for page in range(reader.numPages):
            text += reader.getPage(page).extractText()
    return text

pdf_text = extract_text_from_pdf('example.pdf') # read input file
print(pdf_text)
```

Output: «*Print textual contents of pdf file.*»

Explanation:

- Command `open(pdf_path, 'rb')` opens a file in *read-in-binary* mode. The `with` statement is used to ensure that the file is properly closed after reading. It opens the file in binary mode because PDF files are binary files.
- Command `reader = PyPDF2.PdfFileReader(file)` creates a *PdfFileReader* object reader, which is used to read the PDF file opened in the previous step.
- Command `reader.numPages` gives no of pages available in the input pdf file. A *for* loop is created for no. of pages. (e.g. 1, 2, 3, etc.)
- Command `reader.getPage(page)` gives a single page from the input pdf file, from which its contents are extracted through command.

Ex.16 Mearge two pdf files

```
import PyPDF2

def merge_pdfs(pdf1_path, pdf2_path, output_path):
    # Open the input PDF files
    with open(pdf1_path, 'rb') as pdf1_file, open(pdf2_path, 'rb') as pdf2_file:
        # Create PdfReader objects for the input PDF files
        pdf1_reader = PyPDF2.PdfReader(pdf1_file)
        pdf2_reader = PyPDF2.PdfReader(pdf2_file)
```

```
    # Create a PdfWriter object to write the merged PDF
    pdf_writer = PyPDF2.PdfWriter()

    # Add all pages from the first PDF
    for page in pdf1_reader.pages:
        pdf_writer.add_page(page)

    # Add all pages from the second PDF
    for page in pdf2_reader.pages:
        pdf_writer.add_page(page)

    # Write the merged PDF to the output file
    with open(output_path, 'wb') as output_pdf_file:
        pdf_writer.write(output_pdf_file)

pdf1_path = 'input1.pdf'
pdf2_path = 'input2.pdf'
output_path = 'merged.pdf'
merge_pdfs(pdf1_path, pdf2_path, output_path)
```

Output: «*Print textual contents of pdf file.*»

Explanation:

- Command `open(pdf1_path, 'rb')` and `open(pdf2_path, 'rb')` opens two input files in *read-in-binary* mode. The `with` statement is used to ensure that the file is properly closed after reading. It opens the file in binary mode because PDF files are binary files.
- Command `reader = PyPDF2.PdfFileReader(file)` creates a *PdfFileReader* object reader, which is used to read the PDF file opened in the previous step.
- Command `PyPDF2.PdfWriter()` create a *PdfWriter* object to write the merged PDF. This object is used latter to add pages from the input PDF files and write them to the output PDF file.
- Two for loops are created for each opened pdf file according to number of pages.
- Command `open(output_path, 'wb')` opens a file in write mode and through command `pdf_writer.write(output_pdf_file)` write the contents of the *PdfWriter* object to the output PDF file specified by output_path.

7.5.3 pdf2image

The `pdf2image` library is a powerful Python tool designed for converting PDF documents into images. It offers a simple yet effective way to extract pages from PDF files and convert them into various image formats such as PNG, JPEG, and TIFF. One of the primary features of `pdf2image` is its ability to handle multipage PDFs efficiently, allowing users to convert entire documents into a series of images seamlessly. Moreover, pdf2image offers flexibility in terms of customization, allowing users to specify output resolution, page ranges, and other parameters according to their requirements.

Ex.17 Convert all pages of pdf into image and save to storage

```
from pdf2image import convert_from_path

def extract_pages_as_images(pdf_file_path, output_folder):
    # Convert PDF pages to images
    images = convert_from_path(pdf_file_path)

    # Save each image to the output folder
    for i, image in enumerate(images):
        image_path = f"{output_folder}/page_{i+1}.png"
        image.save(image_path, ``PNG'')

# Example usage
pdf_file_path = 'input_file.pdf'
output_folder = 'images'
extract_pages_as_images(pdf_file_path, output_folder)
```

Output: «*All pages of input pdf file will be converted into images and will be saved in a folder of name "images"*»

Explanation:

- Function convert_from_path converts PDF pages to PIL Image objects.
- A for loop is iterated for each item in images object.
- Command image.save(image_path, "PNG") stores a image in to a specified path. and image type is set as *PNG* here.

Ex.18 Convert each page of PDF file into binary image with specific threshold

```
import os
from pdf2image import convert_from_path
from PIL import Image
from reportlab.lib.pagesizes import letter
from reportlab.pdfgen import canvas

def pdf_to_bw_with_threshold(pdf_path, threshold=128):
    # Convert PDF to images
    pages = convert_from_path(pdf_path, dpi=200)
```

```
    # Create a PDF canvas
    pdf_canvas = canvas.Canvas("merged_file.pdf", pagesize=letter)

    # Iterate through each page
    for i, page in enumerate(pages):
        # Convert the image to grayscale
        gray_im = page.convert('L')

        # Apply threshold to create black and white image
        bw_image = gray_im.point(lambda x: 0 if x < threshold else 255, '1')

        # Save the black and white image
        bw_image_path = f'output_bw_image_page_{i+1}.png'
        bw_image.save(bw_image_path)

        # Draw the image on the PDF canvas
        pdf_canvas.drawImage(bw_image_path, 0, 0, width=letter[0],
                                                   height=letter[1])

        # Add a new page if it's not the last image
        if i < len(pages) - 1:
            pdf_canvas.showPage()

        # Remove the temporary image file
        os.remove(bw_image_path)

    # Save the PDF
    pdf_canvas.save()

# Example usage
pdf_file_path = 'input_file.pdf'
threshold_value = 200  # Adjust threshold value as needed between 0 to 255
pdf_to_bw_with_threshold(pdf_file_path, threshold_value)
```

Output:
A new pdf file with name *merged_file.pdf* whose each pages has been converted into binary image (having only two pixel values: either black or white).

Explanation:
All elements of list `numbers` passed to function `square()` through `map()` function.

8. Object-Oriented Programming (OOP)

8.1 Introduction

Object-Oriented Programming (OOP) is a powerful paradigm used in software development for organizing and designing code. OOP is like organizing a big project into smaller parts, called objects. It fundamentally revolves around the concept of *objects*, which are instances of classes *encapsulating data and behaviors.* OOP promotes modular design, reusability, and maintainability of code, making it a cornerstone of modern software engineering.
Think about a household. In a household, there are different appliances and tools, each with its own purpose and functionality. For example, there's a refrigerator for storing food, a microwave for heating meals, and a vacuum cleaner for cleaning floors. In object-oriented programming (OOP), you can think of each appliance or tool as an object. Each object (appliance or tool) has its own attributes (data) and behaviors (methods). For instance, the refrigerator object might have attributes such as temperature settings and contents, while the vacuum cleaner object might have attributes such as suction power and cleaning mode. Similar to how each appliance in a household serves a specific function but contributes to the overall management of the home, objects in OOP encapsulate specific functionalities that collectively form the program. This structured and modular approach allows for easier organization and maintenance of the code, as well as better scalability and reusability of components.

In the ever-evolving landscape of software development, programmers have devised various methodologies to structure and organize code. These methodologies, known as **programming paradigms**, dictate the fundamental approach to solving problems and building software systems.

Two predominant paradigms are *procedural programming* and *object-oriented programming (OOP).*

8.1.1 Procedural Programming

The traditional approach to programming, emphasizes the sequential execution of instructions. In this paradigm, programs are structured around procedures or functions, which manipulate data stored in variables. While procedural programming is effective for solving small-scale problems, it often becomes unwieldy and difficult to manage in larger projects. As programs grow in complexity, maintaining and modifying procedural code becomes increasingly challenging, leading to code duplication, tight coupling, and reduced reusability.

8.1.2 Object-Oriented Programming

Object-Oriented Programming (OOP) offers a more structured and modular approach to software development. OOP revolves around the concept of objects, which are instances of classes encapsulating data and behaviors. This paradigm promotes code reusability, maintainability, and scalability by organizing code into discrete units that model real-world entities. By encapsulating data and behavior within objects, OOP facilitates abstraction, allowing developers to focus on essential characteristics while hiding implementation details. Difference between a python class and python object is shown in Table 8.1.

Python Class

In Python, a class is a fundamental building block of object-oriented programming serving as a blueprint for creating objects. It encapsulates data and functions that operate on that data within a single unit. The structure of a class typically consists of attributes and methods. Attributes represent the data associated with the class, defining its state, while methods are functions that define the behavior of the class.

To create a class in Python, you use the `class` keyword followed by the class name. After class name, a colon (`:`) is written to mark the beginning of class body. Body of class is written from next line with proper indent. Within the class definition, you can declare attributes using variables and define methods using functions.

Ex.1
```
# Blank structure of a class definition

class Person:
    pass
```

Explanation:
A new class, named `Person` is defined. Nothing is written in the class definition here, therefore a `pass` statement is used as a placeholder for future code.

Python Object

An object in Python, is an instance of a class, embodying the characteristics and behaviors defined by that class. Each object has a state (attributes or properties) and behaviors (methods or functions) associated with it. The state represents the data or information that the object holds, while the behaviors define the actions or operations that the object can perform.

When an object is created from a class, it is instantiated, meaning it becomes a unique instance of that class, with its own state and behaviors. In Python, objects are dynamically typed, meaning the type of an object is determined at runtime based on the class from which it is instantiated. This allows for flexibility and ease of use, as objects can be created and manipulated without specifying their types explicitly. Overall, objects in Python provide a powerful and intuitive way to model real-world entities and build complex software systems.

Ex.2
```
# Object Creation from |\ref{blanckpythonclass}|

MyObject1 = Person()
```

Explanation:
Object is created by writing class name with Opening and closing bracket.

Table 8.1: Comparison between Python classes and objects

Aspect	**Class**	**Object**
Definition	Blueprint/template for creating objects.	Instance of a class.
Creation	Defined using `class` keyword.	Created by instantiating a class.
Purpose	Encapsulates common properties and behaviors.	Represents a specific instance with unique attributes and behavior.
Attributes	Define attributes (variables).	Contains values assigned to attributes.
Methods	Define behaviors (functions)	Accesses/manipulates its own attributes, performs actions defined in class.
Inheritance	Supports inheritance from other classes.	Inherits attributes/methods from its class.
Relationship	Many objects can be created from the same class.	Each object is a separate instance of a class.

8.2 Class Definition

Class is a blueprint for creating objects. It serves as a template or a prototype from which objects are instantiated. Class definitions encapsulate both data (in the form of attributes) and behavior (in the form of methods) that are common to all instances of that class.

8.2.1 Class Declaration

Class declaration is the initial step in defining a blueprint for creating objects with specific attributes and behaviors. The declaration begins with the class keyword followed by the desired class name, typically adhering to *CamelCase* convention. Within the class block, various components such as attributes and methods are defined to represent the state and behavior of objects instantiated from that class:

- *Attributes* define the data associated with the class.
- *Methods* define the operations that can be performed on that data.
- *Constructor* method `__init__()` is defined to initializes the attributes of the class, when an object is created.
- The *self* parameter is a *reference to the current instance* of the class. It is passed as the first parameter to all methods and is used to access attributes and methods of the instance.
- Python supports special methods, also known as *dunder methods* , which are surrounded by double underscores (`__`). These methods provide additional functionality to classes, such as **string representation** (`__str__()`), **equality comparison** (`__eq__()`), and more.
- *Docstrings* are optional but recommended strings that provide documentation for the class, its attributes, and methods. They are enclosed in triple quotes (“') and appear immediately after the class declaration or method definition.

Python's dynamic nature enables flexible class declaration, permitting attributes and methods to be added, modified, or removed during runtime.

Ex.3 `# Constructor in class`

```
class Person:
    def __init__(self, name, age):
        self.name = name
        self.age = age
```

Explanation:

- *class Person:* : This line declares a class named Person.
- `def __init__(self, name, age):` : This is the constructor method (`__init__()`), which is called automatically when an instance of the class is created. It takes three parameters: `self` (a reference to the instance itself), `name`, and `age`.
- `self.name = name` and `self.age = age` : Inside the *constructor*, `self.name` and `self.age` are instance attributes. These attributes are initialized with the values passed as arguments to the constructor. `self.name` will store the name of the person, and `self.age` will store their age.

Ex.4
```
# Method in class

class Circle:
    def __init__(self, radius):
        self.radius = radius

    def calculate_area(self):
        return 3.14 * self.radius ** 2
```

Explanation:

- A class with name *Circle* is declared.
- Inside the constructeor, `self.radius = radius` initializes an attribute (`radius`) for the instance, storing the radius value passed as an argument.
- `def calculate_area(self)` : This is a method named *calculate_area()*, defined within the `Circle` class.
- The method takes one parameter, `self` which is a reference to the instance itself. This parameter allows the method to access the instance's attributes, such as *self.radius.*
- The method `calculate_area()` calculates the area of the circle using the provided formula and returns the result.

Ex.5
```
# Optional Special Method in class

class Book:
    def __init__(self, title, author):
        self.title = title
        self.author = author

    def __str__(self):
        return f"{self.title} by {self.author}"
```

Explanation:

- `def __str__(self):` : This is a special method `def __str__()`, also known as the *string representation* method.
- It is automatically called when the `str()` function is used on an instance of the class or when the object is converted to a string implicitly.
- This method returns a string representation of the object.

8.2.2 Self Parameter

In Python, `self` is a convention rather than a *keyword.* It represents the instance of the class and is used to access instance variables and methods within the class. However, it is *not a reserved keyword*, and you can use any variable name in place of `self`. It is not recommended to use other variable name in place of `self`, because it can lead to confusion for the programmer.

Ex.6
```
# Self parameter without keyword "self"

class MyClass:
    def __init__(obj, x):
        obj.x = x

    def display(obj):
        print("Value of x:", obj.x)
```

Explanation:

- Instead of using `self` as the conventional parameter name, we have used `obj`.

8.2.3 Class Attributes

Attributes are variables that store data associated with the class. These attributes represent the state of the objects created from the class. Attributes are defined within the class body.

- Class attributes are variables defined within a class that are shared by all instances of the class.
- They are declared directly within the class body but outside of any method definitions.
- Class attributes are accessed using the class name itself or through instances of the class.
- They are often used to define properties or characteristics that are common to all instances of the class.
- Class attributes can be initialized with default values, and they can also be modified later if needed.
- Changes made to class attributes are *reflected across all instances* of the class.
- Unlike instance attributes, class attributes are not tied to a specific instance but rather to the class itself.
- Class attributes are defined using the syntax `attribute_name = value` within the class body.
- They are typically accessed using the dot notation (`Class.attribute_name`) or via instance objects (`instance.attribute_name`).
- Class attributes can also be used to define constants or configurations that apply to all instances of the class.

There are multiple ways to access the class attributes.

Directly using class name

Ex.7
```
# Accessing class attribute directly using class name

class MyClass:
    class_var = 10  # Class attribute

print(MyClass.class_var)
```

Output: 10

Explanation:
Class attributes can be accessed using the class name.

Externally using object of class

Ex.8
```
# Accessing class attribute using object of class

class MyClass:
    class_var = 10  # Class attribute

obj = MyClass()
print(obj.class_var)
```

Output: 10

Explanation:
Class attributes can be accessed using object name.

Inside instance method

Ex.9
```
# Accessing class attribute inside instance method

class MyClass:
    class_var = 10  # Class attribute

    def class_method(cls):
        print("Accessing class attribute inside class method:", cls.class_var)

obj = MyClass()
obj.class_method()
```

Output: Accessing class attribute inside class method: 10

Explanation:
Class attributes can be accessed using `cls.class_var` inside a class method.

Ex.10
```
class MyClass:
    class_var = 0 # Class attribute
    def __init__(self, data):
        class_var = data
```

```
    def function1(cls):
        print("Class Attribute:", cls.class_var)


obj = MyClass(10)
obj.function1()
```

Output: 0

Explanation:

- Code `cls.class_var` is used to access the class attribute.
- Code `class_var = data` inside constructor creates a local variable within the constructor, not an instance variable inside the constructor.
- This local variable (created within constructor) is not accessible through other part of the code.

8.2.4 Instance Attributes

Instance attributes are variables specific to each individual instance of a class in Python. They encapsulate the state of each object and can vary from one instance to another. Instance attributes are typically defined within the `__init__()` method or other instance methods using the self parameter. They are accessed and modified using instance objects, allowing each instance to have its own unique values for the attributes. Instance attributes are essential for representing the unique characteristics or properties of objects and play a crucial role in object-oriented programming by providing a way to manage object state.
Instance attributes in Python represent the unique properties or characteristics of individual objects. These attributes are specific to each instance of a class and encapsulate the state of each object. By defining instance attributes within the `__init__()` method or other instance methods using the `self` parameter, Python allows for the creation of objects with distinct and customizable characteristics. Instance attributes provide a means to manage object state dynamically, enabling objects to maintain their unique identity and behavior throughout their lifecycle. Through instance attributes, developers can create flexible and reusable classes that accurately model real-world entities with varying properties and behaviors.

Accessed using Dot operator

Ex.11
```
# Access instance attributes using Dot operator

class MyClass:
    def __init__(self, x):
```

```
        self.var1 = x

obj = MyClass(10)
print(obj.var1)
```

Output: 10

Explanation:
Class attributes can be accessed using Dot operator.

Ex.12
```
# Access instance attributes using Dot operator

class MyClass:
    var1 = 20
    def __init__(self, x):
        self.var1 = x

obj = MyClass(10)
print(obj.var1)
print(MyClass.var1)
```

Output:
10
20

Explanation:

- `var1` is Class variable and `self.var1` is instance variable.
- The class attribute is not affected by the instance attribute `var1` of the `obj` instance.

Access using instance method

Ex.13
```
# Access instance attributes using Dot operator

class MyClass:
    def __init__(self, x):
        self.instance_var = x

    def get_instance_var(self):
        return self.instance_var

obj = MyClass(10)
print(obj.get_instance_var())
```

Output: 10

Explanation:
Class attributes can be accessed using the "*instance method*".

Access using `setattr` and `getattr`

Ex.14
```
# Access instance attributes using Dot operator

class MyClass:
    def __init__(self, x):
        self.instance_var1 = x


obj = MyClass(10)
setattr(obj, `instance_var1', 20)
setattr(obj, `instance_var2', 30)

print(getattr(obj, `instance_var1'))
print(getattr(obj, `instance_var2'))
```

Output:
20
30

Explanation:

- Above code demonstrates the use of `setattr()` and `getattr()` functions to set and get instance variables dynamically.
- The instance attribute `instance_var1` of the `obj` instance has been initialized through constructor .
- Code `setattr(obj, 'instance_var1', 20)` overnight the instance variable generated through constructor.
- Code `setattr(obj, 'instance_var2', 30)` uses the `setattr()` function to set the value of a new instance variable `instance_var2` to 30. This dynamically adds a new instance variable `instance_var2` to the obj instance with the value 30.
- Function `getattr()` is used to get the value of a instance variable.

8.2.5 Private Variables

Private variables in Python are class variables or instance variables that are intended to be inaccessible from outside the class. They are indicated by prefixing the variable name with two underscores (`__`). Private variables help encapsulate data within a class and prevent direct access from external code. While private variables are not enforced access control mechanisms in Python, they serve as a convention to indicate that certain attributes or methods are intended for internal use only. Private variables can only be accessed and modified within the class itself, typically through *accessor* and *mutator* methods, providing a level of data hiding and abstraction to ensure the integrity and encapsulation of class data.

Private variables, denoted by the prefix of two underscores (__) in Python, serve as a mechanism to encapsulate data within a class and restrict direct access from external code. These variables are intended for internal use within the class and are designed to promote data hiding and abstraction. By limiting access to private variables from outside the class, Python encourages encapsulation and modular design, fostering better software engineering practices. Private variables can only be accessed and modified within the class itself. While Python does not enforce strict access control, private variables serve as a convention to indicate that certain attributes or methods are intended for internal use only, enhancing code readability, maintainability, and security.

Ex.15
```
# Accessing private variable

class MyClass:
    var1 = 10
    var2 = 10
    __var3 = 10

    def __init__(self, data):
        self.var1 = data

print(MyClass.__var3)
```

Output:
« *AttributeError: type object 'MyClass' has no attribute 'textunderscore _var3'* »

Explanation:
- `__var3` is a private variable due to the *double underscores prefix.*
- It results in an AttributeError because `__var3` is a private variable.

8.3 Understanding Attributes in Python Classes

Attributes are fundamental components of Python classes that encapsulate data and behavior within objects. They define the characteristics and state of objects, allowing them to store and manipulate data. Table 8.2 represent the summery of the three main types of attributes: class attributes, instance attributes, and private variables. Each type has its own scope, access level, and behavior, providing flexibility and control over how data is managed within a class.

8.4 Name Mangling

Name mangling is a technique used in Python to make class attributes or methods "private" by modifying their names to prevent accidental access or overriding from subclasses. It's achieved

Table 8.2: Properties of Class Attributes, Instance Attributes, and Private Variables

Property	**Class Attribute**	**Instance Attribute**	**Private Variable**
Scope	Shared among all instances.	Unique to each instance.	Unique to class and instances.
Accessible	Through class name or instances.	Through instances only.	Through instances only.
Access Level	Public	Public	Private
Naming Convention	Defined outside methods within class.	Defined within methods or constructor.	Defined with double underscores (__) within class.
Initialization	Initialized outside methods.	Initialized within methods or constructor.	Initialized within methods or constructor.
Modification	Can be modified externally and by instances.	Can be modified only by instances.	Can be modified only within class.
Name Mangling	Not subject to name mangling.	Not subject to name mangling.	Subject to name mangling.

by prefixing a double underscore (`__`) to the attribute or method name. When a name starts with `__` but doesn't end with two or more underscores, Python applies name mangling. By using name mangling, Python ensures that class attributes or methods marked as private are accessible only within the class itself.

Inside the class, mangled names are accessed without modification. However, outside the class, mangled names are accessed by prefixing `_ClassName` to the attribute or method name.

For example, if a class defines a private variable __private_var, outside the class, it is accessed as `_ClassName__private_var`. This prevents naming conflicts with attributes or methods in subclasses.

Here's how name mangling works in Python:

1. Mangling Rules:
   - If a class attribute or method name starts with two underscores (__) but doesn't end with two or more underscores, Python applies name mangling.
   - Python renames the attribute or method by prefixing the class name to it with an additional underscore (_) and the class name. This prevents naming conflicts with attributes or methods in subclasses.
2. Accessing Mangled Names:
   - Inside the class, mangled names are accessed without modification.
   - Outside the class, mangled names are accessed by prefixing _ClassName to the attribute or method name.
3. Purpose:
   - Name mangling is primarily used to make class attributes or methods "private" to the class to prevent accidental access or overriding.
   - It helps encapsulate class internals and maintain data integrity by restricting direct access from outside the class.

Ex.16
```
# Accessing private variable

class MyClass:
    ''' Name Mangling and its access'''
    __var1 = 10

print(MyClass._MyClass__var1)
```

Output:
10

Explanation:

- Docstring "Name Mangling and its access" provides information about the class.
- `__var1` is a private variable due to the *double underscores prefix.*
- Class name is "*MyClass*", and private variable name is *__var1*, so the mangled name becomes `_MyClass__var1`.

8.5 Key Concepts of OOP

Object-Oriented Programming Language is based on *objects* and *class.* Main concept of OOP is to bind the data and the functions together as single unit, so that controlled access to functions may be provided, to be used by other part of code, without giving direct access to the data within the class. OOP encourages the reusing of objects in the same and other programmes. There are four basic concepts of object-oriented programming: (i) inheritance, (ii) polymorphism, (iii) abstraction, and (iv) encapsulation.

8.5.1 Encapsulation

Encapsulation is a fundamental concept of object-oriented programming (OOP) that involves bundling data (attributes or properties) and methods (functions) together within a class to restrict access to the internal state of objects and to hide implementation details from the outside world. Encapsulation in Python is achieved primarily through the use of access modifiers such as public, private, and protected attributes and methods. *By default, all attributes and methods in Python are considered public* and can be accessed from outside the class.

However, Python provides a convention for denoting private attributes and methods by prefixing their names with a double underscore (__). Private attributes and methods can only be accessed within the class itself, effectively encapsulating the internal state of objects and preventing direct modification from external code.

Python also supports protected attributes and methods, denoted by a single underscore (_), which are intended for internal use within the class and its subclasses.

Encapsulation promotes data hiding, abstraction, and information hiding, allowing developers to control access to class members, enforce constraints, and maintain the integrity of the object's state. Additionally, encapsulation enables the implementation of getter and setter methods, which provide controlled access to private attributes and allow validation and manipulation of data before it is stored or retrieved.

Ex.17
```
#---------Class Definition Start------------
class Person:
    def __init__(self, name, age):
        self.name = name                # Public attribute
        self._age = age                 # Protected attribute
        self.__address = "Unknown"     # Private attribute

    def display_info(self):
        print(f"Name: {self.name}, Age: {self._age}, Address: {self.__address}")

    def update_address(self, new_address):
        self.__address = new_address

#---------Class Definition End------------

# Create an instance of the Person class
person1 = Person("Raju", 30)

# Accessing public attributes and methods
print("Public attribute name:", person1.name)

# Accessing protected attribute
print("Protected attribute age:", person1._age)

# Using method to update private attribute
person1.update_address("Raj Path, Delhi")

# Using public method to access private attribute
person1.display_info()
```

Explanation:

- We define a Person class with public, protected, and private attributes `name`, `_age`, and `__address`, respectively.
- The `display_info()` method displays information about the person, including the private attribute `__address`.
- The `update_address()` method allows updating the private attribute `__address`.
- Attempting to directly access the private attribute `__address` from outside the class will raise an `AttributeError`, demonstrating encapsulation's role in protecting internal data.

Ex.18
```
#---------Encapsulation Example------------
class Person:
    def __init__(self, name):
        self.__name = name  # Encapsulated attribute

    def get_name(self):
        return self.__name  # Encapsulated method to get the name

    def set_name(self, new_name):
        self.__name = new_name  # Encapsulated method to set the name

#---------Class Definition End------------

# Creating an instance of the Person class
person = Person("John")

# Accessing the encapsulated attribute using the encapsulated method
print("Original name:", person.get_name())

# Modifying the encapsulated attribute using the encapsulated method
person.set_name("Alice")
print("Modified name:", person.get_name())
```

Explanation:

- The `name` attribute is encapsulated within the `Person` class.
- It is accessed and modified through encapsulated methods (`get_name` and `set_name`) instead of directly accessing it.
- This ensures data encapsulation, as external code cannot directly modify or access the `name` attribute.
- It enforce data integrity and preventing accidental modifications.

8.5.2 Inheritance

Inheritance is a fundamental concept in object-oriented programming (OOP) that allows a new class (called a *subclass* or *derived class*) to inherit attributes and behaviors (methods) from an existing class (called a *superclass* or *base class*). This means that the subclass can reuse and extend the functionality of the superclass, promoting code reuse and modularity. In Python, you can also inherit from multiple parent classes simultaneously, forming what is known as *multiple inheritance*.

The key idea behind inheritance is the creation of a *hierarchy* of classes, where each subclass is a specialized version of its superclass. This relationship is often described using the "`is-a`" relationship. For example, if we have a superclass *Animal*, we can have subclasses like *Dog*,

Cat, and *Bird*, where each subclass inherits characteristics (such as `eat()` or `move()`) from the Animal class.

Inheritance provides several benefits:

- **Code Reusability**: Methods and attributes defined in the superclass can be reused in the subclass without rewriting them.
- **Extensibility**: Subclasses can add new methods or override existing methods from the superclass to tailor functionality to specific needs.
- **Modularity**: By organizing classes into hierarchies, code becomes more modular and easier to manage.

Structure of Inheritance

1. **Superclass (Base Class):**
    - The superclass is the existing class from which attributes and methods are inherited.
    - It serves as the parent class that defines common attributes and behaviors shared by its subclasses.
    - The superclass can also have methods that can be *overridden* by its subclasses.
2. **Subclass (New Class):**
    - The subclass is the new class that inherits attributes and methods from the superclass.
    - It is also known as the derived class because it derives its characteristics from the superclass.
    - Subclasses can *add* new *attributes* or *methods*, *override* existing methods, or *extend* the functionality of the superclass.

Adding New Method/Attribute through Inheritance

A new method can be added in derived class which is not present in the superclass.

Ex.19
```
#---------Adding New Method/Attribute in Inheritance------------
# super class / base class------------
class Animal:
    def __init__(self, species):
        self.species = species

    def make_sound(self):
        return "Some generic sound"

# sub class / derived class------------
class Dog(Animal):
    def __init__(self, breed, name):
        super().__init__("Canine")
        self.breed = breed
        self.name = name
```

```
    def bark(self):
        return "Woof!"

    def get_name(self):
        return self.name

#--------------------Use
my_dog = Dog("Labrador", "Buddy")
# Accessing inherited attribute and methods
print(my_dog.species)       # Output: Canine (inherited attribute)
print(my_dog.make_sound()) # Output: Some generic sound (inherited method)
# Accessing new attribute and method in the subclass
print(my_dog.breed)         # Output: Labrador
print(my_dog.get_name())    # Output: Buddy
print(my_dog.bark())        # Output: Woof!
```

Method Overriding in Inheritance

A specific implementation of a method with same method signature (method name, parameter type list and return type) may be provided in subclass. In this case same method with same signature remains present in both the superclass as well as subclass. The method in the subclass will be called instead of the method in the superclass.

Ex.20

```
#---------Method Overriding in Inheritance------------
# super class / base class------------
class Animal:
    def make_sound(self):
        return "Some generic sound"

# subclass / derived class------------
class Dog(Animal):
    def make_sound(self):
        return "Woof!"

#--------------------Use
my_dog = Dog()
print(my_dog.make_sound())  # Output: Woof!
```

Method Extending in Inheritance

Methods available in super class can be accessed from a base class through feature of method extending. Method extending involves calling the superclass's method from the subclass to

extend its behavior. Method extending (in inheritance) refers to the concept of a subclass enhancing or extending the behavior of a method inherited from its superclass in Python. This approach allows subclasses to leverage existing functionality defined in the superclass while adding specific functionality tailored to the sub class's requirements.
In Python, method extending is typically achieved by calling the superclass's method from within the subclass's method using the super() function. This allows the subclass to inherit and invoke the superclass's method and then customize or augment the behavior by appending additional functionality.

Ex.21
```
#---------Method Extending in Inheritance------------
# super class / base class------------
class Vehicle:
    def start(self):
        return "Engine starting..."

# sub class / derived class------------
class Car(Vehicle):
    def start(self):
        # Extending behavior of superclass method
        start_message = super().start()  # Calling superclass method
        return f"{start_message} Ignition started..."

# Creating an instance of Car
my_car = Car()

# Calling overridden method that extends superclass method
print(my_car.start())  # Output: Engine starting... Ignition started...
```

8.5.3 Abstraction

Abstraction is a fundamental concept in object-oriented programming that focuses on simplifying complex systems by *hiding unnecessary implementation details while emphasizing only the essential features relevant to the user.* In Python, abstraction is typically *achieved through the use of classes and objects.* A class serves as a blueprint for creating objects, encapsulating both data (attributes) and behavior (methods) into a single unit. Through abstraction, the user interacts with objects at a higher level of understanding, without needing to know the intricate internal workings of how those objects are implemented.

Abstraction allows developers to manage complexity by breaking down systems into manageable parts, promoting code reusability, maintainability, and scalability. In Python, abstraction encourages clean, modular code design, facilitating collaboration among developers and enabling easier debugging and testing. By providing a clear separation between interface and implementation, abstraction enhances the overall readability and comprehensibility of code, making it easier to understand and maintain over time.

Abstract Class

In Python, abstraction can be achieved by using abstract classes and interfaces. A class that consists of one or more abstract method is called the abstract class. Abstract methods do not contain their implementation. When a method is declared inside the class *without its implementation*, it is called as *abstract method* and when a method is *completely implemented* inside the abstract class, then it is called as *concrete method* .

Abstract Base Classes (ABC)

Abstract Base Classes (ABCs) in Python are a fundamental part of the language's object-oriented programming paradigm, providing a way to define abstract interfaces that subclasses must implement.

To create abstract methods and abstract classes in Python, we use the `ABC` and `abstractmethod` classes from the `abc` (Abstract Base Class) library. Abstract methods defined in a base class require its child classes to provide implementations for these methods. If we fail to implement any of the abstract methods in a child class, our code will raise an error. In the example below, `method_1` is an abstract method created using the `@abstractmethod` decorator, which signals that any subclass of this base class must define `method_1` to be considered complete. This approach ensures that classes conform to a specific structure or behavior, improving the clarity and reliability of our code.

Ex.22
```
#---------Abstract Class Definition Start------------
from abc import ABC, abstractmethod

# Abstract Base Class (ABC) defining the Vehicle interface
class Vehicle(ABC):
    def __init__(self, make, model):
        self.make = make
        self.model = model

    @abstractmethod
    def start(self):
        pass

    @abstractmethod
    def stop(self):
        pass
```

Explanation:

- Module `abc`, is required to define Abstract Base classes (ABC).

- The `@abstractmethod` decorator marks method `start` and `stop` methods as abstract.
- Any *concrete subclass* of abstract class `Vehicle` must implement both the abstract methods.

Concrete Class

A concrete class in Python is a class that provides complete implementations for all its methods and can be instantiated to create objects directly. Unlike abstract classes, concrete classes do not contain any abstract methods and can stand alone as fully functional entities within a program. Concrete classes are used to represent specific objects or entities with well-defined behaviors and attributes.

Instances of concrete classes can be created using the class name followed by parentheses (`ClassName()`), allowing developers to work with objects that have predefined functionalities. Difference between abstract class and concrete class is shown in Table 8.3.

Table 8.3: Difference between abstract class and concrete class

Aspect	Abstract Class	Concrete Class
Definition	Defines a blueprint for other classes.	Represents a fully implemented class.
Instantiation	Cannot be instantiated directly.	Can be instantiated directly to create objects.
Usage	Provides a template with abstract methods to be implemented by subclasses.	Implements all methods and can be used directly.
Abstract Methods	Contains one or more abstract methods.	Does not contain abstract methods.
Implementation	Subclasses must implement all abstract methods to be concrete.	Provides concrete implementations for all methods.
Example	`ABC` module is used to create abstract classes.	Regular classes without any abstraction.
Purpose	Encourages code reuse and defines a common interface.	Represents specific objects with defined behaviors.
Inheritance	Typically used as a base class for inheritance.	Can inherit from other classes, abstract or not.
Syntax	Uses `@abstractmethod` decorator for abstract methods.	Implements all methods directly within the class.
Object Creation	Cannot create instances directly (must be subclassed).	Instances can be created directly using `ClassName()`.

Ex.23
```
#---------Abstract Class Definition Start------------
from abc import ABC, abstractmethod
import math

class Shape(ABC):
    @abstractmethod
```

```
    def area(self):
        pass

    @abstractmethod
    def perimeter(self):
        pass

#---------Concrete Class Start------------
class Circle(Shape):
    def __init__(self, radius):
        self.radius = radius

    def area(self):
        return math.pi * self.radius**2

    def perimeter(self):
        return 2 * math.pi * self.radius

class Rectangle(Shape):
    def __init__(self, length, width):
        self.length = length
        self.width = width

    def area(self):
        return self.length * self.width

    def perimeter(self):
        return 2 * (self.length + self.width)


# Usage
circle = Circle(5)
print("Circle Area:", circle.area())

rectangle = Rectangle(4, 6)
print("Rectangle Area:", rectangle.area())
print("Rectangle Perimeter:", rectangle.perimeter())
```

Explanation:

- `Shape` is an abstract class defining two abstract methods: `area` and `perimeter`.
- Subclasses like `Circle` and `Rectangle` inherit from `Shape` and provide concrete implementations of these abstract methods.

Inheritance vs Abstraction

The key difference between normal inheritance and abstraction is that *abstraction emphasizes defining abstract methods that subclasses must implement*, allowing for a higher level of interface specification and implementation flexibility. Normal inheritance, on the other hand, focuses on inheriting and extending attributes and methods from a superclass without necessarily requiring method implementation constraints. Table 8.4 summarizes the differences between normal inheritance and abstraction.

Table 8.4: Difference between Normal Inheritance and Abstraction

Aspect	Normal Inheritance	Abstraction
Purpose	Allows a subclass to inherit attributes and methods from a superclass.	Emphasizes defining abstract classes and methods without implementation details.
Involves	Concrete classes inheriting from a base (super) class.	Abstract base classes (ABCs) defining interfaces and abstract methods.
Key Features	Code reuse, hierarchical relationships, method overriding.	Hiding implementation details, enforcing method implementation in subclasses.
Example Use Cases	Animal -> Dog, Cat; Vehicle -> Car, Truck	Shape -> Rectangle, Circle; DatabaseConnection -> MySQLConnection, PostgreSQLConnection
Method Implementation	Subclasses override methods inherited from superclass to provide specific behaviors.	Abstract methods defined in abstract base classes must be implemented by subclasses.
Syntax	No special syntax beyond standard class inheritance.	Uses ABCs from the `abc` module with `@abstractmethod` decorator.
Focus	Extending and specializing behavior inherited from a superclass.	Defining contracts (interfaces) that subclasses must fulfill.
Implementation Constraints	Subclasses are free to implement or override inherited methods.	Subclasses must implement all abstract methods defined in the abstract base class.
Flexibility	Provides flexibility in class design with hierarchical relationships.	Ensures adherence to a predefined interface, promoting code structure and reliability.

8.5.4 Polymorphism

Polymorphism in Python is a key concept in object-oriented programming that allows objects of different types to be treated as objects of a common superclass. It enables methods to be invoked on these objects without knowing their specific types, promoting flexibility, code reusability, and abstraction. Polymorphism is achieved through method overriding, where a subclass provides a specific implementation of a method that is already defined in its superclass. This allows different subclasses to customize behavior inherited from a common superclass while maintaining a consistent interface. Key Points of Polymorphism are:

- Code Reusability: Polymorphism promotes code reuse by allowing methods to be used with different types of objects.

- Flexibility: Polymorphism enables more flexible and generic code that can work with a variety of object types.
- Abstraction: Polymorphism hides implementation details by focusing on object behavior rather than explicit types, enhancing modularity and scalability.

Ex.24
```
#---------Polymorphism------------
#superclass with a speak() method that returns a generic message
class Animal:
    def speak(self):
        return "Animal speaks"

#subclasses of Animal that override the speak() method
class Dog(Animal):
    def speak(self):
        return "Woof!"

#subclasses of Animal that override the speak() method
class Cat(Animal):
    def speak(self):
        return "Meow!"

# Function demonstrating polymorphism
def make_sound(animal):
    return animal.speak()

# Creating instances of Dog and Cat
my_dog = Dog()
my_cat = Cat()

# Calling the function with different objects
print(make_sound(my_dog))  # Output: Woof!
print(make_sound(my_cat))  # Output: Meow!
```

9. Modules and Packages

In the realm of Python programming, modules and packages play a fundamental role in structuring and organizing code. Modules allow you to logically group related functions, classes, and variables together, making your code more modular, reusable, and easier to maintain. Python's rich ecosystem of built-in and third-party modules empowers developers to leverage pre-written functionalities, accelerating development while maintaining code quality.

9.1 Python Modules

A module is a file containing Python definitions and statements. These files have a `.py` extension and can be imported into other Python scripts or modules to make use of their functionality. Modules serve as a way to organize code logically by *grouping related functions, classes, and variables* together. They enable code reuse and promote a modular programming approach, which is crucial for building scalable and maintainable applications.

A Python module is essentially a way to organize Python code into a separate file, allowing for better code organization and reusability. Each module can contain functions, classes, or variables that can be imported into other modules or scripts to be utilized. The primary purpose of modules is to encapsulate code into manageable units, reducing complexity and improving maintainability.

9.1.1 Creating a Module

Creating a module in Python is straightforward—simply write your Python code in a .py file. For example, consider a module named `mymodule1.py` containing some customized functions given in Ex.1. To use this module in another Python script, import it using the `import` statement.

Ex.1
```
#---------mymodule1.py------------
def greet(name):
    return f"Hello, {name}!"

def add_numbers(a, b):
    return a + b
```

9.1.2 Using a Module

Python provides various ways to import modules into scripts:

Importing the entire module

Importing an entire module in Python allows you to access all the definitions (functions, classes, variables) within that module using dot notation. This method imports the entire namespace of the module, meaning all its contents become available under the module's name in the importing script.

Entire module can be imported using the keyword `import` followed by the name of the module. In this way the complete module (all methods, and data) is imported into the script calling this function. After importing, you can use any function or constant defined in the module by prefixing it with a dot (.)

Ex.2
```
#---------using module described in |\ref{moduleexample1}|
import mymodule1

mymodule1.greet("Mahesh")
```

Importing Specific Attributes (Functions, Classes, or Variables) from a Module

Sometimes, you may only need to use specific attributes (functions, classes, or variables) from a module rather than importing the entire namespace. Python allows you to import these specific attributes directly into your script, which can lead to cleaner and more concise code. This method is beneficial when you only need a few specific functionalities from a module and want to avoid potential namespace clashes or unnecessary overhead. For example, to import just the `greet` function from the *mymodule1* module of Ex.1 is shown in Ex.3:

Ex.3
```
#---------using module described in |\ref{moduleexample1}|
from mymodule1 import greet

greet("Mahesh")
```

Renaming Imported Modules or Attributes in Python

Python allows you to rename imported modules or attributes using the `as keyword`. This feature is useful for aliasing module names or shortening attribute names for brevity or clarity in your code. Renaming imported modules or attributes can improve code readability and maintainability, especially when working with third-party libraries or modules with long names. It also helps in avoiding naming conflicts with existing identifiers in your script.

Ex.4
```
#---------using module described in |\ref{moduleexample1}|
import mymodule1 as md

md.greet("Mahesh")
```

9.2 Python Packages

Python packages are a fundamental concept in Python programming for organizing and structuring code into a hierarchical namespace. A package is essentially a directory containing multiple Python modules and an `__init__.py` file, which indicates to Python that the directory should be treated as a package. Packages provide a way to manage and distribute modules more efficiently, enabling better code organization and reusability in large-scale projects. They facilitate a modular approach to programming by allowing developers to group related modules together, thus promoting code maintainability and scalability.

A Python package is a directory structure that contains multiple Python modules and sub-packages. It serves as a container for organizing and distributing related functionalities, making it easier to manage complex projects. They encourage best practices in software design, such as separation of concerns and encapsulation, ultimately leading to more robust and scalable applications.

9.2.1 Structure of a Package

The structure of a Python package follows a specific convention to be recognized by Python's `import` system. Figure 9.1 shows the typical structure of a package. A typical package structure includes:

- Package Directory
  The main directory containing the package.
- __init__.py
  It is an initialization file which is essential to mark the directory as a Python package.

This file can be empty or contain initialization code for the package.

- Python Modules
  One or more modules are organized within the package directory. These modules (python code files) contains the code that defines functions, classes, or variables. Modules can be nested within subdirectories to create sub-packages.

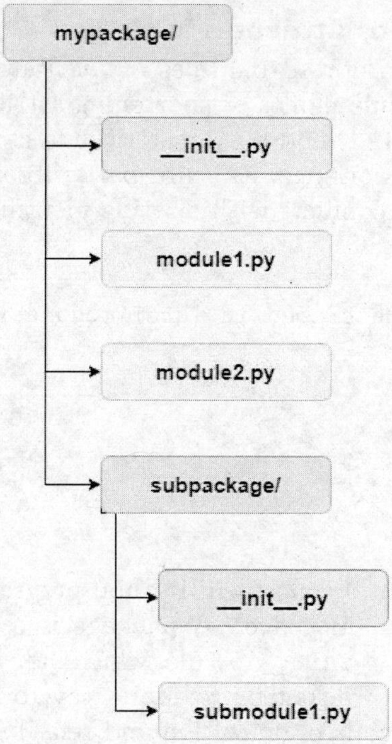

Figure 9.1: Typical structure of a package.

9.2.2 Creating a Package

Creating a Python package involves organizing related modules into a directory structure and including an `__init__.py` file within the directory. To create a package:

- Create a Directory
  Start by creating a directory for your package, naming it appropriately.
- add `__init__.py`:
  Create an empty `__init__.py` file, inside the directory. This file can also contain initialization code if needed.
- Add Modules
  Add Python modules (.py files) to the package directory or create subdirectories for organizing modules into sub-packages.
- Use Packages
  You can then import modules or sub-packages from your package into other Python scripts or packages using dot notation.

Ex.5 Package creation

```
#---------Consider a packeage as shown in Figure  |\ref{Fig:packagestructure}|
# Content of module mymodule1.py

def say_hello(name):
    return f"Hello, {name}!"

#-----------------------------------------------------
# Content of module mymodule2.py

def add(a, b):
    return a + b

def subtract(a, b):
    return a - b
```

Ex.6 Import and Use the Package shown in Ex.5

```
from mypackage.module1 import say_hello
from mypackage.module2.calculator import add, subtract

message = say_hello("Alice")
print(message)  # Output: Hello, Alice!

result_add = add(10, 5)
print("Addition result:", result_add)  # Output: Addition result: 15
```

9.3 Module vs Package

There is a significant difference between a Python module and a Python package.

Python Module:

- A Python module is a single file containing Python code.
- It typically has a `.py` extension and contains definitions (functions, classes, variables) that can be imported and used in other Python scripts or modules.
- Modules help organize code by grouping related functionalities together.
- Modules are imported using the import statement in Python scripts.

Python Module:

- A Python package is a directory (or folder) that contains multiple Python modules and an additional `__init__.py` file.

- The `__init__.py` file indicates to Python that the directory should be treated as a package.
- Packages can contain sub-packages, which are subdirectories containing their own modules and `__init__.py` files.
- Packages are imported similarly to modules but with dot notation to access nested modules or sub-packages.

9.4 Special Variable in Module

There are several special variables and attributes commonly used in Python modules and scripts for various purposes. These special variables help in controlling module behavior, accessing module information, and interacting with the Python runtime environment. Here are some important special variables and attributes used in Python modules:

9.4.1 __main__

This attribute represents the name of the package that the module belongs to.

9.4.2 __name__

The `__name__` variable is a built-in variable in Python that represents the name of the current module. When a Python script or module is executed, Python automatically assigns a value to `__name__` based on how the module is being used:

- If the module is being run as the main program (i.e., directly executed by the interpreter), then `__name__` is set to '`__main__`'.
- If the module is being imported from another module, then `__name__` is set to the name of the module (e.g., 'mymodule').

In Python, `__name__` and `__main__` are special variables that are commonly used in modules and scripts to control the execution flow and behavior of the code.

`if __name__== "__main__":` is commonly used in modules and scripts to control the execution flow and behavior of the code. If the the module is being run as the main program, value of `__name__== "__main__"` is `True`, and code within this `if` block is executed. It isuses when a specific code/function is required to executed when the module is executed standalon as main program and not required to be executed when it is loaded as module in any other program file.

9.4.3 __doc__

This special variable is used to access the *docstring* (documentation string) of a module, function, class, or method.

9.4.4 __file__

This attribute contains the file path of the Python source file from which the module was loaded.

9.4.5 __package__

This attribute represents the name of the package that the module belongs to.

9.4.6 __dict__

This attribute contains the namespace dictionary of the module, which holds all the variables, functions, classes, and imports defined in the module.

9.4.7 __all__

This variable is a list that defines the names to be exported (made available) when `from module import *` is used.

9.4.8 __cached__

This attribute contains the path to the compiled bytecode of the module (*.pyc or *.pyo file), if it is available.

Ex.7 A sample module with `if __name__== "__main__"`

```
# mymodule.py

def say_hello():
    print("Hello from mymodule!")

print("__name__ variable:", __name__)

if __name__ == "__main__":
    # This code block will only execute if this script is run directly
    print("Executing as main program")
    say_hello()
```

Ex.8
```
#---------Consider a module as shown in Figure  |\ref{moduleexample3}|
#Code executed from python terminal

python mymodule.py
```

Output:
__name__variable: __main__
Executing as main program
Hello from mymodule!

Explanation:
Here, module `mymodule.py` is executed as the main program.
Python sets __name__ to '__main__'. Therefore, the condition if __name__== "__main__": evaluates to True, and the code inside this block is executed.

Ex.9
```
import mymodule

print(mymodule.__file__)
```

Output:
« *Path to the source file of mymodule* »

Ex.10
```
import mypackage.module1

print(mypackage.module1.__package__)
```

Output:
« *mypackage* »

Explanation:
Name of the package that the module belongs to.

9.5 ___init___.py

it is called as *Python package directories marker* file, and is required essentially for declaring a folder/subfolder as a package. In the simplest case, `__init__.py` can just be an empty file, but it can also execute initialization code for the package or set the `__all__` variable, described later. This file essentially initializes the package when it is imported, enabling the package to set up any necessary resources, define package-level variables, and control what is exposed to the outside world. When a package is imported, Python first executes the code inside its `__init__.py` file.

Ex.11
```
# Defining Package-Level Variables
#---------Consider a packeage as shown in Figure  |\ref{Fig:packagestructure}|
# mypackage/__init__.py

VERSION = '1.0'
```

Explanation:
Here, `VERSION` is a variable that can be accessed as `mypackage.VERSION` after importing the package.

Ex.12
```
# Importing Submodules
#---------Consider a packeage as shown in Figure  |\ref{Fig:packagestructure}|
# mypackage/__init__.py

from .module1 import some_function
```

Explanation:
The `some_function` from `module1.py` becomes directly accessible via `mypackage.some_functio`
once *mypackage* is imported.

Ex.13
```
# Setting Up Package Initialization
#---------Consider a packeage as shown in Figure  |\ref{Fig:packagestructure}|
# mypackage/__init__.py

print("Initializing my_package")

# Code executed when my_package is imported
```

Explanation:
Printing a message or performing certain tasks upon importing the package can help initialize the package environment.

Ex.14
```
# Controlling Package Exports
#---------Consider a packeage as shown in Figure  |\ref{Fig:packagestructure}|
# mypackage/__init__.py

__all__ = ['module1', 'module2']
```

Explanation:
The `__all__` list specifies which modules should be imported when using `from mypackage import *`. This controls the visibility of package contents.

9.6 Benefits of Modular Programming

Modular programming using Python modules and packages offers numerous advantages that enhance code quality, maintainability, and scalability. Understanding these benefits is essential for leveraging modular design principles in Python development.

9.6.1 Advantages of Using Modules

Python modules provide several key advantages that contribute to efficient software development:

- **Code Reusability:** Modules encapsulate reusable functionalities, allowing developers to reuse code across different parts of an application or in multiple projects.
- **Namespace Isolation:** Modules create a separate namespace for their contents, preventing naming conflicts and promoting cleaner code organization.
- **Improved Maintainability:** Modular code is easier to maintain and update since changes made to one module are isolated from other parts of the codebase.

- **Facilitates Collaboration:** Modules enable multiple developers to work on different parts of a project concurrently without interfering with each other's work.

9.6.2 Encapsulation and Abstraction

Modules encapsulate related functionalities into a cohesive unit, hiding implementation details and exposing only necessary interfaces. This promotes information hiding and reduces complexity, making code more understandable and maintainable.

Modules allow developers to focus on high-level abstractions rather than implementation details. By abstracting complex functionalities behind well-defined interfaces, modules promote code reuse and simplify software design.

9.6.3 Code Organization and Readability

- **Logical Organization:** Modular programming facilitates logical organization of code into manageable units. Modules group related functionalities together, making it easier to locate and understand specific parts of the codebase
- **Enhanced Readability:** Well-organized modules improve code readability by promoting a structured approach to software design. Clear module names and well-defined interfaces make it easier for developers to navigate and comprehend the code.

9.7 Overview of the Python Standard Library

- **Comprehensive Toolkit:** The Python Standard Library provides a comprehensive toolkit of modules and packages covering a wide range of functionalities, including data types, file I/O operations, networking, concurrency, mathematics, and more.
- **Cross-Platform Compatibility:** Standard Library modules are designed to work seamlessly across different operating systems, making Python a versatile language for developing platform-independent applications.
- **Ease of Use:** Python's Standard Library emphasizes simplicity and ease of use, with well-documented APIs and consistent design patterns across modules.

9.8 Utilizing Third-Party Packages with `pip`

The `pip` (Python Package Installer) tool is a powerful utility for managing and installing third-party packages in Python. This section introduces pip and explores best practices for installing, managing, and incorporating external libraries into Python projects. `pip` automatically resolves and installs dependencies required by the specified package, ensuring that all necessary components are installed.

- **Package Management Tool:** `pip` is the standard package manager for Python, providing a convenient way to install, uninstall, and manage Python packages and dependencies.
- **Central Repository:** `pip` interacts with the Python Package Index (PyPI), a central repository that hosts thousands of open-source Python packages, making it easy to discover and install external libraries.

- **Command-Line Interface:** `pip` is operated via the command line, allowing developers to execute various commands for package management (`install`, `uninstall`, `freeze`, `search`, etc.).

9.9 Advance Concept in Module/Package

9.9.1 Namespaces and Scope

- **Namespace Concept:** A namespace is a mapping from names to objects, such as variables, functions, and classes, within a program. Each module in Python has its own namespace, which serves as a container for its defined names.
- **Global and Local Scope:** Python uses a hierarchical scope model, where variables declared outside of functions have global scope, while variables declared within functions have local scope.
- **Accessing Namespaces:** Use the `globals()` and `locals()` functions to access the global and local namespaces, respectively.
- **import Statement and Namespace:** The `import` statement imports names from one module's namespace into another module's namespace, allowing access to imported names using dot notation (module_name.name)

9.9.2 Module-Level Variables and Functions

- **Defining Module-Level Variables:** Variables declared at the top level of a module are considered module-level variables and can be accessed by other modules that import the module.
- **Module-Level Functions:** Functions defined at the top level of a module are module-level functions and can be imported and used by other modules.

9.9.3 Handling Circular Imports

- **Circular Import Problem:** Circular imports occur when two or more modules directly or indirectly import each other, leading to import errors or unexpected behavior. Consider two modules, `module_a.py` and `module_b.py`, where each module tries to import a function from the other module, potentially leading to a circular import problem.

  This approach ensures that the import statements are executed only when the respective functions are called, effectively deferring the imports until they are needed. By using lazy imports within functions, we avoid the circular import problem that would occur if the imports were placed at the top level of the modules.
- **Preventing Circular Imports:** To avoid circular imports, refactor code to minimize dependencies between modules, use *lazy imports* within functions, or move import statements inside functions where possible.
- **Importing Inside Functions:** Importing modules or names inside functions instead of at the top level can defer imports until they are actually needed, helping to avoid circular dependencies at module import time.

Ex.15

```
# module_a.py

def func_a():
    from module_b import func_b
    return func_b()
```

```
# module_b.py

def func_b():
    from module_a import func_a  # Import func_a only when func_b is called
    return func_a()
```

Explanation:

- `module_a.py` defines a function `func_a()` that imports `func_b()` from `module_b` only when `func_a()` is called.
- Similarly, `module_b.py` defines a function `func_b()` that imports `func_a()` from `module_ a` only when `func_b()` is called.

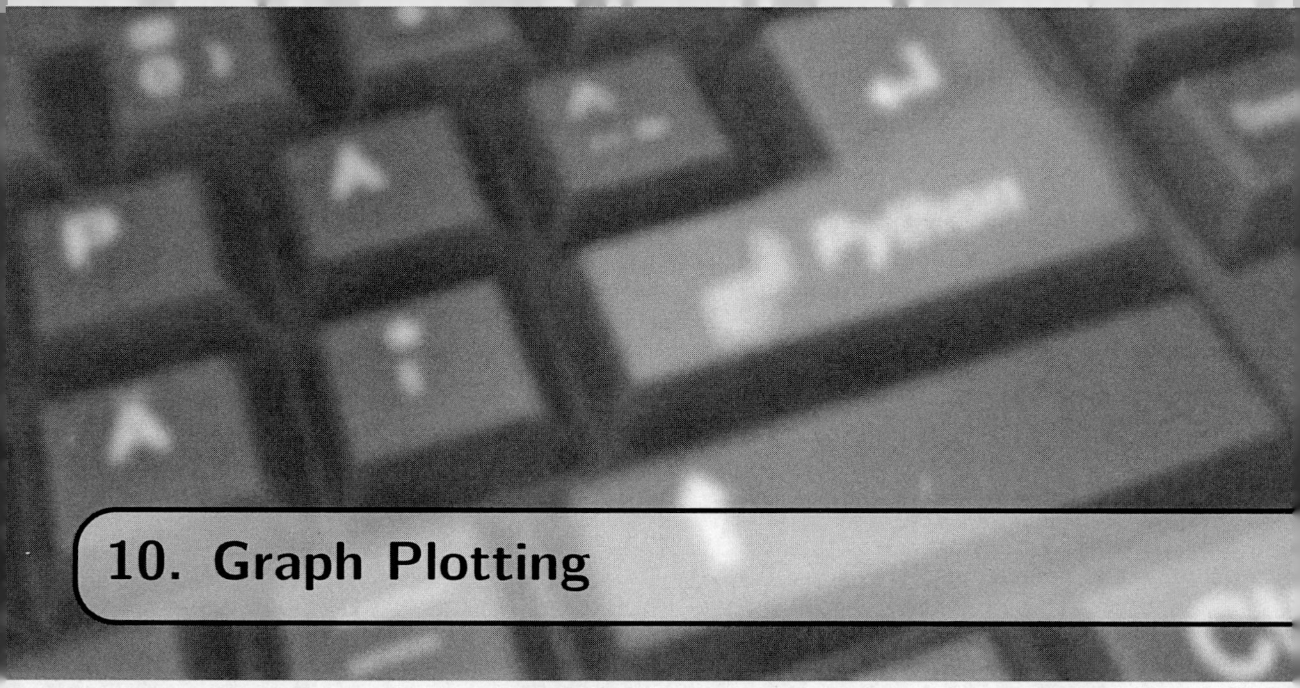

10. Graph Plotting

Graph plotting is a fundamental aspect of data visualization that allows us to represent data in a graphical format. Python offers a rich ecosystem of libraries dedicated to graph plotting and data visualization, empowering users to create stunning and informative graphs for diverse applications. Python provides many open-source plotting library which can be used for plotting different type of graphs. Whether you're a beginner exploring basic plots or an advanced user building complex visualizations, Python offers versatile tools to meet your needs. Python offers a rich ecosystem of libraries dedicated to graph plotting and data visualization, empowering users to create stunning and informative graphs for diverse applications. Each library brings unique strengths and capabilities to the table, catering to different needs and preferences within the data visualization landscape. Each library brings unique strengths and capabilities to the table, catering to different needs and preferences within the data visualization landscape. Python provides powerful libraries like *Matplotlib*, *Plotly*, and *Seaborn* that make it easy to create a wide variety of graphs and charts efficiently.

10.1 Matplotlib

Matplotlib is a comprehensive library for creating static, animated, and interactive visualizations in Python. It was originally developed by John D. Hunter, a neurobiologist, who created the library to facilitate data analysis and visualization in his scientific research. Matplotlib quickly evolved into an open-source project widely adopted by the scientific and data analysis communities. Inspired by MATLAB's plotting capabilities, Matplotlib was designed to provide a similar plotting interface in Python, enabling researchers and analysts to create high-quality, publication-ready plots programmatically. Over the years, Matplotlib has grown into a versatile library with extensive documentation and a large user base. Its flexibility allows users to create a wide range of plots, customize every aspect of their visualizations, and seamlessly integrate plots into scientific papers, presentations, and interactive environments. Table 10.1 shows the list of commands/code snippets, commonly used in Matplotlib to accomplish various tasks related to creating 2D graphs.

```
# Command to install library : Matplotlib

pip install matplotlib
```

10.1.1 Matplotlib.pyplot: A Versatile Tool for Python Plotting

`matplotlib.pyplot` is a fundamental submodule of the Matplotlib library, providing a powerful and intuitive interface for creating a wide range of 2D plots and visualizations in Python. Its simplicity and flexibility make it a popular choice among data scientists, researchers, and developers for generating publication-quality plots programmatically. By importing `matplotlib.pyplot`, users gain access to a comprehensive set of functions and methods for customizing plot elements such as axes, labels, colors, and styles, enabling precise control over the appearance of their visualizations.

Ex.1 Line plot using `Matplotlib`

```
import matplotlib.pyplot as plt

# Sample data
x = [1, 2, 3, 4, 5]
y = [2, 3, 5, 7, 11]

# Create a line plot
plt.plot(x, y, marker='o', linestyle='-', color='b', label='Prime Numbers')

# Customize plot
plt.title('Prime Numbers Plot')
plt.xlabel('X-axis')
plt.ylabel('Y-axis')
plt.legend()

# Display plot
plt.grid(True)
plt.show()
```

Table 10.1: Command /code snippets used to plot 2D graph using Matplotlib

Task	Command/Code
Set Title	`plt.title('Title')`
Set X-Axis Label	`plt.xlabel('Label')`
Set Y-Axis Label	`plt.ylabel('Label')`
Create Line Plot	`plt.plot(x, y)`
Create Scatter Plot	`plt.scatter(x, y)`
Create Bar Graph	`plt.bar(x, height)`
Create Horizontal Bar	`plt.barh(y, width)`
Create Histogram	`plt.hist(data, bins)`
Create Pie Chart	`plt.pie(sizes, labels)`
Create Box Plot	`plt.boxplot(data)`
Create Violin Plot	`plt.violinplot(data)`
Create Area Plot	`plt.fill_between(x, y)`
Create Contour Plot	`plt.contour(X, Y, Z)`
Create Heatmap	`plt.imshow(data, cmap)`
Create Quiver Plot	`plt.quiver(x, y, u, v)`
Create Stream Plot	`plt.streamplot(x, y, u, v)`
Create Errorbar Plot	`plt.errorbar(x, y, yerr)`
Create Stem Plot	`plt.stem(x, y)`
Create Hexbin Plot	`plt.hexbin(x, y)`
Create Polar Plot	`plt.polar(theta, r)`
Create Contourf Plot	`plt.contourf(X, Y, Z)`

Output: Graph of Figure 10.1
Explanation:

- `plt.plot()` is used to create a line plot by passing the x and y data arrays.
- We specify marker style, linestyle, and color for the plot, along with a label for the legend.
- Title of the graph is set using `plt.title()`.
- Labels for x axis and y axis is added using `plt.xlabel()` and `plt.ylabel()` respectively.
- Legends is added in graph using `plt.legend()`. The legend helps to identify which line corresponds to which data series, making the plot more informative and easier to understand.

Ex.2 Multiple Line plot in one figure using `Matplotlib`

```
import matplotlib.pyplot as plt

# Sample data
x = [1, 2, 3, 4, 5]
y = [2, 3, 5, 7, 11]
```

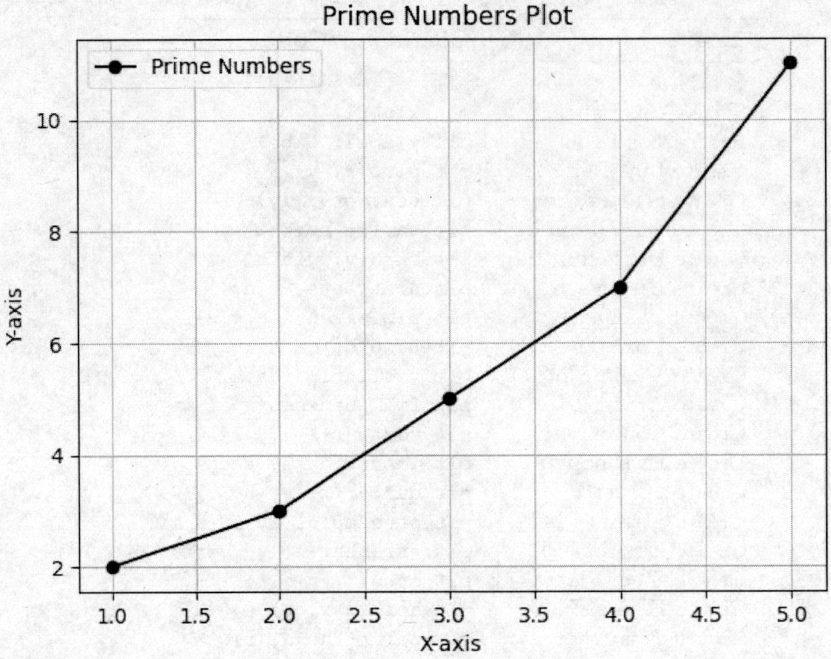

Figure 10.1: Line Graph using Matplotlib

```
z = [1, 4, 9, 16, 25]

# Create a line plot
plt.plot(x, y, marker='o', linestyle='-', color='b', label='Prime Numbers')
plt.plot(x, z, marker='o', linestyle='-', color='g', label='Perfect Square')

# Customize plot
plt.title('My Number Representation Graph')
plt.xlabel('X-axis')
plt.ylabel('Y-axis')
plt.legend()

# Display plot
plt.grid(True)
plt.show()
```

Output: Graph of Figure 10.2

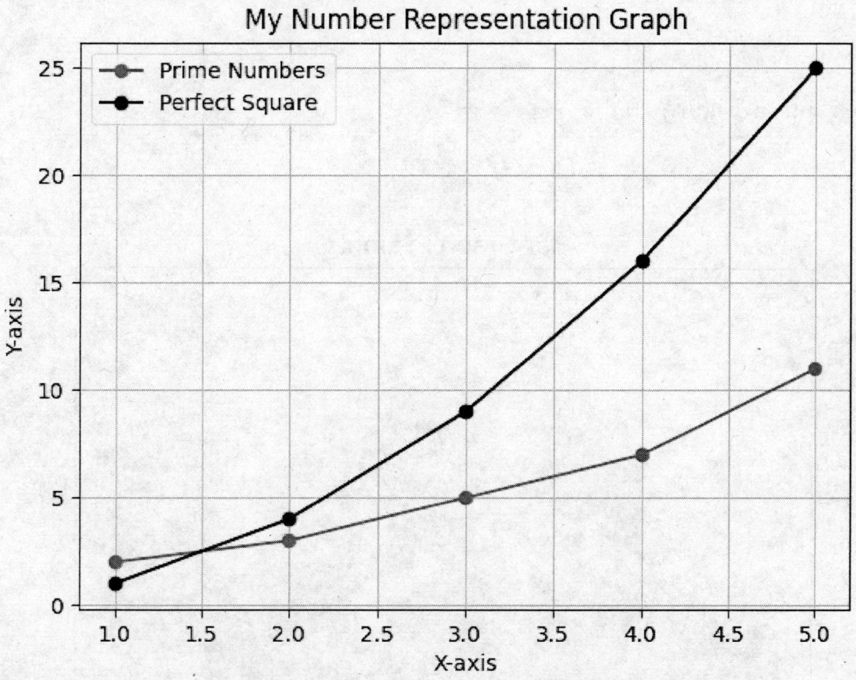

Figure 10.2: Multi-Line Graph using Matplotlib

Explanation:
Multi-line graph may be plotted in same figure using calling function `plt.plot()`, multiple times with different set data.

Ex.3 Bar Graph using `Matplotlib`

```
import matplotlib.pyplot as plt

# Sample data
categories = ['A', 'B', 'C', 'D', 'E']
values = [23, 45, 56, 32, 67]

# Create bar graph
plt.bar(categories, values, color='skyblue')

# Add labels and title
plt.xlabel('Categories')
```

```
plt.ylabel('Values')
plt.title('Bar Graph Example')

# Show plot
plt.show()
```

Output: Graph of Figure 10.3

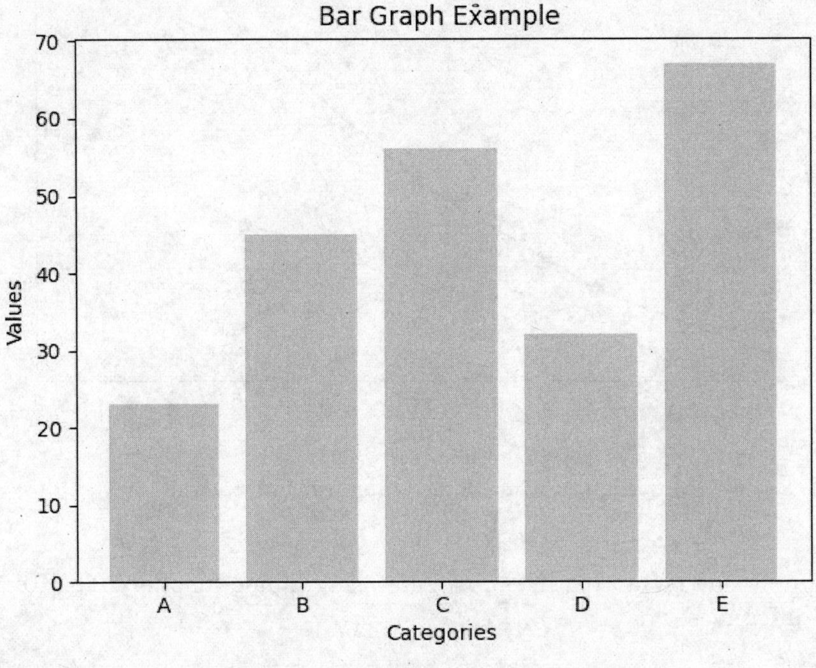

Figure 10.3: Bar graph using Matplotlib

Explanation:
Bar graph is created using `plt.bar()` by passing the categories and values arrays.

Ex.4 Pie Chart using `Matplotlib`

```
import matplotlib.pyplot as plt

# Sample data
myLabels = ['Apples', 'Bananas', 'Oranges', 'Grapes',  'Mangoes']
MyValue = [30, 10, 20, 15, 35]
```

```
# Explode the 2nd and last data (Minimum and Maximum)
exp = (0, 0.1, 0, 0,  0.1)

# Color of each data
myColor = ['skyblue', 'lightgreen', 'orange',  'lightskyblue', 'green']

# Create pie chart
plt.pie(MyValue,labels=myLabels, explode=exp, colors=myColor,
autopct='%1.1f%%')

# Equal aspect ratio ensures that pie is drawn as a circle
plt.axis('equal')

# Add title
plt.title('Fruit Distribution')

# Show plot
plt.show()
```

Output: Graph of Figure 10.4

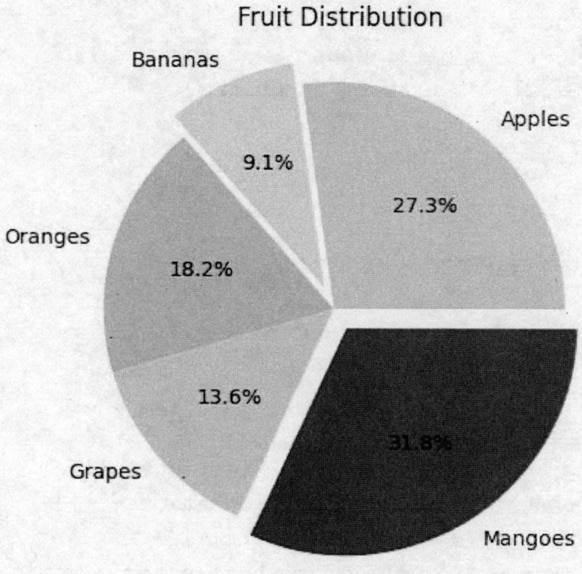

Figure 10.4: Pie chart using Matplotlib

Explanation:

- `myLabels` defines the labels for each segment of the pie chart. Each label corresponds to a category or item represented by a segment in the pie chart.
- `MyValue` defines the values for each segment of the pie chart. The values represent the proportion of each category relative to the whole.
- `exp` defines the *explode* parameter, which is a tuple indicating the fraction of the radius with which to offset each wedge of the pie. A value of 0 means no explosion, while a value greater than 0 results in the corresponding wedge being *exploded* outwards from the center of the pie. Here, the 2nd and last data points (Bananas and Mangoes) are exploded slightly outwards for emphasis.
- `myColor` defines the colors for each segment of the pie chart. Each color corresponds to a segment in the pie chart.
- **plt.pie()** creates the pie chart. It takes in the values, labels, explode, colors, and autopct (formatting for the percentage display) as parameters. This function generates the pie chart based on the provided data.
- `plt.show()` displays the pie chart on the screen. It is the final step in the code, showing the complete visualization generated by the preceding commands.

Ex.5 Gantt Chart using `Matplotlib`

```
import matplotlib.pyplot as plt

# Sample data
tasks = ['Task 1', 'Task 2', 'Task 3', 'Task 4']
startTime = [0, 2, 4, 7]  # Start month (0-based)
durations = [3, 2, 3, 2]  # Duration in months

noOfTasks = len(tasks)

# Plot Gantt chart
fig, ax = plt.subplots(figsize=(10, 6))

# Adjusting bar width and gap between bars
#bar_gap = 0.1  # Reduce the gap between bars

for i in range(noOfTasks):
    ax.barh(tasks[i], width=durations[i], left=startTime[i], color='orange')
    labelText = f"{tasks[i]}, Duration = {durations[i]}"
    labelPosition = startTime[i] + durations[i] / 2
    ax.text(labelPosition, i, labelText, ha='center', va='center')

# Customize plot
```

```
ax.set_xlabel('Month')
ax.set_ylabel('Tasks')
ax.set_title('Gantt Chart Example')

# Show plot
plt.show()
```

Output: Gantt Chart of Figure 10.5

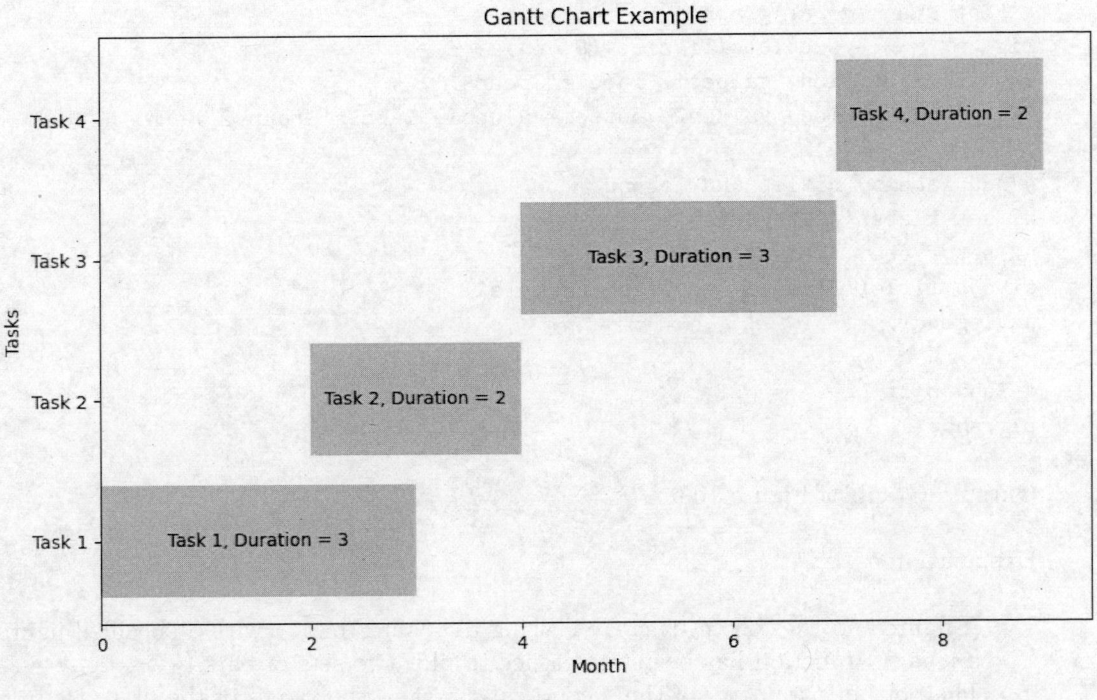

Figure 10.5: Gantt Chart using Matplotlib

Explanation:

- A figure and axes object is created using `plt.subplots()` with a specified figure size.
- `ax.barh` create a horizontal bar graph for each data items available in `tasks`, `startTime`, and `durations`.
- Position of text label inside the horizontal bar graph is calculated using `labelPosition = startTime[i] + durations[i] / 2`, which is placed at the midpoint of the task duration.
- `ax.text` adds the label to the plot at the calculated position. The `ha='center'` and `va='center'` parameters ensure that the label is centered horizontally and vertically with respect to the task bar.
- `plt.show()` displays the Gantt chart.

Ex.6 Gantt Chart using `Matplotlib`

```
import matplotlib.pyplot as plt

# Sample data
categories = ['Category 1', 'Category 2', 'Category 3', 'Category 4']
values1 = [20, 35, 30, 25]
values2 = [15, 25, 20, 30]

# Plot stacked bar graph
fig, ax = plt.subplots(figsize=(8, 6))
ax.bar(categories, values1, label='Group 1')
ax.bar(categories, values2, bottom=values1, label='Group 2')

# Add labels, title, and legend
ax.set_xlabel('Categories')
ax.set_ylabel('Values')
ax.set_title('Stacked Bar Graph Example')
ax.legend()

# Show plot
plt.show()
```

Output: Graph of Figure 10.6

Explanation:

- A figure and axes object is created using `plt.subplots()` with a specified figure size.
- `ax.bar()` function has been used twice to plot two sets of bars.
- The bottom parameter of the second call is set to the values of the first group, which stacks the bars on top of each other.

Ex.7 Grouped Bar graph using `Matplotlib`

```
import matplotlib.pyplot as plt
import numpy as np

# Data
continents = ["Asia", "Africa", "Europe", "North America"]
hindu = [1170, 0, 0, 0]
islam = [1930, 590, 45, 6]
christ = [286, 630, 560, 580]
```

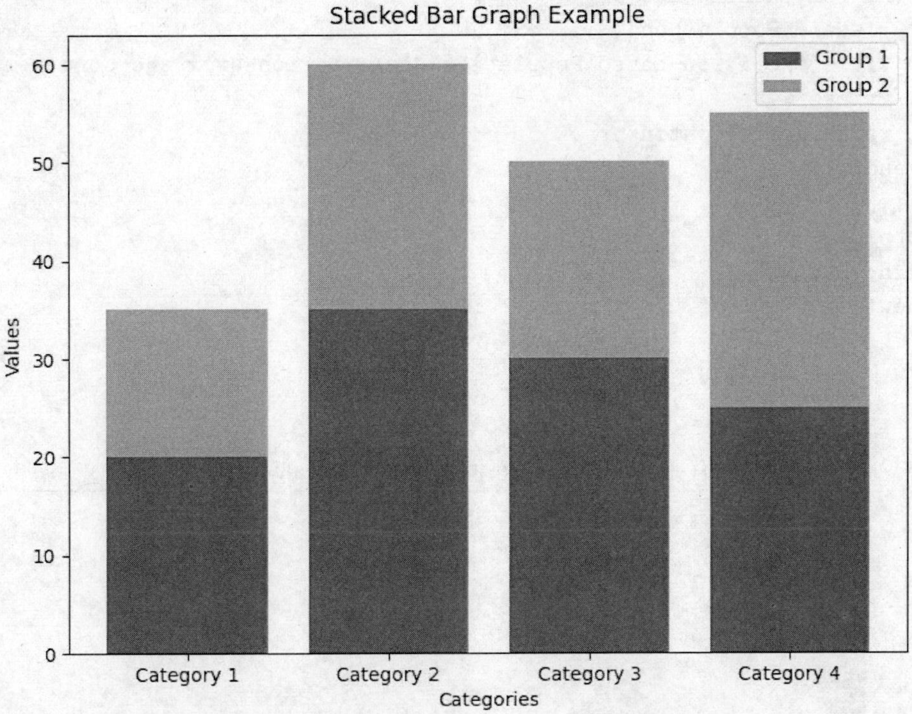

Figure 10.6: Stacked Graph using Matplotlib

```
buddh = [520, 0, 2, 7]

# Set the width of the bars
bw = 0.2 # bar width

# Set the x locations for the groups
x = np.arange(len(continents))

# Plotting
fig, ax = plt.subplots(figsize=(10, 6))


bar1 = ax.bar(x - bw, christ, bw, label='Christianity', color='salmon' )
bar2 = ax.bar(x, islam, bw, label='Islam', color='green' )
bar3 = ax.bar(x + bw, buddh, bw, label='Buddhism')
bar4 = ax.bar(x + 2*bw, hindu, bw, label='Hinduism', color='darkorange' )
```

```
# Add labels, title, and legend
ax.set_xlabel('Continents')
ax.set_ylabel('Population (Million)')
ax.set_title('Religion-based Population distribution over the Continents')
ax.set_xticks(x)
ax.set_xticklabels(continents)
ax.legend()

# Show plot
plt.tight_layout()
plt.show()
```

Output: Graph of Figure 10.6

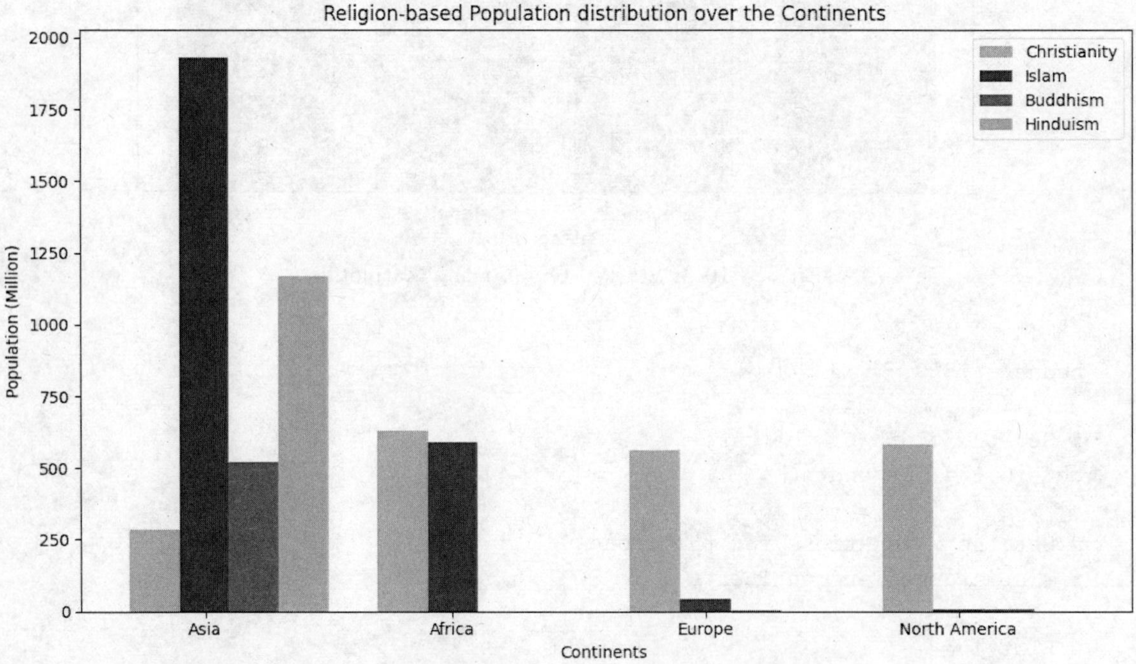

Figure 10.7: Grouped bar graph using Matplotlib

Explanation:

- `bw = 0.2`
  It defines the width of each bar.
- `x = np.arange(len(continents))`
  It creates an array of x-positions for the groups of bars.

- `fig, ax = plt.subplots(figsize=(10, 6))`
  It creates a figure and axis object for the plot.
- `bar1, bar2, bar3, bar4`
  It represent Christianity, Islam, Buddhism, and Hinduism, respectively. The bars are plotted with different colors and positions based on their respective populations and continents.
- `plt.tight_layout()`
  It adjusts subplot parameters to give specified padding.
- `plt.show()`
  It displays the plot.

10.2 Plotly

Plotly is a versatile and interactive plotting library that supports a wide range of graph types, including scatter plots, line plots, bar plots, and 3D plots. It offers capabilities for creating interactive web-based visualizations with features like hover tooltips, zooming, panning, and exporting plots to various formats. Plotly provides online graphing, analytics, and statistics tools for individuals and collaboration, as well as scientific graphing libraries for Python, R, MATLAB, Perl, Julia, Arduino, JavaScript and REST. Table 10.2 shows the difference between Matplotlib and Plotly library.

```
# Command to install library : Plotly

pip install plotly
```

Table 10.2: Difference between Matplotlib and Plotly

Feature	Matplotlib	Plotly
Syntax	More verbose, requires more lines of code.	Concise, especially with Plotly Express.
Interactivity	Limited interactivity (zoom, pan).	Extensive interactivity (hover, zoom, selection).
Output Formats	Generates static images (PNG, PDF, SVG).	Generates interactive HTML plots.
Use Cases	Static, publication-quality plots.	Interactive web-based visualizations, dashboards.
Community	Large and active community.	Strong community with comprehensive documentation.
Support	Mature library with extensive resources.	Commercial support and enterprise solutions.

10.2.1 Package Structure

The Python Plotly package structure encompasses a versatile set of modules and packages designed to facilitate the creation of interactive visualizations and dashboards.

- `plotly.graph_objs`
  It stands as a fundamental component, offering classes and functions for defining and configuring plotly graph objects, including traces, layouts, and annotations.
- `plotly.subplots`
  It is used for generating subplots and grid layouts.
- `plotly.express`
  It is a high-level interface for creating complex plots with minimal code, built on top of `plotly.graph_objs`.
- `plotly.offline`
  It contains functions for generating offline HTML plots and saving plots to files.
- `dash_core_components` and `dash_html_components`
  It provide essential components for building interactive web interfaces.

10.2.2 Graph Plotting Using `plotly.express`

`plotly.express` module can create the entire Figure at once. It uses the `graph_objects` internally and returns the `graph_objects.Figure` instance. Table 10.3 show the list of some commonly used command to generate various types of 2D plots using Plotly Express.

Table 10.3: Difference between Matplotlib and Plotly

`px.line()`	Create a line chart.
`px.scatter()`	Create a scatter plot.
`px.bar()`	Create a bar chart.
`px.histogram()`	Create a histogram.
`px.box()`	Create a box plot.
`px.violin()`	Create a violin plot.
`px.area()`	Create an area chart.
`px.pie()`	Create a pie chart.
`px.scatter_matrix()`	Create a scatter matrix plot.
`px.imshow()`	Create a heatmap.

Ex.8 Pie chart using `plotly`

```
import plotly.express as px

# Sample data
labels = ['Apple', 'Banana', 'Orange', 'Mango']
values = [30, 20, 25, 25]
```

```
# Create pie chart
fig = px.pie(names=labels, values=values, title='Fruit Distribution')

# Show plot
fig.show()
```

Output: Interactive Graph of Figure 10.8 displayed on HTML browser

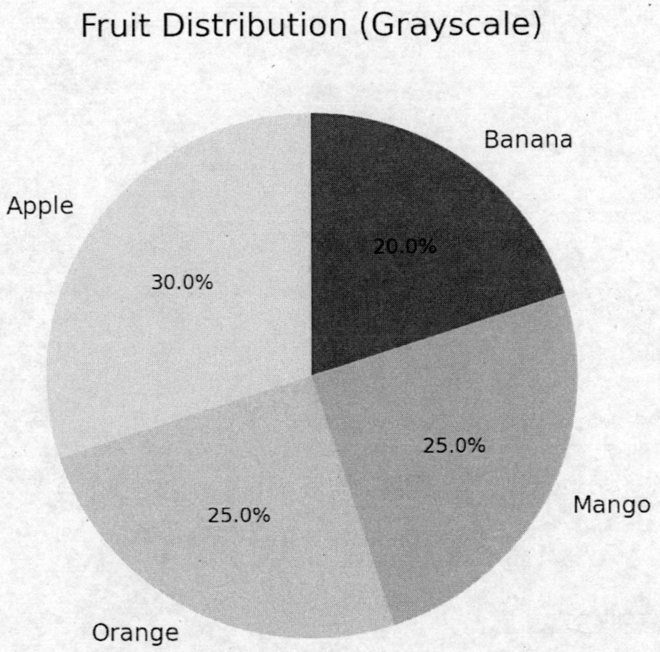

Figure 10.8: Pie chart using Plotly

Explanation:

- We import `plotly.express` as px.
- `labels` representing categories and `values` representing the corresponding values.
- pie chart is created using `px.pie()` and pass the `names` and `values` as parameters.
- pie chart has been assigned to the variable `fig`.
- Finally, the plot is displayed using `show()`.

Ex.9 Box Plot using `plotly`

```
import plotly.express as px

# Load the Iris dataset from Plotly Express
iris = px.data.iris()
```

```
box_fig = px.box(iris, x="species", y="petal_length",
                 title="Box Plot of Petal Length by Species")
box_fig.show()
```

Output: Interactive Graph of Figure 10.9 displayed on HTML browser

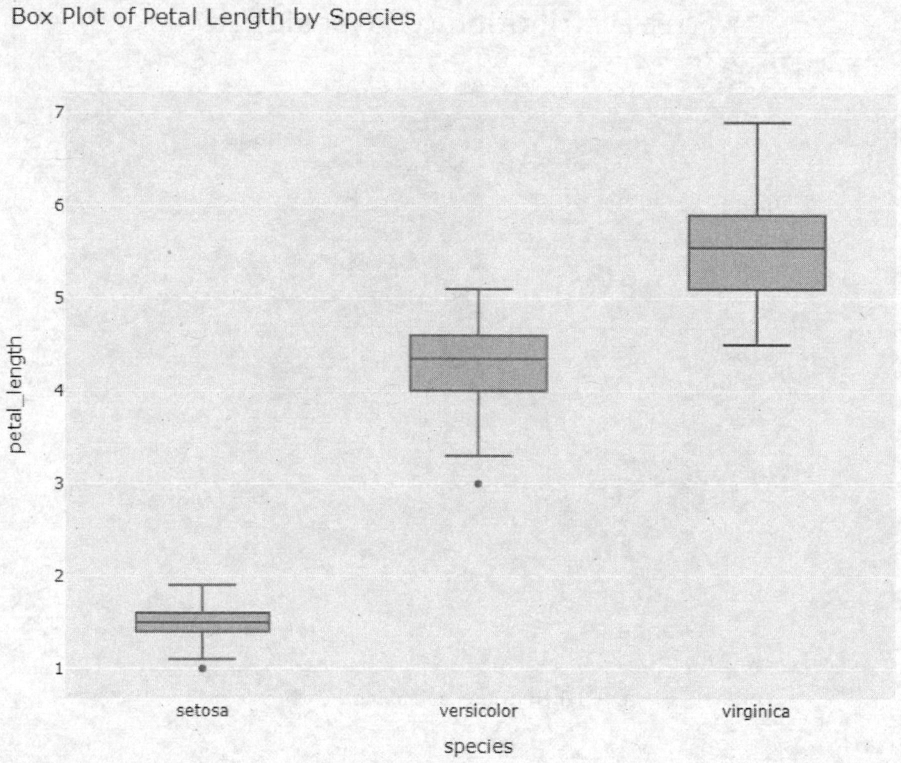

Figure 10.9: Box plot using Plotly

Explanation:

- `iris = px.data.iris()`
  It loads the Iris dataset from Plotly Express. Plotly Express provides several built-in datasets for demonstration purposes, and the Iris dataset is one of them. This dataset contains measurements of sepal and petal lengths and widths for three species of iris flowers: setosa, versicolor, and virginica.
- `px.box()`
  It creates a box plot using the Iris dataset. This function call specifies that the x-axis should represent the species of iris flowers (`x="species"`) and the y-axis should represent the length of the petals (`y="petal_length"`).
- The resulting box plot is then displayed using `box_fig.show()`.

Ex.10 Area chart using `plotly`

```
import plotly.express as px
# Sample data
x = [1, 2, 3, 4, 5]
y1 = [10, 15, 13, 17, 18]
y2 = [12, 14, 11, 16, 17]

# Create area chart
fig = px.area(x=x, y=[y1, y2], labels={'x': 'X-axis', 'y': 'Y-axis'},
                                        title='Area Chart')
fig.show()
```

Output: Interactive Graph of Figure 10.10 displayed on HTML browser

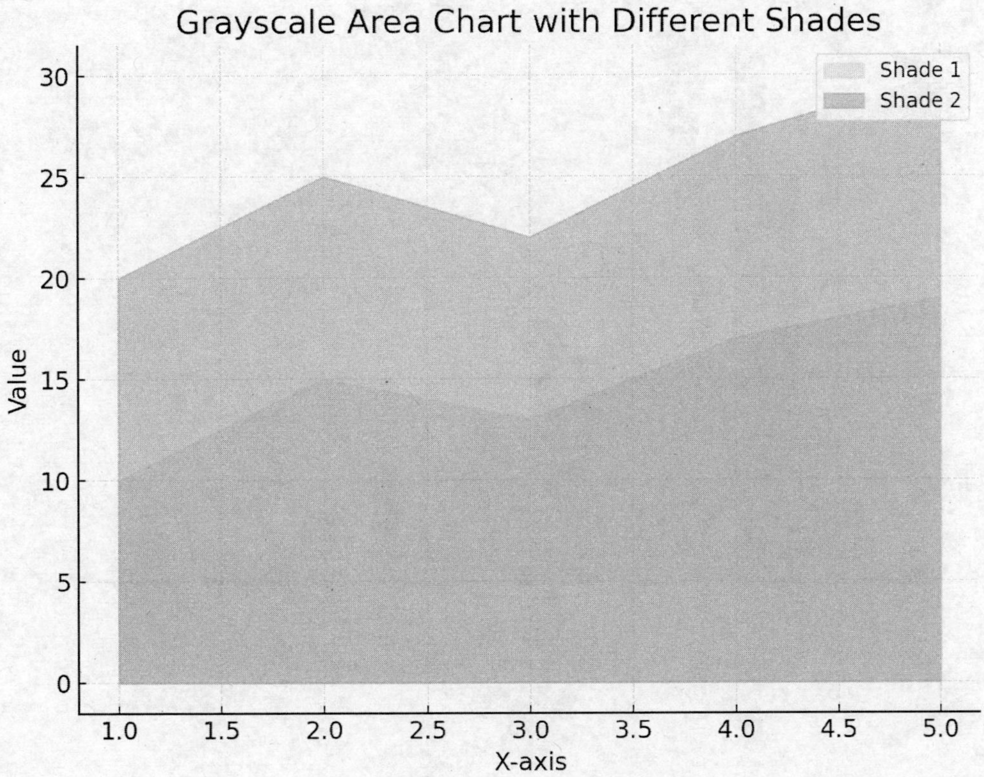

Figure 10.10: Area chart using Plotly

Ex.11 Histogram using `plotly`

```
import plotly.express as px
# Load the Tips dataset from Plotly Express
tips = px.data.tips()

# Create histogram
fig = px.histogram(tips, x="total_bill",
                   title="Histogram of Total Bill (Tips Dataset)")
fig.show()
```

Output: Interactive Graph of Figure 10.11 displayed on HTML browser

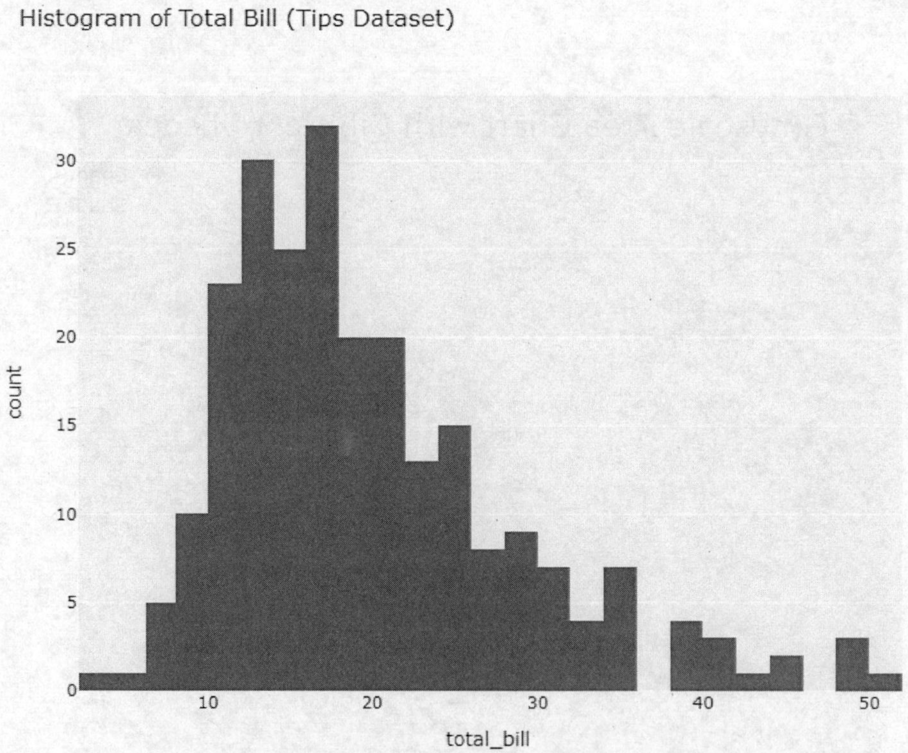

Figure 10.11: Histogram chart using Plotly

Facetting

Facet plots are figure, made up of multiple subplots having the same set of axes. Each subplot shows a subset of the data. Plotly Express functions provides the built-in argument `facet_row` and `facet_col` to easily generate the facet.

Ex.12 Facet with scatter plots.

```
import plotly.express as px
df = px.data.tips()
fig = px.scatter(df, x="total_bill", y="tip", color="smoker"
                                        , facet_col="sex", facet_row="time" )
fig.show()
```

Output: Interactive Graph of Figure 10.12 displayed on HTML browser

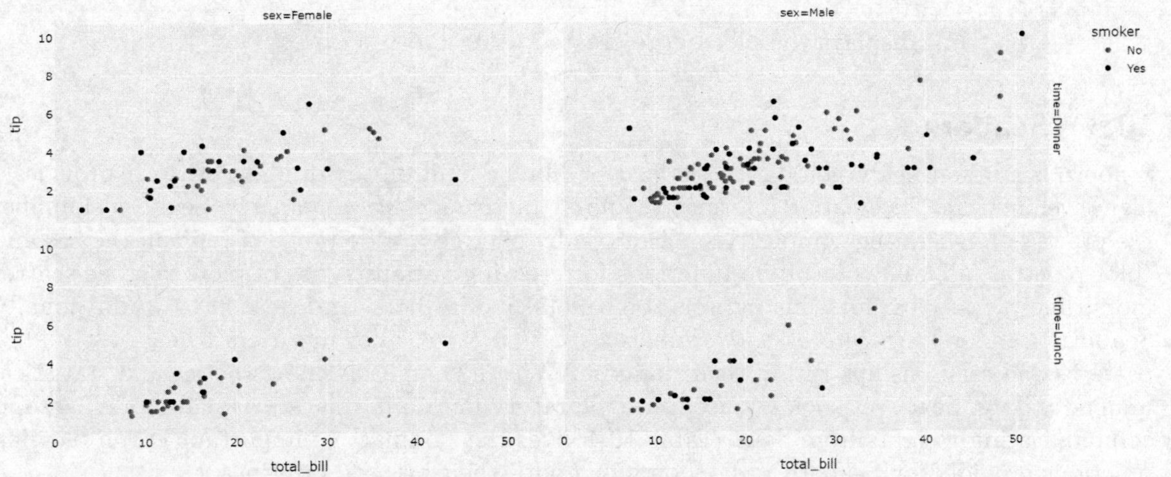

Figure 10.12: Scatter Plot with Facet using Plotly

Explanation:

- `df = px.data.tips()`
  This line loads a sample dataset called "tips" from the Plotly Express datasets. This dataset contains information about tips in a restaurant, including the total bill, tip amount, whether the customer is a smoker, their gender, and the time of day.
- `fig = px.scatter(df, x="total_bill", y="tip", color="smoker", facet_col="sex", facet_row="time")`
  This line creates a scatter plot figure using the px.scatter() function. It takes several parameters:
  - `df` :
    The DataFrame containing the data to be plotted.
  - `x="total_bill"` :
    Specifies that the x-axis of the scatter plot should represent the "total_bill" column from the DataFrame.
  - `y="tip"` :
    Specifies that the y-axis of the scatter plot should represent the "tip" column from the DataFrame.

  - `color="smoker"` :
    Specifies that the color of the data points should be determined by the "smoker" column from the DataFrame, which indicates whether the customer is a smoker or not.
  - `facet_col="sex"` :
    Divides the data into separate columns based on the "sex" column from the DataFrame. Each column will represent a different gender.
  - `facet_row="time"` :
    Divides the data into separate rows based on the "time" column from the DataFrame. Each row will represent a different time of day.
- `fig.show()` :
  This line displays the plot figure created using Plotly Express.

10.3 Seaborn

Seaborn is a powerful Python data visualization library built on top of Matplotlib. It provides a high-level interface for creating informative and attractive *statistical graphics*. Seaborn simplifies the process of generating complex visualizations by offering a wide range of built-in themes and color palettes, as well as intuitive functions for creating various types of plots such as scatter plots, line plots, bar plots, histograms, box plots, violin plots, and heatmaps. Additionally, Seaborn seamlessly *integrates with Pandas data structures*, allowing users to easily visualize patterns and relationships within their datasets. With its emphasis on aesthetics and statistical understanding, Seaborn is widely used in exploratory data analysis, statistical modeling, and communicating insights from data. Table 10.4 gives the summary of important graph plotting functions provided by Seaborn in Python along with their brief descriptions.

While Seaborn can create plots independently without explicitly importing Matplotlib, it still relies on Matplotlib's functionality under the hood. Seaborn cannot generate plots independently without Matplotlib or Plotly being installed because it utilizes Matplotlib's plotting functions for rendering. When you import Seaborn, it automatically sets up the Matplotlib environment in the background. A comperision between key features of matplotlib, plotly, and seaborn is presented in Table 10.5.

```
# Command to install library : Seaborn
# Seaborn supports Python 3.8+.

pip install seaborn
```

10.3.1 Pairplot

The pairplot is a visualization tool provided by the Seaborn library in Python, specifically designed for exploratory data analysis. It allows users to quickly generate a grid of scatterplots, histograms, and density plots to visualize pairwise relationships in a dataset. Each pair of variables in the dataset is represented by a scatterplot, showing how the variables relate to each

Table 10.4: Key feature Comparison of Matplotlib, Plotly, and Seaborn for plotting graphs in Python

Function	Description
`sns.scatterplot`	Create a scatter plot with optional hue and style semantics.
`sns.lineplot`	Draw a line plot with optional estimation of central tendency and confidence intervals.
`sns.barplot`	Show point estimates and confidence intervals as rectangular bars.
`sns.boxplot`	Draw a box plot to show the distribution of quantitative data in a way that facilitates comparisons between variables or across levels of a categorical variable.
`sns.violinplot`	Draw a combination of boxplot and kernel density estimate.
`sns.swarmplot`	Draw a categorical scatterplot with non-overlapping points.
`sns.countplot`	Show the counts of observations in each categorical bin using bars.
`sns.heatmap`	Plot rectangular data as a color-encoded matrix.
`sns.pairplot`	Plot pairwise relationships in a dataset.
`sns.distplot`	Flexibly plot a univariate distribution of observations.

Table 10.5: Key feature Comparison of Matplotlib, Plotly, and Seaborn for plotting graphs in Python

Feature	Matplotlib	Plotly	Seaborn
Ease of Use	Requires more code for customization and complex plots.	Offers an easy-to-use syntax with interactive capabilities.	Provides a high-level interface for easy plotting with minimal code.
Interactive	Limited interactive features without additional libraries.	Highly interactive with built-in capabilities for interactivity,	Not inherently interactive, but can work with Plotly for interactive plots.
Default Aesthetics	Basic default styles with customization options.	Modern and visually appealing default styles.	Stylish default themes with built-in color palettes.
Plot Types	Supports a wide range of plot types and customizations.	Supports various plot types with interactive features.	Focuses on statistical plots with specialized functions.
Performance	Generally fast for most plotting tasks.	Slower for large datasets due to interactivity.	Fast for most plotting tasks, optimized for statistical plotting.
Integration	Widely used and integrates well with other libraries.	Integrates well with Jupyter Notebooks and web applications.	Seamlessly integrates with Pandas data structures.
Community Support	Large and active community with extensive documentation.	Active community with comprehensive documentation.	Active community with detailed documentation and examples.

other. Additionally, the diagonal of the grid shows a univariate distribution plot for each variable, providing insights into the distribution of individual variables. Pairplots are particularly useful for identifying patterns, correlations, and potential outliers in multidimensional datasets. By providing a comprehensive overview of the relationships between variables, pairplots serve as an invaluable tool for understanding the underlying structure of the data and informing subsequent data analysis tasks such as feature selection and modeling.

Ex.13 Pairplot on IRIS dataset.

```
import seaborn as sns
import matplotlib.pyplot as plt
# Sample dataset
iris = sns.load_dataset("iris")

# Draw pairplot
sns.pairplot(iris, hue="species")

# Show plot
plt.show()
```

Output: A Graph representing the pairwise relationship in Iris dataset as shown in Figure 10.13

Figure 10.13: Drawing pairwise relationships `Irish` dataset using Seaborn.

Explanation:

- Seaborn is used for creating statistical visualizations, while Matplotlib's pyplot provides functionality for displaying plots.
- The *Iris* dataset is loaded using Seaborn's `load_dataset()` function. This dataset contains information about the sepal length, sepal width, petal length, petal width, and species of iris flowers.

- The `sns.pairplot()` function is called to create a pairplot visualization. This function takes the *Iris* dataset `iris` as input. The *hue parameter is set to "species"*, which means that the points in the scatterplots will be colored according to the species of iris flowers.
- Finally, the `plt.show()` function is called to display the generated pairplot.

10.3.2 Swarm Plot

A swarm plot is a type of categorical plot provided by the Seaborn library in Python, designed to visualize the distribution of a continuous variable within different categories. It arranges data points along the categorical axis without overlapping, ensuring that each data point is clearly visible. This plot type is particularly useful for visualizing the distribution of data points when dealing with relatively small datasets or when individual data points are of interest. Swarm plots provide insights into the distribution of the continuous variable across different categories, allowing for easy comparison and identification of patterns or outliers within each category.

Ex.14 Swarm plot on Tips dataset

```
import seaborn as sns
import matplotlib.pyplot as plt

# Sample dataset
tips = sns.load_dataset("tips")

# Draw swarm plot
sns.swarmplot(x="day", y="total_bill", hue="sex", data=tips)

# Show plot
plt.show()
```

Output: A Graph representing the pairwise relationship in Iris dataset as shown in Figure 10.14

Explanation:

- It loads the "*tips*" dataset provided by Seaborn, which contains information about tips in a restaurant, including the *total bill*, the *day of the week*, the *gender* of the payer, and other details.
- `sns.swarmplot()` creates a swarm plot with parameter as:
  - `x="day"`: Specifies that the categorical variable "`day`" will be plotted on the `x-axis`.
  - `y="total_bill"`: Specifies that the continuous variable "`total_bill`" will be plotted on the `y-axis`.
  - `hue="sex"`: Specifies that the points will be colored based on the categorical variable "*sex*".

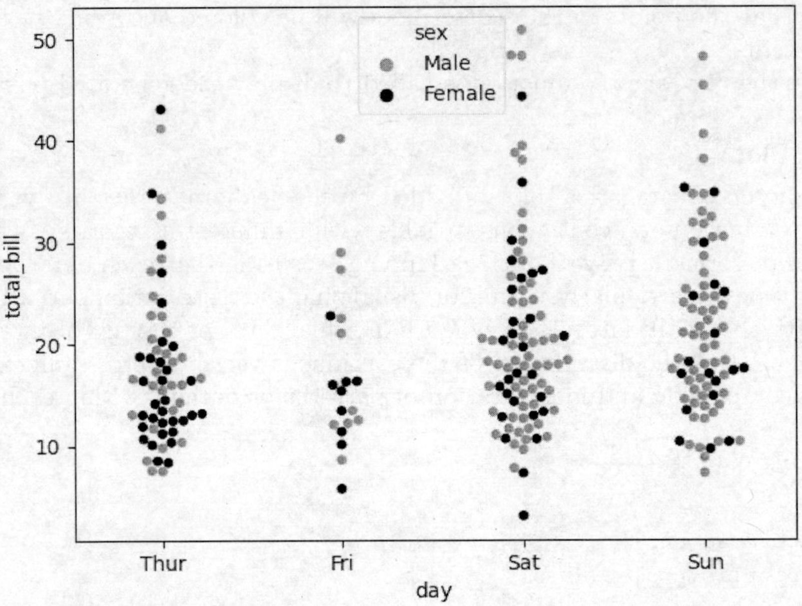

Figure 10.14: Swarm plot visualization based on the "tips" dataset using *seaborn*

- `data=tips`: Specifies the dataset to be used, in this case, the "*tips*" dataset.
- Since we imported `Matplotlib` as *plt*, we use `plt.show()` to display the Seaborn plot.

10.4 Graph Plotting from Excel File

When it comes to plotting graphs from Excel data, there are several libraries and methods available to cater to various needs and preferences. One popular option is to use Python libraries such as *Matplotlib*, *Seaborn*, and *Plotly*. Additionally, tools like `Pandas` offer built-in plotting functionality, allowing users to create plots directly from *DataFrame* objects. Consider a excel file (as shown in Figure 10.15), named as "*mydatafile.xlsx*" for plotting graph.

Ex.15 Read excel file and plot line graph from its data

```
import pandas as pd
import matplotlib.pyplot as plt

# Read Excel file into DataFrame
df = pd.read_excel("mydatafile.xlsx")
plt.figure()
```

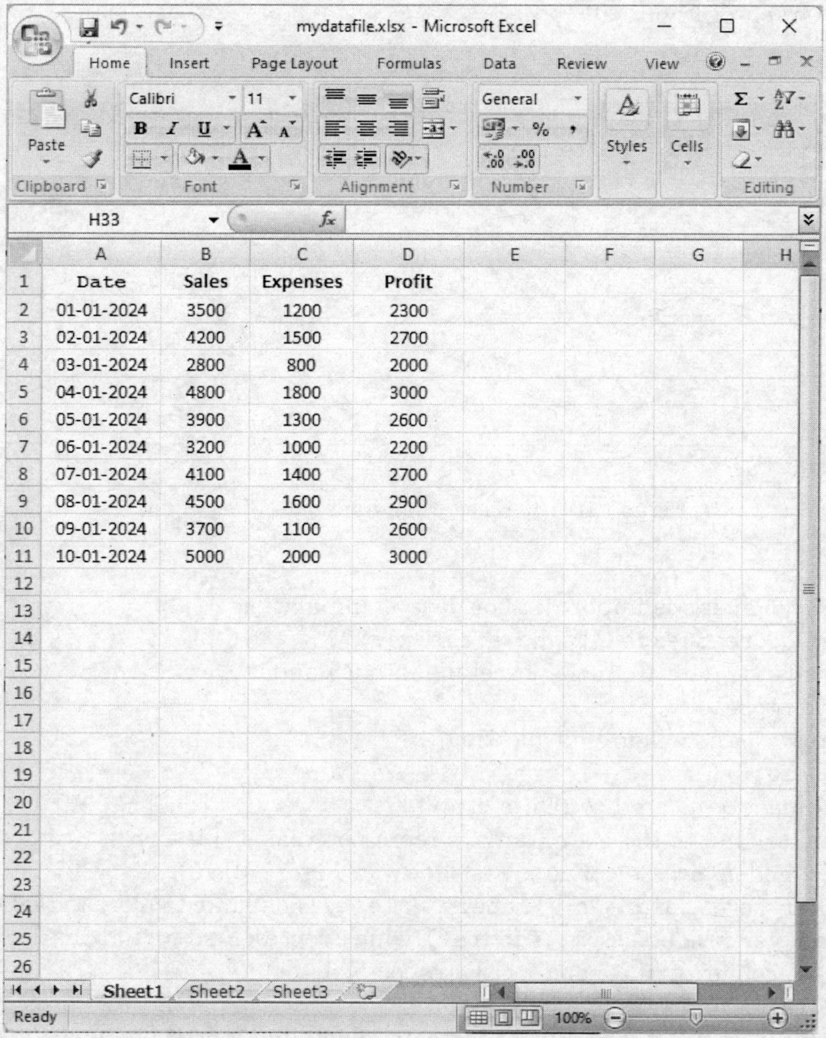

Date	Sales	Expenses	Profit
01-01-2024	3500	1200	2300
02-01-2024	4200	1500	2700
03-01-2024	2800	800	2000
04-01-2024	4800	1800	3000
05-01-2024	3900	1300	2600
06-01-2024	3200	1000	2200
07-01-2024	4100	1400	2700
08-01-2024	4500	1600	2900
09-01-2024	3700	1100	2600
10-01-2024	5000	2000	3000

Figure 10.15: Sample excel file for plotting graph

```
#Plot line graph with marker, different color and labels
plt.plot(df['Date'], df['Profit'], marker='o', color='g', label='Profit')
plt.plot(df['Date'], df['Sales'], marker='o', color='b', label='Sale')
plt.plot(df['Date'], df['Expenses'], marker='o', color='r', label='Expense')

plt.legend()
plt.title('Line Plot')
plt.show()
```

Output: Graph of Figure 10.16

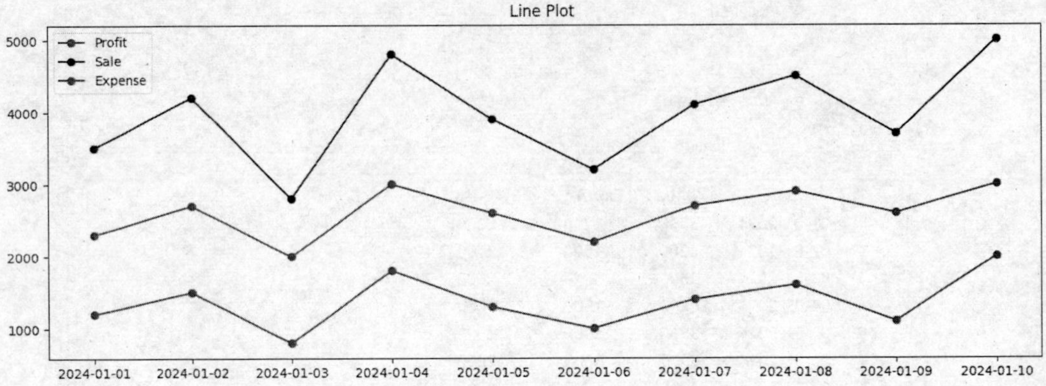

Figure 10.16: Line Graph from data of excel file

Explanation:

- Library `Pandas` is importded for data manipulation.
- `df = pd.read_excel("mydatafile.xlsx")`
  It reads the data from the Excel file into a Pandas DataFrame.
- `plt.figure()`
  It creates a new figure for plotting.
- `plt.plot()`
  This function is used to plot a graph.
- 'Date' column of the DataFrame is represented as `df['Date']` . Similarly the *Profit*, *Sales*, and *Expenses* columns (as shown in Figure 10.15).
- `marker='o', color='b', label='Sale'` : The marker, color, and label are optional parameter inside the `plt.figure()` which represents circular markers ('o')on data points, colour of lines, and labels respectively.
- `plt.legend()`
  It adds a legend to the plot to indicate which line represents which variable.

Ex.16 Read excel file and plot multiple graph in one figure

```
import pandas as pd
import matplotlib.pyplot as plt

# Read Excel file into DataFrame
excel_file = "mydatafile.xlsx"
df = pd.read_excel(excel_file)

# Plot different types of graphs
plt.figure(figsize=(10, 5))

# Scatter plot
plt.subplot(1, 2, 1)
plt.scatter(df['Date'], df['Sales'])
plt.title('Scatter Plot')
plt.xticks(rotation='vertical')

# Bar plot
plt.subplot(1, 2, 2)
plt.bar(df['Date'], df['Profit'])
plt.title('Bar Plot')
plt.xticks(rotation='vertical')

# Adjust layout to prevent overlap
plt.tight_layout()

plt.show()
```

Output: Graph of Figure 10.17

Explanation:

- Library `Pandas` is importded for data manipulation.
- `df = pd.read_excel("mydatafile.xlsx")`
  It reads the data from the Excel file into a Pandas DataFrame.
- `plt.figure(figsize=(10, 5))`
  It creates a new figure with a specified size (10 inches in width and 5 inches in height) for plotting.
- `plt.subplot(1, 2, 1)`
  This line creates a subplot grid with 1 row and 2 columns and selects the first subplot (leftmost).

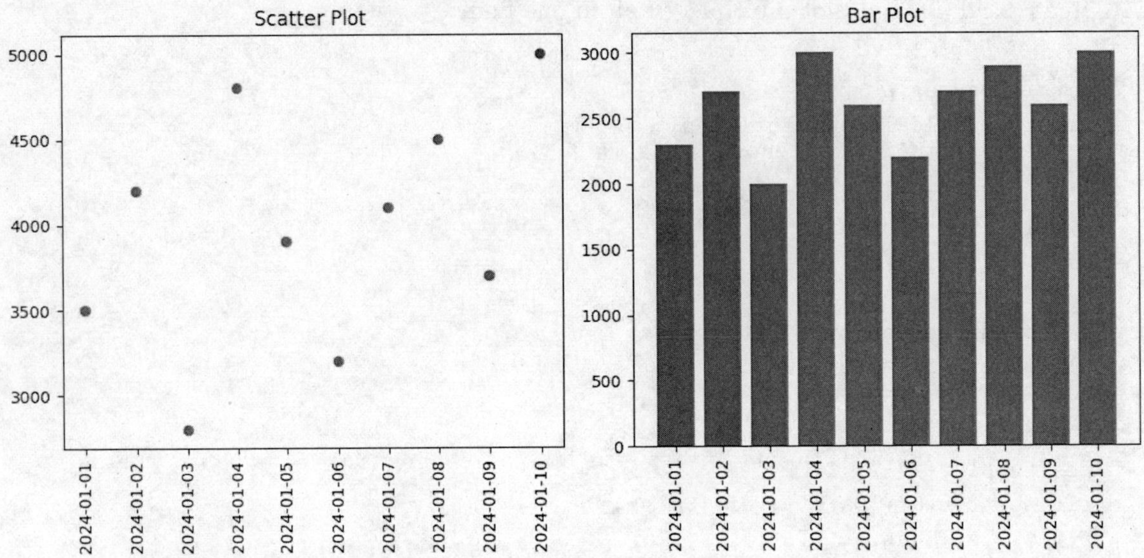

Figure 10.17: `subplot()` : Multiple graph inside one figure, data taken directly from excel file

`plt.scatter(df['Date'], df['Sales'])`
This line plots a scatter plot of 'Sales' against 'Date'. It represents the first type of graph, a scatter plot, in the left subplot.

- `plt.subplot(1, 2, 2)`
  This line creates a subplot grid with 1 row and 2 columns and selects the 2nd subplot (rightmost).
- `plt.bar(df['Date'], df['Profit'])`
  It plots a bar plot of 'Profit' against 'Date'.
- `plt.tight_layout()`
  This line adjusts the layout of subplots to prevent overlap and improve readability.
- `plt.show()`
  This line displays the entire figure containing both subplots with the scatter plot and the bar plot.

PART III MACHINE LEARNING THROUGH PYTHON

11. Introduction to Machine Learning

Machine learning (ML) is a subfield of artificial intelligence (AI) that focuses on the development of algorithms and statistical models that enable computers to learn and improve their performance on a specific task without being explicitly programmed. At its core, machine learning is concerned with the creation of systems that can automatically analyze and interpret data, identify patterns, and make decisions or predictions based on those patterns. Traditional computer programs completely rely on explict instructions given to perform a task, whereas machine learning algorithms learn from experience, adjusting their parameters or structure to optimize performance over time.

One of the key concepts in machine learning is the notion of training data. This data serves as the input to the learning algorithm and consists of examples or instances that are used to teach the system how to perform a specific task. During the training process, the algorithm iteratively processes the training data, making adjustments to its internal parameters to minimize errors or discrepancies between its predictions and the actual outcomes. Through this process of iterative refinement, the algorithm gradually improves its performance and becomes better equipped to generalize to new, unseen data.

Machine learning has a wide range of applications across various domains, including computer vision, natural language processing, healthcare, finance, autonomous vehicles, and many others. It has enabled significant advancements in areas such as image recognition, speech recognition, recommendation systems, and predictive analytics, among others. As the field continues to evolve, researchers are exploring new algorithms, techniques, and methodologies to tackle increasingly complex problems and push the boundaries of what is possible with machine learning.

11.1 Understanding Fundamentals

Machine learning (ML) represents a paradigm shift in computer science, enabling computers to learn from data and improve performance over time without being explicitly programmed.

11.1.1 What is Machine Learning

Machine learning is a subfield of artificial intelligence (AI) focused on the development of algorithms and models that enable computers to learn patterns and make predictions from data. Unlike traditional programming, where rules are explicitly defined by programmers, machine learning algorithms learn patterns and relationships from data through iterative processes.

At its core, machine learning revolves around the concept of learning from data. Algorithms are trained on large datasets, iteratively adjusting their parameters to minimize errors and improve performance on specific tasks. The ultimate goal is to develop models that can generalize well to unseen data, making accurate predictions or decisions.

11.1.2 Importance and Applications

Ability of machine learning to extract meaningful insights from large datasets, recognize patterns, and make predictions has made it an invaluable tool in today's data-driven world.

In healthcare, machine learning is enhancing diagnostics, predicting disease outcomes, and personalizing treatment plans based on individual patient data. From identifying cancerous tumors in medical images to monitoring vital signs and predicting patient readmissions, machine learning algorithms are streamlining healthcare processes and improving patient outcomes.

In finance, machine learning algorithms are used for fraud detection, credit scoring, algorithmic trading, and risk management. These algorithms analyze vast amounts of financial data in real-time, identifying anomalous patterns and making rapid decisions to optimize investment strategies, minimize risks, and enhance overall financial performance.

In e-commerce and digital marketing, machine learning powers recommendation systems, personalized advertising, and customer segmentation. By analyzing user behavior, preferences, and purchase history, these systems deliver targeted recommendations and advertisements, maximizing engagement, and conversion rates.

In manufacturing and supply chain management, machine learning optimizes production processes, predicts equipment failures, and optimizes inventory management. By analyzing sensor data from machinery and supply chain operations, machine learning algorithms identify inefficiencies, minimize downtime, and streamline operations, resulting in cost savings and improved productivity.

In transportation, machine learning enables autonomous vehicles, traffic management systems, and predictive maintenance for vehicles and infrastructure. These technologies enhance safety, reduce congestion, and optimize transportation networks, paving the way for more efficient and sustainable urban mobility.

Across these and many other domains, the importance of machine learning lies in its ability to automate tasks, extract actionable insights from data, and drive innovation. As the volume and complexity of data continue to grow, machine learning will play an increasingly vital role in unlocking value, driving efficiency, and shaping the future of virtually every industry.

11.1.3 Key Terminology

Models

Model refers to the mathematical representation or algorithm used to make predictions based on input data. A model learns patterns and relationships from the training data and uses this knowledge to make predictions on new, unseen data. Models can range from simple linear models (e.g., linear regression) to complex nonlinear models (e.g., neural networks). The choice of model depends on factors such as the nature of the problem, the complexity of the data, and the available computational resources.

Once training is complete, the model can be deployed into production to make predictions on real-world data.

Features

Features are the input variables or attributes that are used to make predictions in a machine learning model. It is also known as *predictors* or *independent variables.* Features represent the characteristics or attributes of the data that are relevant to the learning task. These can include numerical values, categorical variables, text, images, or any other type of data that is relevant to the problem being solved.

Feature selection is important step, where we identify and preprocess the most informative features for model training.

Data

Data is the foundation of machine learning. It representing the raw information used to train, evaluate, and test models. This data can encompass various types, including numerical values, text, images, audio, and more, depending on the nature of the problem being addressed. High-quality data is crucial for producing accurate and reliable machine learning models, as the performance of these models heavily relies on the quality, diversity, and representativeness of the data they are trained on.

Labels

Labels are the ground truth annotations or target values associated with each input example in the training data. In supervised learning tasks, where the algorithm learns from labeled data, labels provide the correct answers or desired outputs for the given inputs. For example, in a binary classification task to distinguish between images of cats and dogs, the labels would indicate whether each image depicts a cat or a dog. These labels guide the learning process, allowing the algorithm to adjust its predictions and internal representations based on the observed discrepancies between its outputs and the true labels.

Training Data

It is subset of whole dataset, used to train the machine learning algorithms to perform a specific task. It consists of input examples paired with their corresponding output labels or target values. The training data serves as the foundation for learning, as machine learning algorithms use this labeled information to adjust their internal parameters or structures, optimizing their performance to minimize errors or discrepancies between their predictions and the true outcomes.

The quality and quantity of training data play a significant role in determining the effectiveness and generalization capabilities of machine learning models.

Test Data

It is a separate subset of whole dataset, used to evaluate the performance of a trained machine learning model. This unseen data serves as a proxy for real-world scenarios, allowing practitioners to assess how well the model generalizes to new, unseen examples. By comparing the model's predictions on the test data against the true labels or target values,we can gauge the model's accuracy, precision, recall, and other performance metrics, providing insights into its effectiveness and potential areas for improvement.

Validation Data

It is an additional subset of the dataset used to fine-tune the hyperparameters of machine learning models and prevent overfitting. During the model development process, the training data is often partition into two subsets: one for actual training and another for validation. The validation data allows practitioners to iteratively adjust the model's hyperparameters, such as learning rate, regularization strength, and network architecture, based on its performance on unseen data. This process helps optimize the model's generalization capabilities and ensures that it performs well on new, unseen examples beyond the training set.

11.2 Types of Machine Learning

Machine learning encompasses various approaches and techniques, each tailored to address specific types of learning tasks and challenges. Machine learning can be classified based on various criteria:

11.2.1 Based on Learning Style

Based on Learning style, the machine learning algorithms is categorized into three parts: Supervised Learning, Unsupervised Learning, and Reinforcement Learning.

11.2.2 Based on Application

Based on application, the machine learning algorithms is categorized into four parts: Classification, Regression, Clustering, and Dimensionality Reduction.

11.3 Supervised Learning

Supervised learning is a fundamental approach in machine learning where the algorithm learns from labeled data, which means that each training data is paired with an output label or target value. The goal is to learn a mapping from inputs to outputs based on the provided examples. Model in this approach learn to map inputs to outputs based on the provided examples. Example of supervised learning algorithms are: Random Forest, Support Vector Machine (SVM), KNN, ANN, etc.

The typical process involve in supervised learning are:

1. **Data Collection:** The first step in supervised learning is to gather a dataset containing labeled examples. These examples consist of input features (also known as independent variables) and corresponding output labels (dependent variables). The quality and representativeness of the dataset are crucial for the success of the learning process.
2. **Data Preprocessing:** Once the dataset is collected, it often undergoes preprocessing to clean, transform, and prepare it for training. This may involve tasks such as handling missing values, scaling or normalizing features, encoding categorical variables, and splitting the data into training and test sets.
3. **Model Selection:** The next step is selecting an appropriate machine learning model or algorithm for the task at hand. The choice of model depends on factors such as the nature of the problem (classification or regression), the complexity of the data, and the available computational resources.
4. **Training:** In this phase, the selected model is fed with the labeled training data, and it learns to map input features to output labels through an iterative optimization process. During training, the model adjusts its internal parameters or weights to minimize the difference between its predictions and the true labels, typically using techniques like gradient descent or its variants.
5. **Evaluation:** Once the model is trained, its performance is evaluated using a separate dataset (test data), which contains examples unseen during training. Matrices like accuracy, precision, recall, f-score, are used for evaluation purpose
6. **Interpretation and Visualization:** Various techniques are employed to interpret the model's predictions, analyze feature importances, and visualize the relationships between input features and output labels. Feature importance plots, such as bar charts or heatmaps, are commonly used to identify the most influential features in the model's decision-making process. Confusion matrices provide a comprehensive summary of the model's performance, showing the counts of true positive, true negative, false positive, and false negative predictions across different classes. Additionally, Receiver Operating Characteristic (ROC) curves and Precision-Recall curves are used to evaluate binary classification models and visualize the trade-off between true positive rate and false positive rate, or precision and recall, respectively.
7. **Fine-tuning and Validation:** In some cases, additional steps such as hyperparameter tuning and cross-validation may be performed to fine-tune the model and improve its generalization performance. This involves adjusting parameters that are not learned during training, such as learning rates, regularization strengths, and model architectures, based on the model's performance on a validation set.

11.3.1 Application of Supervised Learning

Supervised learning has a wide range of applications:

Classification

Classification is a type of supervised learning task where the goal is to categorize input data into discrete classes or categories. In classification problems, the output variable (also known as the target or label) is categorical. The algorithm learns to map input features to predefined classes based on the labeled examples in the training data. Examples of classification tasks include spam email detection (classifying emails as spam or not spam), sentiment analysis (classifying text as positive, negative, or neutral), image recognition (classifying images into different object categories), disease diagnosis, etc.

Machine learning techniques such as Logistic Regression, Decision Trees, Random Forest, SVM, Naive Bayes, K-Nearest Neighbors (KNN) can be applied in classification problem.

Regression

Regression is another type of supervised learning task where the goal is to predict a continuous numeric value or quantity. In regression problems, the output variable is continuous, meaning it can take on any value within a range. The algorithm learns to map input features to continuous target values based on the labeled examples in the training data. Examples of regression tasks include predicting house prices (based on features such as location, size, and number of bedrooms), forecasting stock prices, estimating sales revenue, estimating customer lifetime value, etc.

Machine learning techniques such as Linear Regression, Decision Trees, Random Forest, Neural Networks can be applied in regression problem.

Time-Series Forecasting

Time-series data consists of observations recorded at regular intervals over time. These observations can represent various metrics, such as stock prices, sales figures, temperature readings, or any other time-dependent variable. Time-series forecasting is focused on predicting future values based on past observations, where the data is indexed or ordered chronologically. Time-series forecasting can be considered a specialized form of supervised learning tailored specifically for sequential data with temporal dependencies.

Machine learning techniques such as Linear Regression, Decision Trees, SVM, and Neural Networks can be applied to time-series forecasting tasks.

11.4 Unsupervised Learning

Unsupervised learning is a type of machine learning where the algorithm learns patterns and structures from unlabeled data, without explicit guidance or supervision. Unlike supervised learning, where the algorithm learns from labeled examples with known outcomes, unsupervised learning algorithms explore the data and discover hidden patterns, relationships, and structures on their own. Difference between supervised learning and unsupervised learning is summarized in Table 11.1. Example of unsupervised learning are: K-Means Clustering, Density-Based Spatial Clustering of Applications with Noise (DBSCAN), Principal Component Analysis (PCA), Gaussian Mixture Models (GMM), etc.

The typical process involve in unsupervised learning are:

1. **Data Collection:** The first step in any machine learning task is to gather the data. This may involve collecting data from various sources such as databases, APIs, sensors, etc.

The data collected should be relevant to the problem being addressed and representative of the underlying patterns or structures.
Unsupervised learning deals with unlabeled data, where there are no explicit output labels or target values against any example of data set.

2. **Data Preprocessing:** Similar to that of supervised learning process, collected data requires preprocessing to clean, transform, and prepare it for analysis. This may involve tasks such as handling missing values, removing outliers, scaling or normalizing features, and encoding categorical variables.
3. **Exploratory Data Analysis (EDA):** Exploratory data analysis involves exploring and visualizing the data to gain insights into its characteristics, distributions, and relationships. This step helps identify patterns, trends, and anomalies in the data, guiding subsequent modeling decisions.
4. **Feature Engineering:** Feature engineering involves creating relevant features or predictors from the raw data that can improve the performance of the unsupervised learning algorithms. This may include creating new features, transforming existing features, or selecting informative subsets of features.
5. **Model Selection:** Once the data is preprocessed and features are engineered, the next step is to select an appropriate unsupervised learning algorithm for the task at hand. The choice of algorithm depends on factors such as the nature of the data, the problem being addressed, and the desired outcome.
6. **Training:** In this step, the selected unsupervised learning algorithm is applied to the preprocessed data to learn patterns, structures, or representations from the unlabeled examples. The model parameters are adjusted iteratively to minimize a chosen objective function, such as clustering error or reconstruction error.
7. **Evaluation:** Evaluating unsupervised learning models can be challenging since there are no explicit labels or ground truth to compare predictions against. Instead, evaluation metrics often focus on assessing the quality of the learned representations, the coherence of clusters, or the ability of the model to capture meaningful patterns in the data.
8. **Interpretation and Visualization:** Once the model is trained and evaluated, the learned patterns or structures can be interpreted and visualized to gain insights into the underlying relationships within the data. Visualization techniques such as *scatter plots*, *heatmaps*, and *dendrograms* can help illustrate clusters, associations, or anomalies in the data.

11.4.1 Application of Unsupervised Learning

Common Techniques in Unsupervised Learning are:

Clustering

Clustering algorithms group similar data points together into clusters or segments based on their features or attributes. The goal is to partition the data into distinct groups, where data points within the same cluster are more similar to each other than to those in other clusters.

Examples of clustering algorithms include K-means clustering, hierarchical clustering, and DBSCAN.

Dimensionality Reduction

Dimensionality reduction techniques aim to reduce the complexity of the data by extracting essential features or representations while preserving as much relevant information as possible. These techniques are particularly useful for high-dimensional data where the number of features is large.

Principal Component Analysis (PCA), t-distributed Stochastic Neighbor Embedding (t-SNE), and Autoencoders are common dimensionality reduction methods.

Anomaly Detection

Anomaly detection, also known as outlier detection, involves identifying data points or instances that deviate significantly from the norm or expected behavior. Anomalies may indicate errors, fraud, or novel patterns in the data.

Unsupervised anomaly detection techniques include density-based methods, distance-based methods, and isolation forests.

Table 11.1: Comparison between Supervised and Unsupervised Learning Processes

Aspect	Supervised Learning	Unsupervised Learning
Data Labeling	Data is labeled with corresponding output labels/targets.	Data is unlabeled; no explicit output labels/targets.
Model Training	Model learns to map input features to output labels.	Model discovers patterns, structures, or representations.
Evaluation Metrics	Metrics like accuracy, precision, recall are used.	Evaluation focuses on learned representations, clusters, etc.
Interpretation and Visualization	Interpretation often involves analyzing feature importances, confusion matrices, etc. Visualization methods include ROC curves, Precision-Recall curves, etc.	Visualization used to explore learned patterns, clusters, etc.

11.5 Reinforcement Learning

Reinforcement Learning (RL) is a type of machine learning paradigm inspired by behavioral psychology, where an agent learns to make sequential decisions by interacting with an environment to achieve a certain goal. Unlike supervised learning, where the model is trained on labeled examples, and unsupervised learning, where the model learns from unlabeled data, reinforcement learning is based on the concept of trial and error learning, where the agent learns through experimentation and feedback. One example of a reinforcement learning algorithm is Q-Learning. Q-Learning is a model-free reinforcement learning algorithm that learns the optimal action-selection policy for a given environment by estimating the quality of each action in each state. Q-Learning is a foundational algorithm in reinforcement learning and serves as the basis for many other algorithms and extensions, such as Deep Q-Networks (DQN) and Double Q-Learning. It has applications in various domains, including robotics, gaming, finance, and optimization.

The typical process involve in reinforcement learning are:

1. **Problem Formulation:** The first step in reinforcement learning is to formulate the problem. This involves defining the task or goal that the agent aims to achieve, identifying the environment in which the agent operates, specifying the set of possible states and actions, and defining the reward structure.
2. **Environment Setup:** Once the problem is formulated, the environment is set up to simulate the interactions between the agent and its surroundings. This involves implementing the environment dynamics, including state transitions, action effects, and reward feedback, as well as any additional constraints or parameters.
3. **Agent Initialization:** The agent, which is responsible for making decisions and learning from experience, is initialized with an initial policy or strategy. This policy determines how the agent selects actions based on the current state and any available information.
4. **Exploration vs. Exploitation:** At each time step, the agent must balance between exploration (trying out new actions to learn more about the environment) and exploitation (leveraging known information to maximize rewards). Various exploration strategies, such as *epsilon-greedy* or *softmax*, can be employed to achieve this balance.
5. **Interaction with Environment:** The agent interacts with the environment by observing the current state, selecting actions based on its policy, and receiving feedback in the form of rewards. This process continues iteratively over multiple episodes or time steps.
6. **Learning and Policy Improvement:** During the interaction with the environment, the agent learns from experience and updates its policy to improve performance. This typically involves estimating the value of different state-action pairs, updating the policy based on these estimates, and iteratively refining the policy over time.
7. **Policy Evaluation:** After learning from experience, the agent evaluates the performance of its policy using various evaluation metrics, such as cumulative rewards or average return. This allows the agent to assess the effectiveness of its learned policy and identify areas for improvement.
8. **Policy Improvement:** Based on the evaluation results, the agent may further refine its policy to improve performance. This could involve exploring new strategies, adjusting policy parameters, or incorporating new knowledge gained from experience.
9. **Iteration and Optimization:** The process of interaction, learning, evaluation, and improvement iterates over multiple episodes or time steps until the agent achieves satisfactory performance or convergence to an optimal policy. Various optimization techniques, such as value iteration or policy gradient methods, may be employed to expedite learning and convergence.

11.5.1 Key Concepts of Reinforcement Learning

Agent

It is the learner or decision-maker that interacts with the environment. The agent observes the current state of the environment, selects actions, and receives feedback or rewards based on its actions.

Environment

It is the external system with which the agent interacts. The environment can be anything from a physical system (e.g., a robot navigating a maze) to a virtual simulation (e.g., a video game environment).

State

It is a representation of the current situation or configuration of the environment. The state provides relevant information to the agent to make decisions about which actions to take.

Action

Action is the set of possible choices available to the agent at each state. The agent selects actions based on its current state and policy.

Policy

It is the strategy or set of rules that the agent uses to select actions in different states. The policy defines the behavior of the agent and determines its decision-making process.

Reward

It is the feedback signal provided by the environment to the agent after each action. The reward indicates how favorable or unfavorable the action was in achieving the agent's goal.

11.5.2 Components of Reinforcement Learning

Exploration vs. Exploitation

One of the key challenges in reinforcement learning is the trade-off between exploration and exploitation. Exploration involves trying out different actions to discover new strategies or learn more about the environment, while exploitation involves leveraging known information to maximize rewards. Balancing exploration and exploitation is crucial for effective learning and decision-making.

11.5.3 Learning Algorithms

Reinforcement learning algorithms can be categorized into model-based and model-free approaches. Model-based algorithms learn an explicit model of the environment dynamics, such as transition probabilities and rewards, to make decisions. Model-free algorithms, on the other hand, directly learn the optimal policy or value function without explicitly modeling the environment.

Value Functions

Value functions estimate the expected return or utility of being in a certain state and following a certain policy. They help the agent evaluate the desirability of different states and actions and guide its decision-making process.

Q-Learning and Policy Gradient Methods

Q-Learning is a popular model-free reinforcement learning algorithm that learns the Q-value function, which represents the expected return of taking a particular action in a given state and following a certain policy thereafter. Policy gradient methods directly optimize the policy parameters to maximize cumulative rewards, typically using techniques such as gradient ascent.

11.6 Building Blocks of Machine Learning

Machine learning systems are built upon several fundamental components and methodologies, each serving a crucial role in the process of learning from data and making predictions. The key building blocks of machine learning are:

11.6.1 Algorithms and Models

Algorithms and models form the core of machine learning systems, providing the computational machinery for learning patterns and making predictions from data. There exists a diverse array of algorithms and models, each with its unique characteristics, strengths, weaknesses, and use cases.

Each algorithm has its strengths, weaknesses, and ideal use cases. For example, linear regression is well-suited for tasks with linear relationships between features and targets, while decision trees are effective for handling non-linear relationships and capturing interactions between features. Neural networks excel at learning intricate patterns and representations from high-dimensional data but may require large amounts of data and computational resources for training.

11.6.2 Optimization Techniques

Optimization techniques play a crucial role in training machine learning models, enabling the adjustment of model parameters to minimize errors or loss functions and improve performance. Some common optimization techniques include:

- **Gradient Descent:** An iterative optimization algorithm that updates model parameters in the direction of the steepest descent of the loss function with respect to the parameters. Gradient descent is widely used in training neural networks and other parameterized models.
- **Stochastic Gradient Descent (SGD):** A variant of gradient descent that updates model parameters using a random subset of training examples (mini-batch) at each iteration. SGD is computationally efficient and well-suited for large-scale and online learning tasks.
- **Hyperparameter Tuning:** The process of searching for the optimal set of hyperparameters (e.g., learning rate, regularization strength) that govern the behavior and performance of machine learning models. Techniques such as *grid search* , *random search* , and *Bayesian optimization* are commonly used for hyperparameter tuning.

11.6.3 Tools and Frameworks

Machine learning practitioners rely on a variety of tools and frameworks to implement, train, and deploy machine learning models efficiently. These tools encompass programming languages, libraries, and frameworks that provide support for various tasks, such as data preprocessing, model training, evaluation, and deployment. Some popular tools and frameworks include:

- **Programming Languages: Python** and **R** are two of the most widely used programming languages for machine learning due to their rich ecosystem of libraries, ease of use, and extensive community support.
- **Libraries:** Libraries such as Scikit-learn, TensorFlow, PyTorch, and Keras provide high-level interfaces and abstractions for building and training machine learning models. Scikit-learn offers a comprehensive set of algorithms and utilities for classical machine learning tasks, while TensorFlow and PyTorch are popular frameworks for deep learning and neural network-based models.

11.7 Future Trends and Challenges

As the field of machine learning continues to evolve rapidly, driven by advancements in technology, research, and applications, several key trends and challenges are shaping the future landscape of machine learning.

11.7.1 Advancements in Research

Advancements in research are fueling innovation and pushing the boundaries of what is possible in machine learning. Key areas of advancement include:

- **Deep Learning:** Deep learning, powered by neural networks with multiple layers, has revolutionized machine learning in recent years, enabling breakthroughs in areas such as computer vision, natural language processing, and reinforcement learning. Ongoing research in deep learning focuses on improving model architectures, training techniques, and scalability to handle increasingly complex tasks and datasets.
- **Generative Models:** Generative models, such as generative adversarial networks (GANs) and variational autoencoders (VAEs), are gaining traction for their ability to generate realistic data samples, images, and text. These models have applications in image synthesis, data augmentation, and unsupervised learning, and are being explored for creative applications such as art generation and content creation.

11.7.2 Emerging Applications

Machine learning is finding applications in a wide range of domains, from traditional fields such as healthcare and finance to emerging areas enabled by technological advancements. Some emerging applications include: Edge Computing, and Federated Learning. The difference between edge computing and federated learning is summarized in Table 11.2.

- **Edge Computing:** Edge computing is a distributed computing paradigm that brings computation and data storage closer to the location where it is needed, often at the "edge" of the network, such as IoT devices, sensors, and mobile devices. In edge computing, data

processing and analysis are performed locally on the edge devices or in nearby edge servers, rather than relying solely on centralized data centers or cloud computing resources. This enables real-time processing, low-latency communication, and reduced bandwidth usage, making it ideal for applications that require rapid response times, efficient use of network resources, and autonomous decision-making at the edge.
The proliferation of edge computing devices, such as smartphones, IoT devices, and autonomous vehicles, is driving the demand for machine learning models that can run efficiently on resource-constrained devices. Edge computing enables real-time, low-latency inference and decision-making at the edge of the network, enabling applications, such as smart cities, autonomous vehicles, and personalized healthcare.

- **Federated Learning:** Federated learning is a machine learning paradigm that enables collaborative model training across decentralized and distributed data sources while preserving data privacy and security. In federated learning, instead of aggregating data in a central repository for model training, computation is performed locally on individual devices or edge servers, and only model updates are exchanged between the devices and a central server or aggregator. This allows multiple parties to collaboratively train a shared model without sharing their raw data, thereby addressing privacy concerns and data security risks associated with centralized data collection and processing.
Federated learning enables collaborative model training across distributed data sources while preserving data privacy and security. By training models locally on user devices or edge servers and aggregating updates centrally, federated learning enables scalable, privacy-preserving machine learning applications in domains such as healthcare, finance, and IoT.

Table 11.2: Comparison between Edge Computing and Federated Learning

Aspect	**Edge Computing**	**Federated Learning**
Data Processing	Data processing occurs locally on devices or edge servers.	Model training occurs locally, but model updates are sent to a central server or aggregator for aggregation.
Data Sharing	Data may be shared or processed locally without leaving the edge device.	Data remains decentralized, and only model updates are shared with a central server or aggregator.
Privacy Concerns	Privacy concerns may arise if sensitive data is processed locally on edge devices.	Designed to address privacy concerns by keeping raw data decentralized and private.
Centralization	Decentralized approach with processing closer to data sources.	Semi-centralized approach with model updates aggregated at a central server.
Communication	Emphasizes local communication and processing to reduce latency and bandwidth usage.	Requires communication between edge devices and a central server or aggregator for model updates.
Applications	Commonly used for real-time processing, IoT, and low-latency applications.	Used for collaborative model training across distributed data sources while preserving privacy.

11.7.3 Addressing Limitations and Risks

Despite the promise and potential of machine learning, several limitations and risks need to be addressed to realize its full benefits. Some key challenges include:

- **Overcoming Data Scarcity and Quality Issues:** Machine learning models rely on large volumes of high-quality data for training and generalization. However, in many domains, data scarcity, imbalance, and noise pose significant challenges for model development and deployment. Addressing data scarcity and quality issues requires innovative techniques for data augmentation, transfer learning, and domain adaptation.
- **Ensuring Robustness and Reliability:** Machine learning models are susceptible to adversarial attacks, robustness issues, and failures in real-world scenarios. Ensuring the robustness and reliability of machine learning systems requires techniques for adversarial defense, uncertainty estimation, model interpretability, and verification and validation. Additionally, designing systems with fail-safe mechanisms and human oversight can mitigate the risks associated with machine learning failures.

11.8 Steps of Machine Learning Implementation

Different steps of applying machine learning on a data is:

1. **Data Collection:** Gather the raw data required for the task. This data can come from various sources such as databases, online repositories, or through direct data acquisition methods like surveys and sensors.
2. **Data Preprocessing:** Clean and transform the raw data into a format suitable for analysis. This includes handling missing values, removing duplicates, normalizing data, encoding categorical variables, and feature scaling.
3. **Exploratory Data Analysis (EDA):** Perform a thorough analysis of the data to understand its underlying patterns, distributions, and relationships. This step often involves visualizations and summary statistics to gain insights into the data.
4. **Feature Engineering:** Create new features or modify existing ones to improve the performance of the machine learning model. This can involve domain-specific knowledge and various techniques like polynomial features, interaction terms, or dimensionality reduction.
5. **Model Selection and Training:** Choose the appropriate machine learning algorithms that are well-suited to the problem at hand. This involves understanding the strengths and limitations of different models. After selecting a model, use the preprocessed data to train the selected machine learning models. This step involves fitting the model to the data and learning the underlying patterns.
6. **Model Evaluation:** Assess the performance of the trained models using evaluation metrics such as accuracy, precision, recall, F1-score, and ROC-AUC. This step often includes cross-validation to ensure the model's generalizability.
7. **Hyperparameter Tuning:** Optimize the model's performance by fine-tuning the hyperparameters.
8. **Model Deployment:** Implement the trained and validated model into a production environment where it can make predictions on new, unseen data.

12. Data Preprocessing

Data preprocessing is a crucial step in the machine learning pipeline, serving as the foundation for creating robust and effective models. It involves transforming raw data into a clean, organized, and analyzable format, addressing issues such as missing values, noise, and inconsistencies. By ensuring that the data is of high quality and suitable for analysis, preprocessing enhances the accuracy, efficiency, and generalizability of machine learning algorithms.

12.1 Introduction

Data preprocessing is a crucial step in the machine learning pipeline that directly impacts the performance and reliability of machine learning models. Raw data often comes with inconsistencies, noise, and irrelevant information, which can significantly degrade the model's ability to learn and make accurate predictions. Proper preprocessing ensures that the data is clean, consistent, and in a format that machine learning algorithms can effectively process.

12.1.1 Common Challenges in Raw Data

Raw data often presents several challenges that need to be addressed before it can be used for training machine learning models. Common challenges and issues encountered in raw data are:

1. **Missing Values:** Missing values occur when no data value is stored for a variable in an observation. This can happen due to various reasons such as data entry errors, equipment malfunctions, or respondents skipping questions in surveys. Incomplete data can lead to

biased models and incorrect conclusions because the absence of data might not be random and can systematically affect the outcomes.
For example, if income data is missing more frequently for higher earners, a model predicting purchasing power would be skewed.

2. **Inconsistent Data Formats:** Inconsistent data formats refer to variations in how data is recorded or represented. This can include differences in date formats (MM/DD/YYYY vs. DD/MM/YYYY), units of measurement (inches vs. centimeters), or categorical values (Yes/No vs. Y/N). These inconsistencies can hinder the analysis process by making it difficult to combine and compare data, potentially leading to errors and misinterpretations.
3. **Noise and Outliers:** Noise refers to random variations or errors in data that do not convey useful information, while outliers are extreme values that deviate significantly from the rest of the data. Noise and outliers can distort model training and evaluation by misleading the learning algorithm, leading to poor model performance and unreliable predictions.
For instance, an outlier in housing price data can disproportionately affect the estimated relationship between features and prices.
4. **Redundant and Duplicate Records:** Redundant and duplicate records occur when the same data point is recorded multiple times. This can happen due to errors in data collection or merging datasets. Repeated entries can mislead the learning algorithm by over-representing certain data points, leading to biased models and inaccurate predictions.
For example, if customer purchase records are duplicated, a sales prediction model may overestimate demand.
5. **Imbalanced Data:** Imbalanced data refers to a dataset where the distribution of classes is not uniform. This is common in classification tasks where one class is significantly more frequent than others, such as fraud detection (fraudulent vs. non-fraudulent transactions). Skewed class distributions can affect the model's ability to generalize because the model may become biased towards the majority class, leading to poor performance in predicting the minority class.

12.1.2 Data Preprocessing Steps

Data preprocessing involves a series of systematic steps designed to prepare raw data for analysis. Overview of key steps are:

Data Cleaning

Data cleaning involves identifying and rectifying errors and inconsistencies in the data to ensure that it is accurate and ready for analysis. This step is critical because errors and inconsistencies in the data can lead to misleading results and poor model performance. Key tasks under this step are:

- **Addressing Missing Values:** Handle missing data through imputation (e.g., filling with mean, median, or using algorithms like k-nearest neighbors), deletion (removing records with missing values), or using models that can handle missing values inherently.

- **Removing Duplicates:** Identify and eliminate duplicate records to avoid bias and redundancy, ensuring each data point is unique.
- **Correcting Errors:** Identify and correct inaccuracies such as typographical errors, incorrect values, or inconsistencies in data formats.

Data Transformation

Data transformation involves converting data into a suitable format for analysis. This step is crucial for ensuring that data is consistent, normalized, and ready for machine learning algorithms, which often require data to be in specific formats. Key tasks under this step are:

- **Normalizing and Scaling:** Standardize the range of independent variables or features of data. Normalization typically scales data to a range of [0, 1], while standardization transforms data to have a mean of 0 and a standard deviation of 1.
- **Encoding Categorical Data:** Convert categorical variables into a numerical format using techniques such as one-hot encoding, label encoding, or target encoding, ensuring that machine learning algorithms can process these features.

Feature Engineering

Feature engineering involves creating new features or modifying existing ones to improve model performance. This step leverages domain knowledge to extract more meaningful information from raw data. Key tasks under this step are:

- **Creating New Features:** Generate new features from existing data, such as interaction terms, polynomial features, or aggregations (e.g., sum, mean).
- **Feature Selection:** Identify and select the most relevant features for model training using methods like filter methods (correlation, chi-square), wrapper methods (recursive feature elimination), or embedded methods (LASSO, tree-based feature importance).
- **Dimensionality Reduction:** Reduce the number of features to simplify models and avoid overfitting using techniques like Principal Component Analysis (PCA) or Linear Discriminant Analysis (LDA).

Data Splitting

Data splitting involves dividing the dataset into separate sets for training, validation, and testing to ensure that the model can generalize well to new, unseen data.

- **Train-Test Split:** Divide the dataset into a training set, which will be used to train the model and a test set, which will be used to evaluate the model's performance on unseen data.
- **Validation Set:** Further split the training set into a validation set to fine-tune model parameters and select the best model configuration.
- **Cross-Validation:** Use techniques like *k-fold cross-validation* to evaluate model performance more robustly by training and validating the model multiple times on different subsets of the data.

Data Augmentation

Data augmentation involves generating additional data to improve model robustness. It is particularly useful in domains with limited data such as image, text, and time series data. Key tasks under this step are:

- **Techniques for Image Data:** Apply transformations such as rotation, scaling, flipping, and cropping to generate new images from existing ones, enhancing the diversity of the training dataset.
- **Techniques for Text Data:** Use methods such as synonym replacement, random insertion, and back-translation to create variations of text data, increasing the training data size and variety.
- **Techniques for Time Series Data:** Generate additional time series data through methods like jittering (adding small noise), scaling, and window slicing to create more training samples.

12.2 Data Cleaning

12.2.1 Imputation Techniques

Ex.1 Handling Missing Values : Mean Imputation

```
import pandas as pd
from sklearn.impute import SimpleImputer

# Sample DataFrame with missing values
data = {'age': [25, 30, 35, None, 40, None, 50]}
df = pd.DataFrame(data)

# Impute missing values with mean
imputer = SimpleImputer(strategy='mean')
df['age'] = imputer.fit_transform(df[['age']])

print(df)
```

Output:

```
    age
0   25.0
1   30.0
2   35.0
3   36.0
4   40.0
5   36.0
6   50.0
```

Explanation:
`pandas` is a powerful library for data manipulation and analysis. `SimpleImputer` is a class from `sklearn` used to *impute (fill in) missing* values.

- **df = pd.DataFrame(data):** This dictionary is converted into a DataFrame `df` using `pd.DataFrame(data)`.
- **imputer = SimpleImputer(strategy='mean'):** An instance of `SimpleImputer` is created with the strategy set to '`mean`'. This means missing values will be replaced with the mean of the column.
- **df['age'] = imputer.fit_transform(df[['age']]):** The `fit_transform` method is called on the `imputer` with the `[['age']]` DataFrame. The double brackets ensure it's treated as a 2D array. It calculates the mean of the non-missing values in the '`age`' column and replaces the missing values with this mean.
- **print(df):** It prints the `DataFrame` after imputation.

The mean of the non-missing values [25, 30, 35, 40, 50] is calculated as (25 + 30 + 35 + 40 + 50) / 5 = 36. The missing values (`None`) are replaced with this mean (36).

12.2.2 Deletion Strategies

Ex.2 Removing Rows with Missing Values

```
import pandas as pd

# Sample DataFrame with missing values
data = {'age': [25, 30, 35, None, 40, None, 50]}
df = pd.DataFrame(data)

# Remove rows with missing values
df_cleaned = df.dropna()

print(df_cleaned)
```

Output:

```
    gender
     age
0    25.0
1    30.0
2    35.0
4    40.0
6    50.0
```

Explanation:
Necessary library pandas is imported for data cleaning operation. DataFrame named df with one column named 'age'. The column 'age' contains a list of ages, with two missing values represented as None.

- **df = pd.DataFrame(data):** The dictionary is converted into a DataFrame df using pd.DataFrame(data).
- **df_cleaned = df.dropna():** This line uses the dropna() function to remove rows containing any missing values (NaN or None) from the DataFrame df. The resulting DataFrame with missing values removed is assigned to the variable df_cleaned.
- **df_cleaned:** It prints the DataFrame after imputation.

The output of this code will be the DataFrame with missing values removed. Rows containing missing values (None) have been removed from the DataFrame.

Ex.3 Removing Columns with Missing Values

```
import pandas as pd

# Sample DataFrame with missing values
data = {'gender': ['M', 'F', 'F', 'M', 'M', 'M', 'F'],
    'age': [25, 30, 35, None, 40, None, 50],
        'income': [50000, 60000, None, 80000, 90000, 100000, None]}
df = pd.DataFrame(data)

# Remove columns with missing values
df_cleaned = df.dropna(axis=1)

print(df_cleaned)
```

Output:

	gender
0	M
1	F
2	F
3	M
4	M
5	M
6	F

Explanation:
Necessary library pandas is imported for data cleaning operation. DataFrame named df with one column named 'age'. The column 'age' contains a list of ages, with two missing values represented as None.

- **df_cleaned = df.dropna(axis=1):** It uses the `dropna()` function to remove columns containing any missing values ((`NaN` or `None`) from the DataFrame df.
  The parameter `axis=1` specifies that columns (not rows) with missing values should be removed.
  The resulting DataFrame with missing value columns removed is assigned to the variable `df_cleaned`.
- **df_cleaned:** It prints the cleaned DataFrame texttt df_cleaned to the console.

12.2.3 Outlier Detection and Treatment

Ex.4 Handling Outlier : Using Z-Score

```
import pandas as pd
import numpy as np
# Sample DataFrame with potential outliers
data = {'age': [25, 30, 35, 40, 45, 100, 50]}
df = pd.DataFrame(data)

# Calculate Z-scores
z_scores = np.abs((df['age'] - df['age'].mean()) / df['age'].std())

# Remove outliers (Z-score > 2)
df_cleaned = df[z_scores < 2]

print(df_cleaned)
```

Output:

	age
0	25.0
1	30.0
2	35.0
3	40.0
4	45.0
6	50.0

Explanation:
It demonstrates how to detect and remove outliers from a DataFrame using Z-scores. `pandas` is used for data manipulation and analysis. `numpy` is used for numerical operations, particularly for calculating Z-scores.

- **df = pd.DataFrame(data)**
  It creates a DataFrame named `df` with one column, '`age`', containing age values. The value 100 is a potential outlier.
- **df['age'].mean()**
  It calculates the mean of the 'age' column.

- **df['age'].std()**
  It calculates the standard deviation of the 'age' column.
- **z_scores = np.abs((df['age'] - df['age'].mean()) / df['age'].std())**
  It calculates the Z-scores for each value in the 'age' column. The Z-score indicates how many standard deviations a value is from the mean.
- **df_cleaned = df[z_scores < 2]**
  It filters out rows where the Z-score is greater than 2.
- **df[z_scores < 2]**
  It selects rows where the Z-score is less than 2, effectively removing outliers.
- **print(df_cleaned)**
  It prints the cleaned DataFrame `df_cleaned` to the console.

Z-score Threshold 2 is commonly used, but it can be adjusted depending on the specific context and the distribution of the data. For example, a threshold of 3 is sometimes used for more lenient outlier detection.

Ex.5 Isolation Forest for Outlier Detection

```
import pandas as pd
from sklearn.ensemble import IsolationForest

# Sample DataFrame with potential outliers
data = {'age': [25, 30, 35, 40, 45, 100, 50]}
df = pd.DataFrame(data)

# Apply Isolation Forest
iso_forest = IsolationForest(contamination=0.1)
df['outlier'] = iso_forest.fit_predict(df[['age']])

# Remove outliers
df_cleaned = df[df['outlier'] == 1].drop(columns=['outlier'])

print(df_cleaned)
```

Output:

	age
0	25.0
1	30.0
2	35.0
3	40.0
4	45.0
6	50.0

Explanation:
It demonstrates how to detect and remove outliers from a DataFrame using the Isolation Forest algorithm. `pandas` is used for data manipulation and analysis. `IsolationForest` is used foroutlier detection using the Isolation Forest algorithm.

- **df = pd.DataFrame(data)**
  It creates a DataFrame named `df` with one column, '`age`', containing age values. The value 100 is a potential outlier.
- **iso_forest = IsolationForest(contamination=0.1)**
  It creates an instance of IsolationForest with a contamination parameter of 0.1, indicating that 10 % of the data is expected to be outliers.
- **df['outlier'] = iso_forest.fit_predict(df[['age']])**
  The `fit_predict` method is called on the 'age' column to fit the Isolation Forest model and predict outliers.
  The predictions are added as a new column, '`outlier`', in the DataFrame `df`. The `fit_predict` method returns 1 for inliers and -1 for outliers.
- **df[df['outlier'] == 1]**
  It selects rows where the 'outlier' column value is 1 (indicating inliers).
- **.drop(columns=['outlier'])**
  It removes the 'outlier' column from the resulting DataFrame. The resulting cleaned DataFrame is assigned to the variable `df_cleaned`
- **df_cleaned = df[df['outlier'] == 1].drop(columns=['outlier'])**
  It removes outliers.
- **print(df_cleaned)**
  It prints the cleaned DataFrame `df_cleaned` to the console.

12.3 Data Transformation

12.3.1 Normalization and Scaling

Feature scaling is a technique used to standardize the range of independent variables or features in data. In machine learning, it is essential because features in different ranges can cause models to perform poorly or take longer to converge. Models that rely on distance calculations or gradient descent optimization benefit significantly from feature scaling.

Min-Max Scaling scales the data to a fixed range, usually 0 to 1. The formula for Min-Max scaling is:

$$X_{scaled} = \frac{X - X_{min}}{X_{max} - X_{min}}$$

Z-score Normalization scales the data so that it has a mean of 0 and a standard deviation of 1. The formula is:

$$X_{normalized} = \frac{X - \mu}{\sigma}$$

Ex.6 Data Scaling : Min-Max Scaling

```
import pandas as pd
from sklearn.preprocessing import MinMaxScaler

# Sample DataFrame
data = {'age': [25, 30, 35, 40, 45, 50]}
df = pd.DataFrame(data)

# Apply Min-Max Scaling
scaler = MinMaxScaler()
df['age_scaled'] = scaler.fit_transform(df[['age']])

print(df)
```

Output:

	age	age_scaled
0	25	0.0
1	30	0.2
2	35	0.4
3	40	0.6
4	45	0.8
5	50	1.0

Explanation:
It scales the data to a range of [0, 1]by transforming the values such that the minimum and maximum values of the feature become 0 and 1 respectively. `MinMaxScaler` is a preprocessing utility in `sklearn` that scales features to a given range, typically [0, 1].

- **data = 'age': [25, 30, 35, 40, 45, 50]**
  A dictionary named `data`is created where the key is 'age' and the value is a list of integers.
- **df = pd.DataFrame(data)**
  The pandas DataFrame constructor is used to convert the dictionary data into a DataFrame. The resulting DataFrame is stored in the variable `df`.
- **scaler = MinMaxScaler()**
  It Initialize the Min-Max Scaler.
- **df['age_scaled'] = scaler.fit_transform(df[['age']])**
  It fits the scaler to the 'age' data and transforms it. The fit operation calculates the minimum and maximum values of the data and the transform operation scales the data to the range [0, 1].
  The scaled data is stored in a new column '`age_scaled`' in the DataFrame `df`.
- **print(df)**
  This line prints the modified DataFrame `df` to the console.

Ex.7 Data Scaling : Z-score Normalization

```
import pandas as pd
from sklearn.preprocessing import StandardScaler

# Sample DataFrame
data = {'age': [25, 30, 35, 40, 45, 50]}
df = pd.DataFrame(data)

# Apply Z-score Normalization
scaler = StandardScaler()
df['age_normalized'] = scaler.fit_transform(df[['age']])

print(df)
```

Output:

	age	age_normalized
0	25	–1.46385
1	30	–0.87831
2	35	–0.29277
3	40	0.29277
4	45	0.87831
5	50	1.46385

Explanation:
It transforms the data to have a mean of 0 and a standard deviation of 1, which helps in making the data distribution more standardized. `StandardScaler` is a tool from the `sklearn.preprocessing` module used for standardizing features by removing the mean and scaling to unit variance (Z-score normalization).

- **data = 'age': [25, 30, 35, 40, 45, 50]**
  A dictionary named `data`is created where the key is 'age' and the value is a list of integers.
- **df = pd.DataFrame(data)**
  The pandas DataFrame constructor is used to convert the dictionary data into a DataFrame. The resulting DataFrame is stored in the variable `df`.
- **scaler = StandardScaler()**
  It creates an instance of `StandardScaler` and assign it to the variable `scaler`.
- **df['age_normalized'] = scaler.fit_transform(df[['age']])**
  The `fit_transform` method of scaler is called on the 'age' column of the DataFrame, which performs the standardization.
- **print(df)**
  This line prints the modified DataFrame `df` to the console.

12.3.2 Encoding Categorical Variables

Ex.8 One-Hot Encoding : Converts categorical variables into a series of binary variables

```
import pandas as pd

# Sample DataFrame
data = {'color': ['red', 'blue', 'green', 'blue', 'red']}
df = pd.DataFrame(data)

# Apply One-Hot Encoding
df_encoded = pd.get_dummies(df, columns=['color'])

print(df_encoded)
```

Output:

	color_blue	color_green	color_red
0	False	False	True
1	True	False	False
2	False	True	False
3	True	False	False
4	False	False	True

Explanation:
This Python code demonstrates how to perform one-hot encoding on a categorical variable using the `pd.getdummies()` function from the pandas library.

- **df_encoded = pd.get_dummies(df, columns=['color'])**
  The `pd.get_dummies()` function is called on the DataFrame `df`, with the column '`color`' specified in the columns parameter. This function converts the categorical values in the '`color`' column into a series of binary columns, each representing one of the unique categories in the original column.
- **print(df_encoded)**
  It outputs the one-hot encoded DataFrame `df_encoded` to the console.

One-Hot Encoding creates binary columns for each unique category in the original categorical column. Each row has a 1 (True) in the column corresponding to its original category and 0 (False) in all other columns.

Ex.9 Label Encoding : Converts categorical variables into integer codes

```
import pandas as pd
from sklearn.preprocessing import LabelEncoder

# Sample DataFrame
```

```
data = {'color': ['red', 'blue', 'green', 'blue', 'red']}
df = pd.DataFrame(data)

# Apply Label Encoding
encoder = LabelEncoder()
df['color_encoded'] = encoder.fit_transform(df['color'])

print(df)
```

Output:

	color	color_encoded
0	red	2
1	blue	0
2	green	1
3	blue	0
4	red	2

Explanation:
This Python code demonstrates how to perform label encoding on a categorical variable using the `LabelEncoder` from the `sklearn.preprocessing` module. `LabelEncoder` is a tool from the `sklearn.preprocessing` module, which is used for converting categorical labels into integer codes.

- **encoder = LabelEncoder()**
  It create an instance of `LabelEncoder` and is assigned to the variable `encoder`.
- **df['color_encoded'] = encoder.fit_transform(df['color'])**
  The `fit_transform` method of encoder is called on the '`color`' column of the DataFrame, which converts the categorical values into numerical labels. The encoded values are stored in a new column '`color_encoded`' in the DataFrame `df`.
- **print(df)**
  It outputs the DataFrame `df` to the console, showing both the original and the encoded values.

The `LabelEncoder` assigns a unique integer to each unique value in the '`color`' column. The unique categories are sorted alphabetically before encoding. '`Blue`' comes first alphabetically and is assigned 0, '`green`' is next and is assigned 1. The encoded values replace the original categorical values in a new column '`color_encoded`'.

Ex.10 Target Encoding : Encodes categorical variables based on the mean of the target variable for each category

```
import pandas as pd

# Sample DataFrame
data = {'color': ['red', 'blue', 'green', 'blue', 'red'],
        'price': [10, 20, 15, 25, 30]}
df = pd.DataFrame(data)
```

```
# Apply Target Encoding
mean_price = df.groupby('color')['price'].mean()
df['color_encoded'] = df['color'].map(mean_price)

print(df)
```

Output:

	color	price	color_encoded
0	red	10	20.0
1	blue	20	22.5
2	green	15	15.0
3	blue	25	22.5
4	red	30	20.0

Explanation:
Target encoding replaces categorical values with the mean of the *price* for each category.

- **mean_price = df.groupby('color')['price'].mean()**
  - The `groupby` method groups the DataFrame by the '`color`' column.
  - The `mean` method calculates the mean price for each color category.
  - he result is a Series `mean_price` with the mean price for each unique color.
- **df['color_encoded'] = df['color'].map(mean_price)**
  The map method replaces each value in the '`color`' column with the corresponding mean price from the `mean_price` Series. The encoded values are stored in a new column '`color_encoded`' in the DataFrame `df`.
- **print(df)**
  It outputs the DataFrame `df` to the console, showing both the original and the encoded values.

The `groupby` and `mean` methods calculate the mean price for each unique color: blue = (20+25) / 2 = 22.5, red = (10+30) / 2 = 20, green = (15) / 1 = 15.

12.4 Feature Engineering

Feature engineering involves creating new features or modifying existing ones to improve model performance. This step leverages domain knowledge to extract more meaningful information from raw data. Key Tasks under feature engineering are: Creating New Features, Feature Selection, Dimensionality Reduction.

12.4.1 Creating New Features

Ex.11 Creating polynomial feature from a given dataset

```
import pandas as pd
from sklearn.preprocessing import PolynomialFeatures

# Sample DataFrame
data = {'age': [25, 30, 35, 40, 45, 50],
        'salary': [50000, 60000, 70000, 80000, 90000, 100000]}
df = pd.DataFrame(data)

# Creating polynomial features
poly = PolynomialFeatures(degree=2, include_bias=False)
poly_features = poly.fit_transform(df)
poly_feature_names = poly.get_feature_names_out(['age', 'salary'])

df_poly = pd.DataFrame(poly_features, columns=poly_feature_names)

print(df_poly)
```

Output:

	age	salary	age^2	age salary	$salary^2$
0	25.0	50000.0	625.0	1250000.0	2.500000e+09
1	30.0	60000.0	900.0	1800000.0	3.600000e+09
2	35.0	70000.0	1225.0	2450000.0	4.900000e+09
3	40.0	80000.0	1600.0	3200000.0	6.400000e+09
4	45.0	90000.0	2025.0	4050000.0	8.100000e+09
5	50.0	100000.0	2500.0	5000000.0	1.000000e+10

Explanation:
Polynomial features are generated by taking combinations of the original features by squaring and multiplying with each other. This allows the model to capture non-linear or complex relationships between features.

- **poly = PolynomialFeatures(degree=2, include_bias=False)**
  This initializes the PolynomialFeatures transformer to generate polynomial features of degree 2. Setting `include_bias=False` excludes the bias (intercept) term. The **bias** is an intercept term in the model to account for the baseline value of the target variable when all features are zero. It is set as `True` when model does not has any default intercept term (e.g. linear regression, logistic regression).
- **poly_features = poly.fit_transform(df)**
  It generates the polynomial features for the DataFrame `df`.

- **poly.get_feature_names_out(['age', 'salary'])**
  It retrieves the names of the newly created features.
- **f_poly = pd.DataFrame(poly_features, columns=poly_feature_names)**
  It creates a new DataFrame `df_poly` with the generated polynomial features.

Ex.12 Dimensionality Reduction

```
import pandas as pd
from sklearn.decomposition import PCA

# Sample DataFrame
data = {'feature1': [2, 8, 5, 6, 1, 3],
        'feature2': [8, 5, 6, 2, 5, 9],
        'feature3': [5, 1, 8, 9, 4, 2]}
df = pd.DataFrame(data)

# Apply PCA for dimensionality reduction
pca = PCA(n_components=2)
principal_components = pca.fit_transform(df)
df_pca = pd.DataFrame(principal_components, columns=['PC1', 'PC2'])

print(df_pca)
```

Output:

	PC1	PC2
0	–1.786921	–2.401795
1	–1.235889	5.340164
2	2.572041	–1.041471
3	5.924062	0.276039
4	–1.150970	–1.904761
5	–4.322323	–0.268176

Explanation:
PCA is used to reduce the dimensionality of the dataset while retaining as much variance as possible. By using PCA, you can transform your dataset into a lower-dimensional space while preserving the most important aspects of the data, making it a powerful tool for feature engineering and data analysis.
In above example, the DataFrame `df` has three features: feature1, feature2, and feature3.

- **pca = PCA(n_components=2)**
  It initialize the PCA transformer to reduce the dataset to 2 principal components.
- **pca.fit_transform(df)**
  It fits the PCA model to the DataFrame `df` and transforms the data into the new reduced dimensions.

- **df_pca = pd.DataFrame(principal_components, columns=['PC1', 'PC2'])**
  This creates a new DataFrame `df_pca` with the principal components as columns.
- **print(df_pca)**
  It prints the DataFrame `df_pca` containing the first two principal components (`PC1` and `PC2`) of the original dataset. These principal components are linear combinations of the original features that capture the most variance in the data.

12.5 Data Splitting

Data splitting is the process of dividing a dataset into distinct subsets, typically for the purposes of training, validating, and testing machine learning models. The primary aim is to ensure that the model's performance is evaluated on unseen data, providing an unbiased estimate of its generalization capabilities.

12.5.1 Importance of Data Splitting

The primary aim of Data splitting is to ensure that the model's performance is evaluated on unseen data, providing an unbiased estimate of its generalization capabilities. Data splitting is a crucial step in the machine learning workflow for several reasons:

- The training set is used to train the model, allowing it to learn patterns, relationships, and features from the data.
- The validation set is used to fine-tune the model, helping in selecting the best hyperparameters and preventing overfitting by providing feedback on model performance during the training process.
- The test set is used to evaluate the final model, providing an unbiased assessment of its performance on new, unseen data. This step ensures that the model can generalize well to real-world scenarios.
- By splitting the data, we ensure that the model does not simply memorize the training data but learns to generalize from it. This is critical for the model's ability to perform well on new data.
- Splitting the data allows for the calculation of reliable performance metrics, as the model's evaluation is based on data it hasn't seen during training.

12.5.2 Data Splitting Techniques

Train-Test Split

The dataset in this method is divided into two subsets: a training set and a test set, usually in a ratio like 70/30 or 80/20. The purpose of train-test split is to train the model on one portion and evaluate it on another so that accuracy may be evaluated unbiased.

Ex.13 Data splitting through train-test split

```
import pandas as pd
from sklearn.model_selection import train_test_split
```

```
# Sample data
data = {'feature1': [1, 2, 3, 4, 5],
        'feature2': [5, 4, 3, 2, 1],
        'target': [0, 1, 0, 1, 0]}
df = pd.DataFrame(data)

# Features and target variable
X = df[['feature1', 'feature2']]
y = df['target']

# Train-test split
X_train, X_test, y_train, y_test = train_test_split(X, y,
                              test_size=0.3, random_state=42)

print("All Data:\n", df)
print("Training features:\n", X_train)
print("Testing features:\n", X_test)

print("Training labels:\n", y_train)
print("Testing labels:\n", y_test
```

Output:

All Data:

	feature1	feature2	target
0	1	5	0
1	2	4	1
2	3	3	0
3	4	2	1
4	5	1	0

Training features:

	feature1	feature2
2	3	3
0	1	5
3	4	2

Testing features:

	feature1	feature2
1	2	4
4	5	1

```
Training labels:
2    0
0    0
3    1

Testing labels:
1    1
4    0
```

Explanation:

- A dictionary `data` is defined with keys `feature1`, `feature2`, and `target`, each associated with a list of values.
- **pd.DataFrame(data):**
  It converts the dictionary into a pandas *DataFrame* `df`.
- All features has been stored in to a variable `X`, and searies of target has been assigned in to another variable y.
- **train_test_split(X, y, test_size=0.3, random_state=42):**
  It split X and y into training and testing sets.
  - **test_size=0.3:**
    It specifies that 30% of the data should be used as the test set.
  - **random_state=42:**
    Here 42 is provided as seed to produce random number. When ever same seed is provided, the sequence of random number generated will be same.
  - `X_train` and `X_test` contain the training and testing features, respectively.
  - `y_train` and `y_test` contain the training and testing labels, respectively.

Stratified Splitting

It is a type of train-test split in which proportions of the target variable are preserved in both the training and testing sets. It ensures that the train and test sets have a similar distribution of the target variable. This is particularly useful when dealing with imbalanced datasets, where some classes are underrepresented. Stratified splitting helps maintain the same proportion of each class in both the training and testing sets, leading to more reliable model evaluation.

Ex.14 Data splitting through train-test split with Stratification

```
X_train, X_test, y_train, y_test = train_test_split(X, y, test_size=0.3,
                                                    stratify=y, random_state=42)
```

Explanation:
Stratified ensures that the target variable y is evenly distributed in both the training and testing sets. This means that the proportion of each class in y will be the same in `y_train` and `y_test`. This is especially important for imbalanced datasets.

Cross-Validation

Cross-validation involves dividing the dataset into multiple subsets (folds). Model is trained multiple times, each time using a different fold as the validation set and the remaining folds as the training set. The final performance result is calculated as the average of the performance obtained from each fold. The most common type of cross-validation is *k-fold cross-validation*, where the dataset is divided into k equal-sized folds.

Ex.15 Data splitting and model evaluation through cross-validation.

```
from sklearn.model_selection import cross_val_score

cv_scores = cross_val_score(model, X, y, cv=5)
```

Explanation:

- Here `model` is the machine learning model.
- It Split the data into 5 folds.(**cv=5**).
- It train the model on 4 folds and test on the remaining one fold. Repeat this process 5 times.
- Scores for each fold is stored into `cv_scores`.

13. Supervised Learning

Supervised learning is a type of machine learning where the model is trained on labeled data. The goal is to learn a mapping from inputs to outputs, allowing the model to make predictions on new, unseen data. This approach is widely used in various applications such as spam detection, medical diagnosis, and financial forecasting.

Supervised learning task is categorized into two subcategory: (i) Classification, and (ii) Regression. Classification is a type of supervised learning where the goal is to predict a discrete label or category for a given input. The output variable in classification is categorical, meaning it belongs to a specific set of classes or groups. Classification problems can be binary (two classes) or multi-class (more than two classes). Regression is a type of supervised learning where the goal is to predict a continuous numerical value for a given input. The output variable in regression is continuous, meaning it can take any value within a range. Table 13.1 show the difference between classification and regression task.

13.1 K-Nearest Neighbors (KNN)

K-Nearest Neighbors (KNN) is one of the simplest classification algorithms in machine learning. KNN can be used in classification task as well as regression tasks. It is a non-parametric, lazy learning algorithm that classifies data points based on their similarity to other data points in the dataset.

Here `K` in KNN stands for number of neighbors to be used for class prediction of new data. When predicting the class label for a new instance in classification, the algorithm identifies the `k`

Table 13.1: Difference Between Classification and Regression

Feature	Classification	Regression
Output Type	Discrete labels or categories.	Continuous numerical values.
Examples	Email spam detection, image classification, sentiment analysis.	House price prediction, weather forecasting, stock price prediction.
Goal	Assign inputs to predefined classes.	Predict a continuous value.
Types	Binary classification (two classes), Multiclass classification (more than two classes).	Simple regression, multiple regression, polynomial regression.
Common Algorithms	K-Nearest Neighbors (KNN), Decision Trees, Random Forest, Logistic Regression, Support Vector Machines (SVM), Naive Bayes.	Linear Regression, Polynomial Regression, Decision Tree Regression, Random Forest Regression, Ridge and Lasso Regression, Support Vector Regression (SVR).
Evaluation Metrics	Accuracy, Precision, Recall, F1-Score, Confusion Matrix.	Mean Absolute Error (MAE), Mean Squared Error (MSE), Root Mean Squared Error (RMSE), R-Squared (R^2).
Output Example	"Spam" or "Not Spam" for an email.	Predicting the price of a house (e.g., $300,000).
Decision Boundary	Creates boundaries between classes.	Fits a curve or line through the data points.
Application Areas	Text classification, medical diagnosis, fraud detection.	Real estate pricing, financial forecasting, temperature prediction.

instances in the training data that are closest to the new instance. Closeness is measured using a distance metric such as Euclidean distance. The predicted class is determined by a majority vote among the `k` nearest neighbors.
The value of `k` is a crucial hyperparameter that significantly influences the performance of the KNN algorithm. Its value is chosen as odd number because there will always be a clear majority class, which helps avoid ties. If `k` were even, such as 4, and the nearest neighbors were split evenly (e.g., 2 from Class A and 2 from Class B), there would be a tie, making it difficult to determine the class.
KNN is a *non-parametric algorithm* because it does not make any assumption on underlying data. It is also called as *lazy learner algorithm* because it does not learn from the training set immediately, instead it stores the dataset and at the time of classification, it performs an action on the dataset.

13.1.1 KNN Algorithm : Illustration of Classification

Consider a dataset (shown in Table 13.2) with two classes: `Class A` and `Class B`. The dataset is represented with two features: `Feature 1` and `Feature 2`. We want to predict the class of a new data point with the following features: **Feature 1**: 5, **Feature 2**: 5.

Let us use KNN with $k = 5$. We will consider the 5 nearest neighbors to make the prediction. Calculate Euclidean distance between the new data point and all instances in the dataset.

Table 13.2: Dataset with two features and two classes.

Feature 1	Feature 2	Class
2	3	Class A
3	3	Class A
4	4	Class A
6	5	Class B
7	6	Class B
8	6	Class B
7	4	Class B

The Euclidean distance formula is given by:

$$\text{distance} = \sqrt{(x_1 - x_2)^2 + (y_1 - y_2)^2}$$

where (x_1, y_1) and (x_2, y_2) are the coordinates of the two points.

For the new point (**Feature 1** = 5, **Feature 2** = 5):

$$\text{Distance to (2, 3)} = \sqrt{(5-2)^2 + (5-3)^2} = \sqrt{9+4} = \sqrt{13} \approx 3.61$$

$$\text{Distance to (3, 3)} = \sqrt{(5-3)^2 + (5-3)^2} = \sqrt{4+4} = \sqrt{8} \approx 2.83$$

$$\text{Distance to (4, 4)} = \sqrt{(5-4)^2 + (5-4)^2} = \sqrt{1+1} = \sqrt{2} \approx 1.41$$

$$\text{Distance to (6, 5)} = \sqrt{(5-6)^2 + (5-5)^2} = \sqrt{1} = 1.00$$

$$\text{Distance to (7, 6)} = \sqrt{(5-7)^2 + (5-6)^2} = \sqrt{4+1} = \sqrt{5} \approx 2.24$$

$$\text{Distance to (8, 6)} = \sqrt{(5-8)^2 + (5-6)^2} = \sqrt{9+1} = \sqrt{10} \approx 3.16$$

$$\text{Distance to (7, 4)} = \sqrt{(5-7)^2 + (5-4)^2} = \sqrt{4+1} = \sqrt{5} \approx 2.24$$

Table 13.3: Dataset with Euclidean distance from test data and selected 3 nearest neighbors

Feature 1	Feature 2	Class	Distance	selected 5 nearest neighbors
2	3	Class A	3.64	
3	3	Class A	2.83	✓
4	4	Class A	1.41	✓
6	5	Class B	1.0	✓
7	6	Class B	2.24	✓
8	6	Class B	3.16	
7	4	Class B	2.24	✓

Now Table 13.3 shows the euclidean distance of all data points from test data point (feature1=5, feature2=5). It also shows the tick mark in column (*selected 5 nearest neighbors*) which are selected as nearest neighbor (5 nearest model). As per selection of nearest neighbor,

3 neighbor indicate output as class-B where as 2 neighbor indicate output as class B. Here majority is with class-B, so predicted output is class-B.

Ex.1 Classification using KNN algorithm (with k=5 neighbors) on *iris* data

```
from sklearn.datasets import load_iris
from sklearn.model_selection import train_test_split
from sklearn.neighbors import KNeighborsClassifier
from sklearn.metrics import accuracy_score, classification_report

iris = load_iris()
X, y = iris.data, iris.target

# Split the dataset into training and testing sets
X_train, X_test, y_train, y_test = train_test_split(X, y, test_size=0.2,
                                                    random_state=42)

knn = KNeighborsClassifier(n_neighbors=3)
knn.fit(X_train, y_train)
y_pred = knn.predict(X_test)

accuracy = accuracy_score(y_test, y_pred)

print(f'Accuracy: {accuracy:.2f}')
print('Classification Report:')
print(classification_report(y_test, y_pred))
```

Explanation:

- **from sklearn.datasets import load_iris:**
  Required to use *iris* data available in *sklearn* package.
- **from sklearn.model_selection import train_test_split** :
  Required to Splits the dataset into training and testing sets.
- **from sklearn.neighbors import KNeighborsClassifier:**
  Required to implement K-Nearest Neighbors Classifier.
- **from sklearn.metrics import accuracy_score, classification_report:**
  `accuracy_score` and `classification_report` are used for evaluating the classifier's performance.
- **iris = load_iris()** :
  It load the dataset into variable `iris` which contains both the feature data and the output data (target).
- **X, y = iris.data, iris.target** :
  Input features of *iris* data is stored into variable '`X`', and the class labels is stored into variable 'y'.

- **X_train, X_test, y_train, y_test = train_test_split(X, y, test_size=0.2, random_state=42) :**
  It splits the data into training and testing sets, having 20% data in test class, and remaining data in training class. Here `X_train`, `y_train` contains training data and training label respectively which will be used for training the model. Here `X_test`, `y_test` contains testing data and testing label respectively which will be used for accuracy calculation purpose.
- **knn = KNeighborsClassifier(n_neighbors=3) :**
  It creates a KNN classifier with $k = 3$.
- **knn.fit(X_train, y_train):**
  This command train the KNN classifier on training data `X_train` and training target `y_train`.
- **y_pred = knn.predict(X_test):**
  This command predict output for test data `X_test` and store predicted output in vector array `y_pred`.
- **accuracy = accuracy_score(y_test, y_pred):**
  Accuracy is calculated by comparing the predicted output and already provided target.
- **classification_report(y_test, y_pred):**
  Generates a detailed report showing the precision, recall, and F1-score for each class.

13.1.2 KNN Algorithm : Illustration of Regression

KNN can also be used for regression task, the algorithm can predicts a continuous value. Consider a dataset (shown in Table 13.4) with continuous target variable shown in column *Target*. The dataset is represented with two features: `Feature 1` and `Feature 2`. We want to predict the target value for the new data point with the following features: **Feature 1**: 4.5, **Feature 2**: 2.5 using KNN with $k = 3$. Here, we will consider the 3 nearest neighbors to make the prediction.

Table 13.4: Dataset with two features and a continuous target as output

Feature 1	Feature 2	Target
1	2	1.5
2	1	2.0
3	3	2.5
4	4	4.0
5	2	4.5
6	3	5.0
7	1	6.0

The Euclidean distance formula is given by:

$$\text{distance} = \sqrt{(x_1 - x_2)^2 + (y_1 - y_2)^2}$$

where (x_1, y_1) and (x_2, y_2) are the coordinates of the two points.

For the new point (Feature 1 = 4.5, Feature 2 = 2.5):

$$\text{Distance to (1.0, 2.0)} = \sqrt{(4.5-1.0)^2+(2.5-2.0)^2} = \sqrt{12.25+0.25} = \sqrt{12.5} \approx 3.54$$

$$\text{Distance to (2.0, 1.0)} = \sqrt{(4.5-2.0)^2+(2.5-1.0)^2} = \sqrt{6.25+2.25} = \sqrt{8.5} \approx 2.92$$

$$\text{Distance to (3.0, 3.0)} = \sqrt{(4.5-3.0)^2+(2.5-3.0)^2} = \sqrt{2.25+0.25} = \sqrt{2.5} \approx 1.58$$

$$\text{Distance to (4.0, 4.0)} = \sqrt{(4.5-4.0)^2+(2.5-4.0)^2} = \sqrt{0.25+2.25} = \sqrt{2.5} \approx 1.58$$

$$\text{Distance to (5.0, 2.0)} = \sqrt{(4.5-5.0)^2+(2.5-2.0)^2} = \sqrt{0.25+0.25} = \sqrt{0.5} \approx 0.71$$

$$\text{Distance to (6.0, 3.0)} = \sqrt{(4.5-6.0)^2+(2.5-3.0)^2} = \sqrt{2.25+0.25} = \sqrt{2.5} \approx 1.58$$

$$\text{Distance to (7.0, 1.0)} = \sqrt{(4.5-7.0)^2+(2.5-1.0)^2} = \sqrt{6.25+2.25} = \sqrt{8.5} \approx 2.92$$

Sort the distances and select the $k = 3$ smallest ones:

- Distances:

$$3.54, 2.92, 1.58, 1.58, 0.71, 1.58, 2.92$$

- Nearest neighbors (sorted by distance):

$$(5.0, 2.0)\ (\text{Target } 4.5), (3.0, 3.0)\ (\text{Target } 2.5), (4.0, 4.0)\ (\text{Target } 4.0)$$

For regression, compute the average of the target values of the k nearest neighbors.

- Nearest neighbors:

$$(5.0, 2.0)\ (\text{Target } 4.5), (3.0, 3.0)\ (\text{Target } 2.5), (4.0, 4.0)\ (\text{Target } 4.0)$$

- Average target value: $\frac{4.5+2.5+4.0}{3} = \frac{11.0}{3} \approx 3.67$

Prediction: The predicted target value for the new data point (Feature 1 = 4.5, Feature 2 = 2.5) is approximately 3.67.

Ex.2 Regression using KNN algorithm (with k=3 neighbors)

```
import numpy as np
from sklearn.neighbors import KNeighborsRegressor

X = np.array([
    [1.0, 2.0],
    [2.0, 1.0],
    [3.0, 3.0],
    [4.0, 4.0],
    [5.0, 2.0],
```

```
    [6.0, 3.0],
    [7.0, 1.0]
])
y = np.array([1.5, 2.0, 2.5, 4.0, 4.5, 5.0, 6.0])

new_data = np.array([[4.5, 2.5]])

knn_regressor = KNeighborsRegressor(n_neighbors=3)
knn_regressor.fit(X, y)
prediction = knn_regressor.predict(new_data)

print(f'Predicted target value for {new_data[0]}: {prediction[0]:.2f}')
```

Explanation:

- **from sklearn.neighbors import KNeighborsRegressor**
  Required to implement K-Nearest Neighbors Regression.
- **knn_regressor = KNeighborsRegressor(n_neighbors=3)**:
  It creates a KNN regressor with $k = 3$.
- **knn_regressor.fit(X, y)**:
  This command starts training the regressor on the dataset X and target y.
- **prediction = knn_regressor.predict(new_data)**:
  It Predict the target value for the new data point.

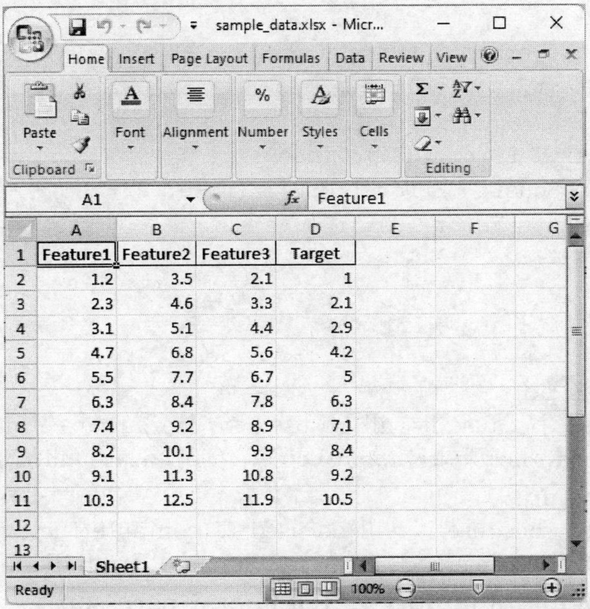

	A	B	C	D
1	Feature1	Feature2	Feature3	Target
2	1.2	3.5	2.1	1
3	2.3	4.6	3.3	2.1
4	3.1	5.1	4.4	2.9
5	4.7	6.8	5.6	4.2
6	5.5	7.7	6.7	5
7	6.3	8.4	7.8	6.3
8	7.4	9.2	8.9	7.1
9	8.2	10.1	9.9	8.4
10	9.1	11.3	10.8	9.2
11	10.3	12.5	11.9	10.5

Figure 13.1: Sample excel data for Regression

Ex.3 Regression using KNN algorithm on own data, stored in excel file (Figure 13.1).

```
import pandas as pd
import numpy as np
from sklearn.neighbors import KNeighborsRegressor
from sklearn.metrics import mean_squared_error, mean_absolute_error, r2_score
from sklearn.model_selection import train_test_split

file_path = 'sample_data.xlsx'
data = pd.read_excel(file_path)

X = data[['Feature1', 'Feature2', 'Feature3']]
y = data['Target']

X_train, X_test, y_train, y_test = train_test_split(X, y, test_size=0.2,
                                                     random_state=42)


knn_regressor = KNeighborsRegressor(n_neighbors=3)
knn_regressor.fit(X_train, y_train)
y_pred = knn_regressor.predict(X_test)

mse = mean_squared_error(y_test, y_pred)
rmse = np.sqrt(mse)
mae = mean_absolute_error(y_test, y_pred)
r2 = r2_score(y_test, y_pred)

print(f'Mean Squared Error (MSE): {mse:.2f}')
print(f'Root Mean Squared Error (RMSE): {rmse:.2f}')
print(f'Mean Absolute Error (MAE): {mae:.2f}')
print(f'R^2 Score: {r2:.2f}')
```

Explanation:

- **import pandas as pd**:
  Pandas is imported, because it will be used for loading excel data and in to selecting specific columns from the *DataFrame* to create the feature matrix.
- **import numpy as np**:
  Numpy is imported, because it will be used to compute the square root of the Mean Squared Error (MSE) to get the Root Mean Squared Error (RMSE).
- **from sklearn.neighbors import KNeighborsRegressor**:
  Required to implement K-Nearest Neighbors Regression.

- **mean_squared_error, mean_absolute_error, r2_score:**
Theses libraries will be used to evaluate the performance of the regression model.
- **data = pd.read_excel(file_path) :**
This command loads the data from the Excel file into a pandas DataFrame.
- **X = data[['Feature1', 'Feature2', 'Feature3']]:**
Features from the data form is loaded into variable X. Here, Feature1, Feature2, and Feature3 are the features.
- **y = data['Target']:**
The target value from the dataframe is loaded into variable y.
- **X_train, X_test, y_train, y_test = train_test_split(X, y, test_size=0.2, random_state=42) :**
It splits the data into training and testing sets, having 20% data in test class, and remaining data in training class. Here `X_train`, `y_train` contains features and target of training dataset respectively. Here `X_test`, `y_test` contains features and target of test data respectively.
- **knn_regressor = KNeighborsRegressor(n_neighbors=3):**
It Creates a KNN regressor with $k = 3$.
- **knn_regressor.fit(X, y):**
This command starts training the regressor on the training dataset X_train and target y_train.
- **y_pred = knn_regressor.predict(X_test):**
This command predict the output for the test data (`X_test`) through the trained model. The predicted value is stored into variable `y_pred`.
- **mse = mean_squared_error(y_test, y_pred):**
It calculates the Mean Squared Error (MSE) between the actual and predicted target values.
- **rmse = np.sqrt(mse) :**
It calculates the Root Mean Squared Error (RMSE).
- **mean_absolute_error(y_test, y_pred):**
It calculates the Mean Absolute Error (MAE).
- **r2_score(y_test, y_pred):**
Icalculates the R^2 score, which indicates how well the model explains the variability of the target variable.

13.2 Decision Tree

Decision tree is a supervised learning method used for classification and regression. It works by recursively splitting the dataset into subsets based on feature values, creating a tree-like model of decisions. Imagine a tree where each branch represents a choice based on a question about a feature of the data. As you move down the tree, you keep making choices until you reach a leaf, which gives you the final answer or prediction.

13.2.1 Decision Tree : Illustration of Classification

Consider a dataset (shown in Table 13.5) for classification of email as spam or not a spam. Output classes are: `Spam` and `Not Spam`. The dataset is represented with four features: `Contains text "Free"`, `Contains text "Urgent"`, `Has Attachments`, and `Whether sender is known`.

Table 13.5: Dataset for email classification as 'spam' or 'not spam'

Contains "Free"	Contains "Urgent"	Contains "Offer"	Spam
Yes	Yes	Yes	Yes
Yes	Yes	No	Yes
Yes	No	Yes	Yes
Yes	No	No	Yes
No	Yes	Yes	Yes
No	Yes	No	No
No	No	Yes	Yes
No	No	No	No

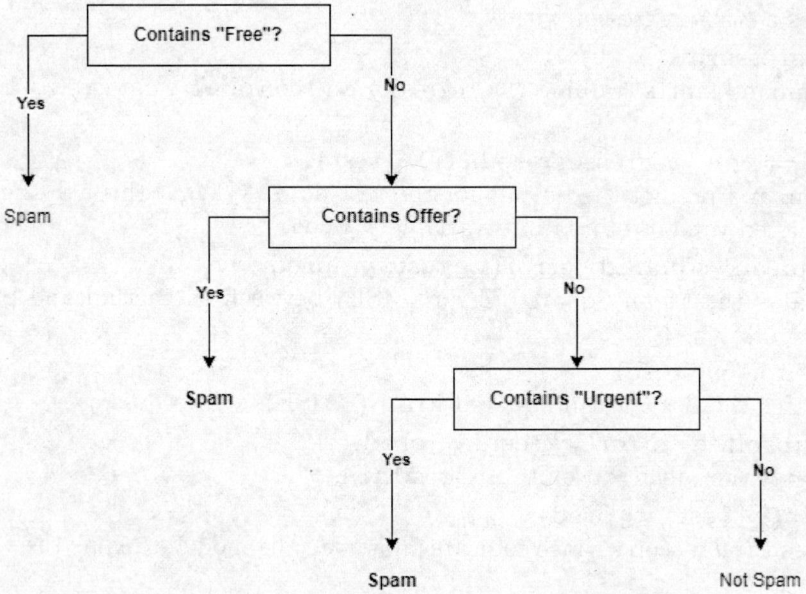

Figure 13.2: Simple Decision Tree for email classification

Working of Decision

1. **Start with the Root Node:**
   - The tree starts with all the data at the root.
2. **Choose the Best Feature to Split on:**
   - Calculate metrics such as *Information Gain* or *Gini Impurity* to determine the best feature to split the data.

- The algorithm evaluates all features (like "Contains 'Free'", "Contains 'Urgent'", etc.) and chooses the one that best separates the data. For example, the tree might first split on whether the email contains the word "Free".

3. **Create Subnodes:**
   - If "Contains 'Free'" is the first split, the tree creates two branches: one for emails that contain "Free" and one for those that do not.
4. **Repeat the Process:**
   - The process is repeated for each subnode, choosing the next best feature to split the data further. For example, if an email contains "Free", the next question might be whether it also contains "Urgent".
5. **Assign Labels at the Leaves:**
   - Once the data subsets are homogeneous or further splitting is not beneficial, assign the most frequent label in each leaf node.
   - The leaves of the tree are labeled with the final prediction. For example, if an email contains both "Free" and "Urgent", the leaf might be labeled "Spam".

13.2.2 Information Gain

When training a Decision Tree, the algorithm needs to determine the best feature to split the data at each node. Two commonly used criteria for making this decision are Information Gain and Gini Impurity. Both measure how well a feature separates the classes in the dataset, but they do so in different ways.

Information Gain measures how much uncertainty or disorder is reduced by splitting the data on a particular feature. It is based on the concept of *Entropy*, which quantifies the impurity or randomness in the dataset.

Entropy

Entropy for a dataset D is calculated as follows:

$$H(D) = -\sum_{i=1}^{n} p_i \log_2 p_i$$

where p_i is the proportion of instances in class i, and n is the number of classes.

Information Gain

Information Gain for a feature A is defined as the reduction in entropy after the dataset D is split based on feature A. It is calculated as:

$$IG(D, A) = H(D) - H(D|A)$$

where $H(D)$ is the entropy of the original dataset, and $H(D|A)$ is the weighted entropy of the dataset after the split by feature A.

Example Calculation

Consider the dataset given in Table 13.5

- Step 1: Calculate the Entropy for the Entire Dataset
  - Spam: 6 instances
  - Not Spam: 2 instances

  $$p_{\text{Spam}} = \frac{6}{8} = 0.75, \quad p_{\text{Not Spam}} = \frac{2}{8} = 0.25$$

  Entropy of the dataset:

  $$H(D) = -(0.75\log_2 0.75 + 0.25\log_2 0.25) = -(0.75 * -0.415 + 0.25 * -2) \approx 1.311$$

- Step 2: Calculate Entropy for Each Feature Split

  For feature: *Contains "Free"*
  Yes = 4 (Spam = 4, not spam=0)
  No = 4 (Spam = 2, not spam=2)

  $$H(Yes) = -\left(\frac{4}{4}\log_2\frac{4}{4} + \frac{0}{4}\log_2\frac{0}{4}\right) = 0$$

  $$H(No) = -\left(\frac{2}{4}\log_2\frac{2}{4} + \frac{2}{4}\log_2\frac{2}{4}\right) = -(0.5 * -1 + 0.5 * -1) = 1$$

  Weighted Entropy After Split:

  $$H(\text{Contain Free}) = \frac{4}{8}H(Yes) + \frac{4}{8}H(No) = 0.5 * 0 + 0.5 * 1 = 0.5$$

  Information Gain:

  $$IG(\text{Contain Free}) = H(D) - H(\text{Contain Free}) = 1.311 - 0.5 = 0.811$$

  For feature: *Contains "Urgent"*
  Yes = 4 (Spam = 3, not spam=1)
  No = 4 (Spam = 3, not spam=1)

  $$H(Yes) = -\left(\frac{3}{4}\log_2\frac{3}{4} + \frac{1}{4}\log_2\frac{1}{4}\right) \approx 0.811$$

  $$H(No) = -\left(\frac{3}{4}\log_2\frac{3}{4} + \frac{1}{4}\log_2\frac{1}{4}\right) \approx 0.811$$

  Weighted Entropy After Split:

  $$H(\text{Contain Urgent}) = \frac{4}{8}H(Yes) + \frac{4}{8}H(No) = 0.5 * 0.811 + 0.5 * 0.811 = 0.811$$

  Information Gain:

  $$IG(\text{Contain Urgent}) = H(D) - H(\text{Contain Urgent}) = 1.311 - 0.811 = 0.5$$

For feature: *Contains "Offer"*
Yes = 4 (Spam = 4, not spam=0)
No = 4 (Spam = 2, not spam=2)

$$H(Yes) = -\left(\frac{4}{4}\log_2\frac{4}{4} + \frac{0}{4}\log_2\frac{0}{4}\right) = 0$$

$$H(No) = -\left(\frac{2}{4}\log_2\frac{2}{4} + \frac{2}{4}\log_2\frac{2}{4}\right) = -(0.5*-1+0.5*-1) = 1$$

Weighted Entropy After Split:

$$H(\text{Contain Offer}) = \frac{4}{8}H(Yes) + \frac{4}{8}H(No) = 0.5*0+0.5*1 = 0.5$$

Information Gain:

$$IG(\text{Contain Offer}) = H(D) - H(\text{Contain Offer}) = 1.311 - 0.5 = 0.811$$

Conclusion: Feature with higher information gain is chosen to split first. In our case both "Contains 'Free'" and "Contains 'Offer'" provide the highest Information Gain, making them the best features for the first split in a decision tree.

13.2.3 Gini Impurity

Gini Impurity is another measure used to assess the quality of a split. It measures how often a randomly chosen element from the set would be incorrectly labeled if it were randomly labeled according to the distribution of labels in the set. Gini Impurity measures the purity of a dataset, focusing on the probability of incorrectly classifying a randomly chosen element. It is defined as:

$$G(D) = 1 - \sum_{i=1}^{n} p_i^2$$

where p_i is the proportion of instances in class i.

After splitting the dataset by a feature, the Gini Impurity of each subset is calculated. The weighted Gini Impurity of the dataset after the split is:

$$G(D|A) = \sum_{i=1}^{n} \frac{|D_{\text{Subset i}}|}{|D|} G(D_{\text{Subset i}}))$$

Example Calculation

Consider the dataset given in Table 13.5

- Step 1: Calculate Gini Impurity for the Entire Dataset
  Total instances: 8 (6 Spam, 2 Not Spam)

$$p_{\text{Spam}} = \frac{6}{8} = 0.75, \quad p_{\text{Not Spam}} = \frac{2}{8} = 0.25$$

Gini Impurity of the dataset:

$$G(D) = 1 - \left((0.75)^2 + (0.25)^2\right) = 1 - 0.625 = 0.375$$

- Step 2: Calculate Gini Impurity for each feature split
  For feature: *Contains "Free"*
  Yes = 4 (Spam = 4, not spam=0)
  No = 4 (Spam = 2, not spam=2)

$$G(Yes) = 1 - \left(\left(\frac{4}{4}\right)^2 + \left(\frac{0}{4}\right)^2\right) = 1 - (1^2 - 0^2) = 0$$

$$G(No) = 1 - \left(\left(\frac{2}{4}\right)^2 + \left(\frac{2}{4}\right)^2\right) = 1 - (0.5^2 + 0.5^2) = 0.5$$

Weighted Gini impurity after the split:

$$G(\text{Contain Free}) = \frac{4}{8}G(Yes) + \frac{4}{8}G(No) = 0.5 * 0 + 0.5 * 0.5 = 0.25$$

For feature: *Contains "Urgent"*
Yes = 4 (Spam = 3, not spam=1)
No = 4 (Spam = 3, not spam=1)

$$G(Yes) = 1 - \left(\left(\frac{3}{4}\right)^2 + \left(\frac{1}{4}\right)^2\right) = 1 - (0.75^2 + 0.25^2) = 1 - (0.5625 + 0.0625) = 1 - 0.625 = 0.375$$

$$G(No) = 1 - \left(\left(\frac{3}{4}\right)^2 + \left(\frac{1}{4}\right)^2\right) = 1 - (0.75^2 + 0.25^2) = 1 - (0.5625 + 0.0625) = 1 - 0.625 = 0.375$$

Weighted Gini impurity after the split:

$$G(\text{Contain Free}) = \frac{4}{8}G(Yes) + \frac{4}{8}G(No) = 0.5 * 0.375 + 0.5 * 0.375 = 0.375$$

For feature: *Contains "Offer"*
Yes = 4 (Spam = 4, not spam=0)
No = 4 (Spam = 2, not spam=2)

$$G(Yes) = 1 - \left(\left(\frac{4}{4}\right)^2 + \left(\frac{0}{4}\right)^2\right) = 1 - (1^2 - 0^2) = 0$$

$$G(No) = 1 - \left(\left(\frac{2}{4}\right)^2 + \left(\frac{2}{4}\right)^2\right) = 1 - (0.5^2 + 0.5^2) = 0.5$$

Weighted Gini impurity after the split:

$$G(\text{Contain Offer}) = \frac{4}{8}G(Yes) + \frac{4}{8}G(No) = 0.5*0+0.5*0.5 = 0.25$$

Conclusion: Based on the Gini impurity, "Contains 'Free' " and "Contains 'Offer' " are the best features for splitting, as they result in the lowest impurity (0.25).

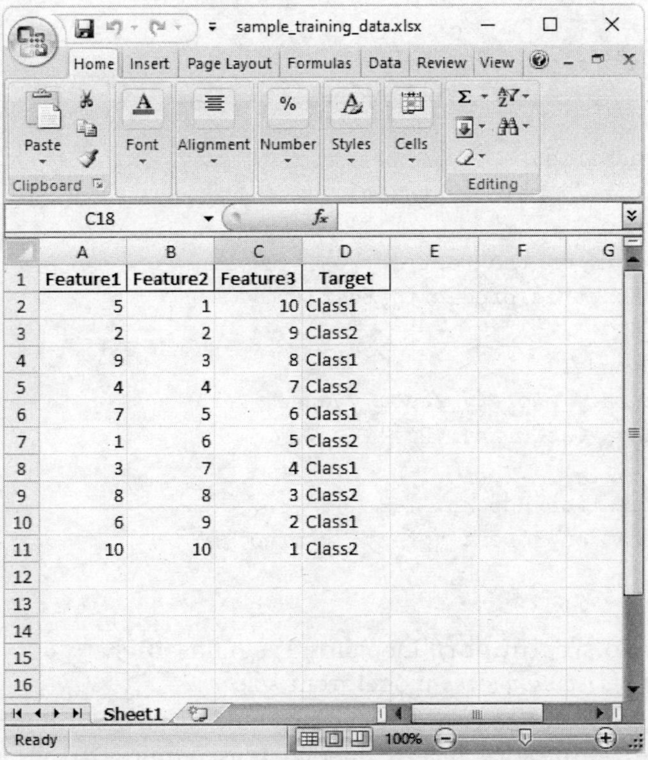

Feature1	Feature2	Feature3	Target
5	1	10	Class1
2	2	9	Class2
9	3	8	Class1
4	4	7	Class2
7	5	6	Class1
1	6	5	Class2
3	7	4	Class1
8	8	3	Class2
6	9	2	Class1
10	10	1	Class2

Figure 13.3: Sample excel data for Classification

Ex.4 Classification using Decisition Tree algorithm from excel data shown in Figure 13.3

```
# Import necessary libraries
import pandas as pd
from sklearn.model_selection import train_test_split
from sklearn.tree import DecisionTreeClassifier
from sklearn.metrics import accuracy_score , classification_report

file_path = 'sample_training_data.xlsx'
data = pd.read_excel(file_path)
```

```
# Dropping the target column to create feature matrix
X = data.drop('Target', axis=1)
y = data['Target']                    # Extracting the target column

# Split the dataset into training and testing sets
X_train, X_test, y_train, y_test = train_test_split(X, y, test_size=0.2,
                                                    random_state=42)

# Create a Decision Tree classifier
decision_tree = DecisionTreeClassifier(random_state=42)

# Train the classifier
decision_tree.fit(X_train, y_train)

# Make predictions on the test set
y_pred = decision_tree.predict(X_test)

# Evaluate the model
accuracy = accuracy_score(y_test, y_pred)
print(f'Accuracy: {accuracy:.2f}')

print('Classification Report:')
print(classification_report(y_test, y_pred))
```

Explanation:

- **from sklearn.tree import DecisionTreeClassifier**
  It import the *Decision Tree* model from *sklearn.*
- **from sklearn.metrics import accuracy_score, classification_report**
  To evaluate the performance of model, it is required to import: *accuracy_score*, *classification_report.*
- **X = data.drop('Target', axis=1)**
  After importing the excel file, feature matrix is created by dropping the *Target* column from the dataset.
- **y = data['Target']**
  The target vector is created from imported excel file.
- **decision_tree = DecisionTreeClassifier(random_state=42)**
  Decision Tree classifier is initialied.
  - Decision trees can involve randomness in several aspects, such as deciding how to split nodes when multiple splits have the same information gain or Gini impurity.
  - By default, these processes are influenced by a random seed, which means that if you run the same code multiple times without setting `random_state`, you could get different trees each time.

– By setting the `random_state` parameter to a fixed value (like 42), you ensure that the randomness is consistent every time the code is run.

- **decision_tree.fit(X_train, y_train)**
  The *DecisionTreeClassifier* object is created and trained on the training data (`X_train, y_train`).
- **y_pred = decision_tree.predict(X_test)**
  The trained model makes predictions on the test set (X_test), and the results are stored in y_pred.
- **accuracy = accuracy_score(y_test, y_pred)**
  Prediction accuracy is calculated by comparing predicted value and ground truth value.
- **classification_report(y_test, y_pred)**
  It provides detailed metrics like precision, recall, F1-score, and support for each class in the target variable.

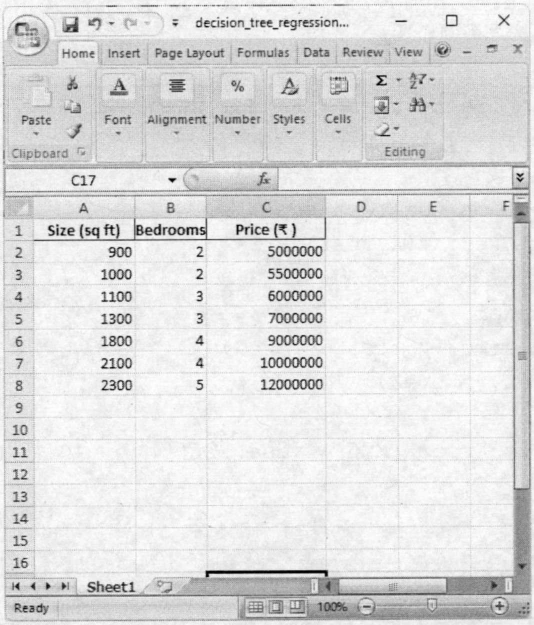

Size (sq ft)	Bedrooms	Price (₹)
900	2	5000000
1000	2	5500000
1100	3	6000000
1300	3	7000000
1800	4	9000000
2100	4	10000000
2300	5	12000000

Figure 13.4: Sample excel data for Regression

Ex.5 Regression using Decision Tree algorithm from excel data shown in Figure 13.4

```
import numpy as np
import pandas as pd
from sklearn.model_selection import train_test_split
from sklearn.tree import DecisionTreeRegressor
from sklearn.metrics import mean_squared_error, r2_score
```

```
# Load sample data from an Excel file
file_path = 'decision_tree_regression_data.xlsx'
data = pd.read_excel(file_path)


X = data.drop('Price', axis=1)  # create the feature matrix
y = data['Price']               # Extracting the target column

# Split the dataset into training and testing sets
X_train, X_test, y_train, y_test = train_test_split(X, y, test_size=0.2,
                                                     random_state=42)

# Convert the training data to numpy arrays with float32 dtype
X_train_np = X_train.to_numpy().astype(np.float32)
y_train_np = y_train.to_numpy()

# Creating and training the Decision Tree Regressor
regressor = DecisionTreeRegressor(random_state=42)
regressor.fit(X_train, y_train)

# Making predictions on the test set
y_pred = regressor.predict(X_test)

# Evaluating the model
mse = mean_squared_error(y_test, y_pred)
r2 = r2_score(y_test, y_pred)

print(f'Mean Squared Error (MSE): {mse:.2f}')
print(f'R^2 Score: {r2:.2f}')
```

Explanation:

- **regressor = DecisionTreeRegressor(random_state=42)**
  A DecisionTreeRegressor model is created with random_state=42 for reproducibility.
- **regressor.fit(X_train, y_train)**
  The model is trained using the fit method on the training data (X_train, y_train).
- **y_pred = regressor.predict(X_test)**
  The trained model is used to make predictions on the test set (X_test), and the predicted values are stored in y_pred.
- **mse = mean_squared_error(y_test, y_pred)**
  It is used to calculate the mean square error. It measures the average squared difference between the actual and predicted values. Lower values indicate a better fit.

- **r2 = r2_score(y_test, y_pred)**
  It calculate R^2 score. It represents the proportion of the variance in the dependent variable that is predictable from the independent variables. An R^2 value closer to 1 indicates a better fit.

13.3 Linear Regression

Linear Regression is a fundamental supervised learning algorithm which models the relationship between a dependent variable (target) and one or more independent variables (features) by fitting a linear equation to observed data. The simplest form, Simple Linear Regression, involves one feature and fits a straight line (`y = mx + c`) where m is the slope and c is the intercept. Multiple Linear Regression extends this to multiple features.
The goal of Linear Regression is to find the best-fitting line by minimizing the sum of the squared differences between the actual and predicted values. This line is known as the line of best fit. Linear Regression is widely used for tasks like predicting house prices, stock prices, and other scenarios where the outcome is a continuous variable.

Ex.6 Linear regression on Diabetes Dataset having 10 features.

```
# Import necessary libraries
from sklearn.datasets import load_diabetes
from sklearn.model_selection import train_test_split
from sklearn.linear_model import LinearRegression
from sklearn.metrics import mean_squared_error, r2_score

# Load the Diabetes dataset
diabetes = load_diabetes()

#display features name
print(f"Feature Names: {diabetes.feature_names}")

X = diabetes.data  # Features
y = diabetes.target  # Target

# Split the data into training and testing sets
X_train, X_test, y_train, y_test = train_test_split(X, y, test_size=0.2)

# Initialize the Linear Regression model
model = LinearRegression()

# Fit the model on the training data
model.fit(X_train, y_train)
```

```
# Make predictions on the testing data
y_pred = model.predict(X_test)

# Evaluate the model
mse = mean_squared_error(y_test, y_pred)  # Mean Squared Error
r2 = r2_score(y_test, y_pred)  # R-squared score

# Print the results
print(f"Mean Squared Error: {mse:.2f}")
print(f"R-squared Score: {r2:.2f}")
```

Explanation:

- **sklearn.datasets.load_diabetes**
  It loads the built-in Diabetes dataset.
- **from sklearn.linear_model import LinearRegression**
  It imports a class that implements the Linear Regression algorithm.
- **from sklearn.metrics import mean_squared_error, r2_score**
  It imports necessary functions used to evaluate the performance of the regression model.
- **model = LinearRegression()**
  It initializes the Linear Regression model.
- **model.fit(X_train, y_train)**
  This function trains the model using the training data (X_train and y_train).
- **y_pred = model.predict(X_test)**
  `model.predict(X_test)` uses the trained model to make predictions on the testing data `(X_test)`. The predicted values are stored in `y_` pred.
- **mse = mean_squared_error(y_test, y_pred)**
  Calculates the Mean Squared Error (MSE), which measures the average squared difference between the actual and predicted values. A lower MSE indicates better performance.
- **r2 = r2_score(y_test, y_pred)**
  Computes the R-squared (R^2) score, which indicates how well the model explains the variability of the target variable. An R^2 score closer to 1 indicates a better fit.

13.4 Syntax of Supervised Learning Code

Generalized code for supervised learning algorithm implementation can be summarized as in 5 following steps:

Step 1: Load required library for: (1) excel data loading, (2) train-test splitting, (3) performance evaluation, etc.

Step 2: Load excel file and extract Features in variable X and output/Result/Target in variable y.

Step 3: Split data and target into training dataset (X_train, y_train) and test dataset (X_test, y_test).

Step 4: Initialize Classifier/Regressor based on chosen algorithm.

Step 5: Perform Training using `.fit(X_train, y_train)`.

Step 6: Perform prediction for evaluation of trained algorithm using test `.predict(X_test)`.

Step 7: Compute evaluation parameter from predicted data (obtained from previous step) and test target data (`y_test`).

While changing algorithm for implementation, the code under step-1 and step-4 will have to change. The Table 13.6 gives the code section which is required to import the classifier and the codes required to initialize the corresponding to different classification algorithms along with training. After training of a specific classification algorithm, prediction is performed through code `y_pred = clf.predict(X_test)`. Similarly Table 13.7 presents the code sections for different regression algorithms.

Table 13.6: Code snippet for implementing supervised machine learning for classification

Algorithm Name	Library to Import	Initialize Regressor & Training
Logistic Regression	`from sklearn.linear_model import LogisticRegression`	`clf = LogisticRegression()` `clf.fit(X_train, y_train)`
Decision Tree	`from sklearn.tree import DecisionTreeClassifier`	`clf = DecisionTreeClassifier()` `clf.fit(X_train, y_train)`
Random Forest	`from sklearn.ensemble import RandomForestClassifier`	`clf = RandomForestClassifier()` `clf.fit(X_train, y_train)`
Support Vector Machine	`from sklearn.svm import SVC`	`clf = SVC()` `clf.fit(X_train, y_train)`
K-Nearest Neighbors	`from sklearn.neighbors import KNeighborsClassifier`	`clf = KNeighborsClassifier()` `clf.fit(X_train, y_train)`
Naive Bayes	`from sklearn.naive_bayes import GaussianNB`	`clf = GaussianNB()` `clf.fit(X_train, y_train)`
Gradient Boosting	`from sklearn.ensemble import GradientBoostingClassifier`	`clf = GradientBoostingClassifier()` `clf.fit(X_train, y_train)`

Table 13.7: Code snippet for implementing supervised machine learning for regression

Algorithm Name	Library to Import	Initialize Regressor & Training
Linear Regression	`from sklearn.linear_model import LinearRegression`	`reg = LinearRegression()` `reg.fit(X_train, y_train)`
Decision Tree Regression	`from sklearn.tree import DecisionTreeRegressor`	`reg = DecisionTreeRegressor()` `reg.fit(X_train, y_train)`
Random Forest Regression	`from sklearn.ensemble import RandomForestRegressor`	`reg = RandomForestRegressor()` `reg.fit(X_train, y_train)`
Support Vector Regression	`from sklearn.svm import SVR`	`reg = SVR()` `reg.fit(X_train, y_train)`
K-Nearest Neighbors Regression	`from sklearn.neighbors import KNeighborsRegressor`	`reg = KNeighborsRegressor()` `reg.fit(X_train, y_train)`
Gradient Boosting Regression	`from sklearn.ensemble import GradientBoostingRegressor`	`reg = GradientBoostingRegressor()` `reg.fit(X_train, y_train)`
Ridge Regression	`from sklearn.linear_model import Ridge`	`reg = Ridge()` `reg.fit(X_train, y_train)`

14. Unsupervised Learning

Unsupervised learning is a type of machine learning where the model is not provided with labeled data. Instead, it is tasked with identifying patterns, relationships, or groupings in the data purely on its structure. Unlike supervised learning, where the goal is to predict a target variable, unsupervised learning tries to uncover hidden structures in the data. Unsupervised learning deals with unlabeled data, meaning there is no "correct" output to guide the learning process. Unsupervised learning plays a crucial role in various fields where labeled data is scarce or expensive to obtain. Some real-world applications include:

- **Customer Segmentation:** Grouping customers based on buying behaviors for targeted marketing.
- **Anomaly Detection:** Identifying unusual patterns in data, useful in fraud detection or network security.
- **Market Basket Analysis:** Finding associations between products customers frequently buy together.
- **Dimensionality Reduction:** Reducing the number of features in data to simplify models and improve performance, commonly used in image processing and text mining.

14.1 K-Means Clustering

K-Means is one of the simplest and most widely used algorithms in unsupervised learning. It is a clustering algorithm that groups data into a predefined number of clusters based on their similarity. The goal is to partition the data into K clusters in which each data point belongs to the cluster with the nearest mean.

14.1.1 Working of K-Means Algorithm

Imagine you have a basket of fruits, and you want to group them into 3 clusters based on their weight and size. The goal is to place similar fruits into the same cluster.

Step 1: Choose the Number of Clusters (K)
First, you decide how many clusters you want. Let's say you want to divide the fruits into **3 clusters**, based on their size and weight. So, $\mathbf{K = 3}$.

Step 2: Randomly Place 3 Centroids
Randomly picks 3 centroids placed anywhere in the space of the fruit data (e.g., the size and weight chart).

Step 3: Assign Each Fruit to the Nearest Centroid
Now, each fruit is assigned to the centroid it is closest to. The closeness is measured by how similar the fruit's weight and size are to the centroid. At the end of this step, you have 3 clusters of fruits, each grouped around one of the randomly placed centroids.

Step 4: Move the Centroids
After assigning all the fruits to the nearest centroid, the algorithm updates the position of each centroid. For this, it moves each centroid to the average position of all the fruits in that cluster.

Step 5: Repeat Steps 3 and 4
This process is repeated until the centroids stop moving or move very little, meaning the clusters are stable.

Step 6: Final Clusters
Once the centroids stop moving, the algorithm ends. You now have 3 final clusters, each containing fruits that are similar in terms of size and weight.

14.1.2 Illustration of K-Means Algorithm

Illustration of working of K-means algorithm is explained using Figure 14.1. We have fruit data with size and weight as feature, having distribution as shown in the first part of figure (Fruit Data). We want to segregate it into three groups (say), so we have to start with three initial guess (random). These initial guesses are shown in *Iteration-0* of the figure. Centroids of these groups are shown with cross '(X)' marks. Now the *euclidean* distance is calculated for each fruits for the data set with reference to each of the three centroids, and the fruit is associated with the centroid it is closest to. Now the cetroid of each group is re-calculated from the fruits of each group through average of the each fruits under the groups. Re-adjusted centroid of *illustration-0* is shown in *illustration-1*. Shifting of centroids is gradually represented in *illustration-1* to *illustration-9*. This shifting is repeated until change of centroid in not less than the fixed offset value. The final value of centroid is shown in last part of Figure 14.1.

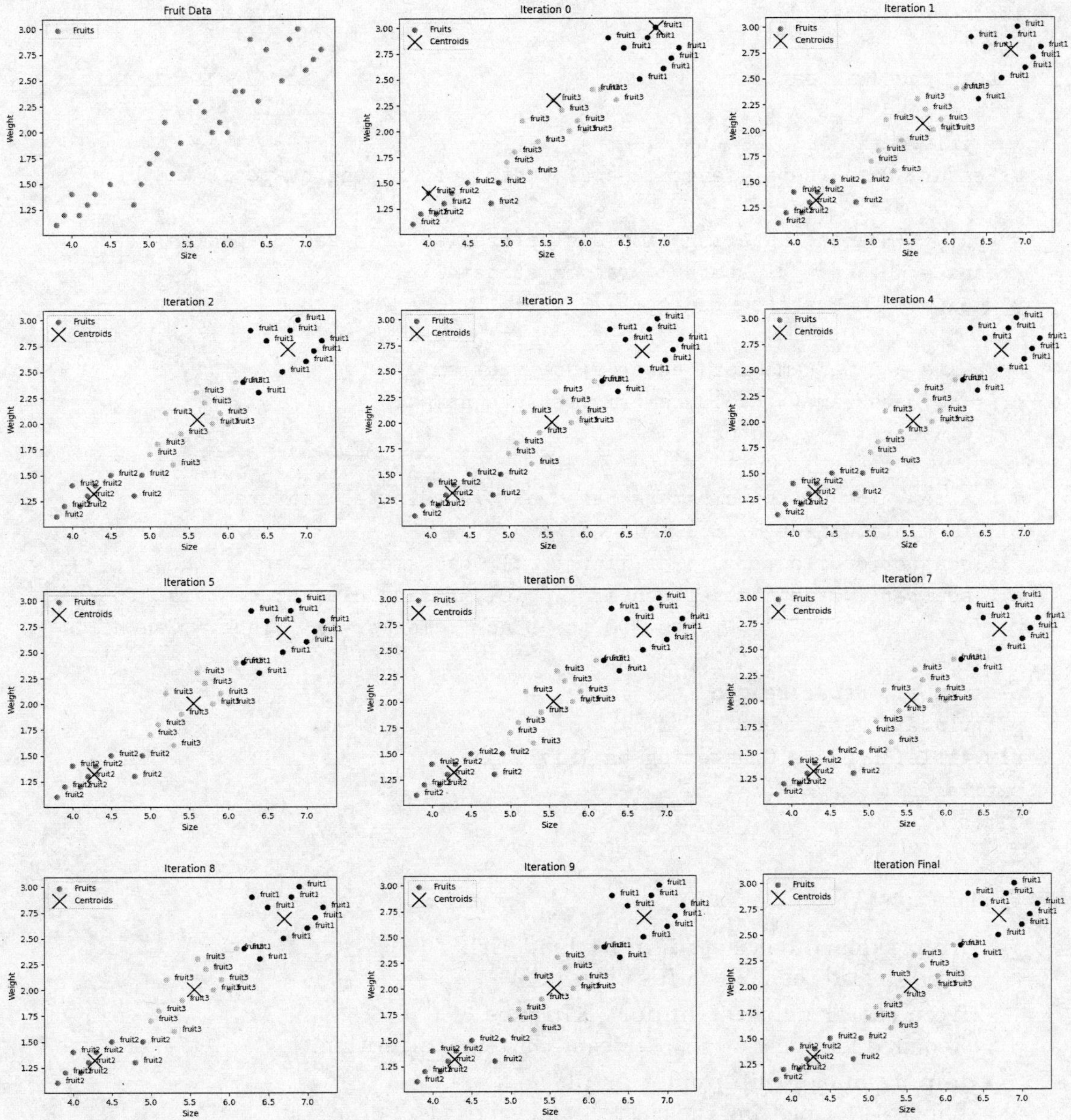

Figure 14.1: Steps of Shifting centroids through K-means algorithm

Ex.1 Clustering using K-means algorithm (3-clusters) on *iris* data

```
from sklearn.datasets import load_iris
from sklearn.cluster import KMeans
import matplotlib.pyplot as plt
```

```
import pandas as pd

# Load the Iris dataset
iris = load_iris()
X = iris.data
# Feature data (sepal length, sepal width, petal length, petal width)

# Apply K-Means clustering with 3 clusters (as Iris has 3 species)
kmeans = KMeans(n_clusters=3, random_state=42)
y_kmeans = kmeans.fit_predict(X)

# Create a DataFrame for better visualization
df = pd.DataFrame(X, columns=iris.feature_names)
df['Cluster'] = y_kmeans

# Scatter plot of the clusters based on two selected features
plt.figure(figsize=(8, 6))
plt.scatter(df.iloc[:, 0], df.iloc[:, 2], c=y_kmeans, cmap='rainbow')
plt.scatter(kmeans.cluster_centers_[:, 0], kmeans.cluster_centers_[:, 2],
                          s=300, c='black', marker='x', label='Centroids')

plt.xlabel('Sepal Length (cm)')
plt.ylabel('Petal Length (cm)')
plt.title('K-Means Clustering on Iris Dataset')
plt.legend()
plt.show()
```

Explanation:

- **from sklearn.datasets import load_iris**
  Used to load the built-in Iris dataset.
- **from sklearn.cluster import KMeans**
  Required for applying the K-Means clustering algorithm.
- **import matplotlib.pyplot as plt**
  Imported for plotting the clusters and centroids.
- **import pandas as pd**
  Used to create a *DataFrame* for easy visualization and manipulation of data.
- **iris = load_iris()**
  It loads the Iris data. The *iris* contains the feature data (4 measurements for each flower) and the true labels (species).
- **X = iris.data**
  This line of code extracts the feature data from the dataset.

- **kmeans = KMeans(n_clusters=3, random_state=42)**
This line of code asks K-Means to create 3 clusters (because the Iris dataset contains 3 species of flowers). K-Means initializes cluster centroids randomly during the start. Different runs may result in different clusters if centroids are initialized in different locations. The `random_state` ensures that the random initialization is the same every time the code is run, producing consistent results. You can use any integer as the seed, but using the same seed ensures the same clusters and centroids across multiple runs of the algorithm. If you don't set random_state, K-Means might produce slightly different clusters each time you run the code due to varying centroid initialization.
- **y_kmeans = kmeans.fit_predict(X)**
This line of code fits the K-Means algorithm on the feature data X and assigns a cluster label to each data point (stored in y_kmeans).
- **df = pd.DataFrame()**
It creates a DataFrame for Visualization. The dataframe Stores the feature data with proper column names.
- **df['Cluster'] = y_kmeans**
Cluster column Stores the predicted cluster label for each data point from *y_kmeans.*
- **plt.figure(figsize=(8, 6))**
It specifies the width=8 inch and height= 6 inch of the figure for plotting the clusters.
- **plt.scatter()**
It is used for scatter ploting, which displays individual data points in a $2D$ space, with one feature mapped to the x-axis and another to the y-axis.
  - `df.iloc[:, 0]` is Sepal Length and is used in x-axis while plotting scatter graph.
  - `df.iloc[:, 2]` is Petal Length and is used in Y-axis while plotting scatter graph.
  - `c=y_kmeans`: The `y_kmeans` is the cluster label assigned to each data point by the K-Means algorithm. If the clusters are [0, 1, 2], the data points are labeled according to the cluster they belong to. When you pass c=y_kmeans to plt.scatter(), each point is colored based on its assigned cluster label.
  - `cmap='rainbow'`: The *'rainbow'* is a predefined colormap in Matplotlib that assigns vibrant colors to the data points.
- **plt.scatter(kmeans.cluster_centers_[:, 0], kmeans.cluster_centers_[:, 2], s=300, c='black', marker='x', label='Centroids')**
  - `kmeans.cluster_centers_[:, 0]` retrieves the x-coordinates of the centroids from the K-Means clustering result.
  - `kmeans.cluster_centers_` returns a 2D array where each row corresponds to a cluster centroid and each column corresponds to a feature.
  - `[:, 0]` selects all rows for the first feature (e.g., Sepal Length).
  - `kmeans.cluster_centers_[:, 2]` retrieves the y-coordinates of the centroids from the K-Means clustering result.
  - `[:, 2]` selects all rows for the 3rd feature (e.g., Petal Length).
  - `s=300` specifies the size of the centroid markers in the plot.

- c='black' sets the color of the centroid markers as black.
- marker='x' specifies the shape of the centroid markers.
- label='Centroids' adds a label to the markers for the legend. It allows users to identify that the black crosses in the plot represent the centroids of the clusters.

Output:
The K-means clustering will be performed on the *iris* dataset to divide it into three clusters. After clustering, it creates a scatter plot using two features (sepal length and petal length) to visually display the clusters with different colors (Fig 14.2). The centroids of the clusters are marked as large black crosses.

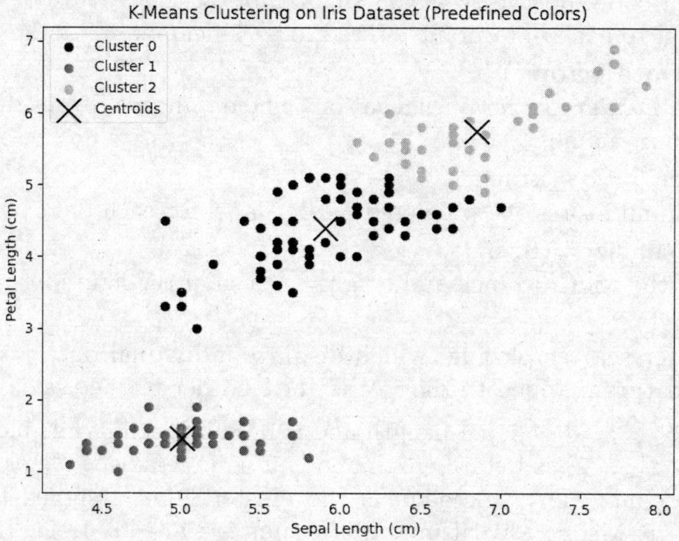

Figure 14.2: Classification using K-means on iris dataset

Ex.2 K-means clustering (3-clusters) on custom excel dataset shown in Figure 14.3, and prediction for new data

```
import pandas as pd
from sklearn.cluster import KMeans
import matplotlib.pyplot as plt

data = pd.read_excel('kmeans_dataset.xlsx')
X = data[['Feature1', 'Feature2']]

# Apply K-Means clustering
kmeans = KMeans(n_clusters=3, random_state=42)
data['Cluster'] = kmeans.fit_predict(X)
```

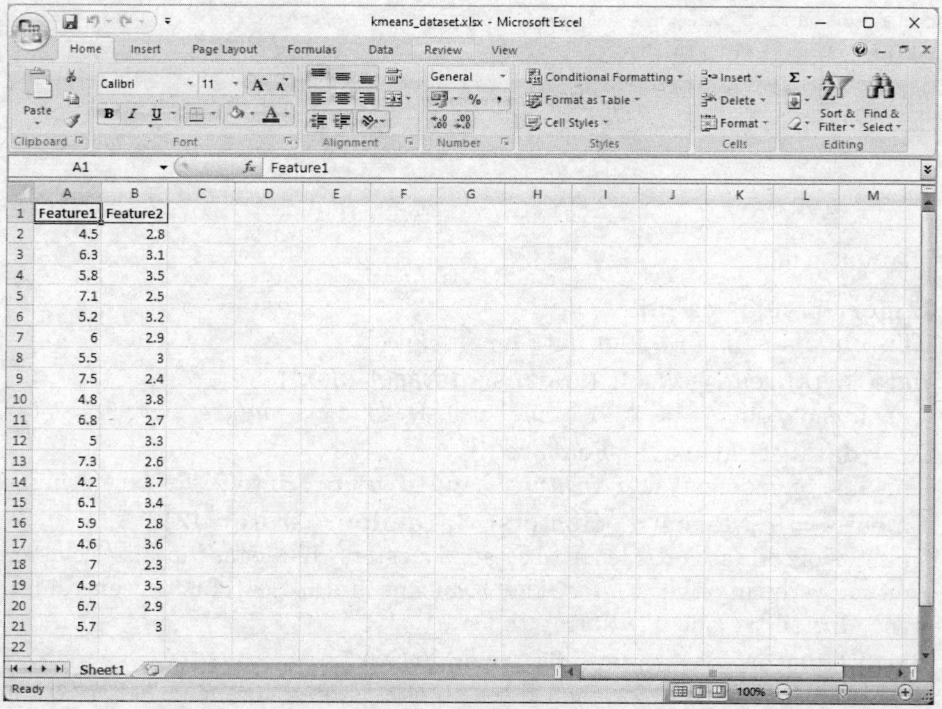

Figure 14.3: Custom datset for K-means classification.

```
# Predict the cluster for new data points
new_data = pd.DataFrame({'Feature1': [5.1,6.7], 'Feature2': [3.2,2.9]})
new_data['Cluster']  = kmeans.predict(new_data)

# Print new data and predicted clusters
print("Test Data and Clusters: \n", new_data)


# Plot the clusters
plt.figure(figsize=(8, 6))
plt.scatter(X['Feature1'], X['Feature2'], c=data['Cluster'])

# Plot the centroids
plt.scatter(kmeans.cluster_centers_[:, 0], kmeans.cluster_centers_[:, 1],
            c='red', marker='x', label='Centroids')

# Plot the predicted new data points
plt.scatter(new_data['Feature1'], new_data['Feature2'],
            s=200, c=new_data['Cluster'], marker='*', label='New Data')
```

```
# Add labels and title
plt.xlabel('Feature 1')
plt.ylabel('Feature 2')
plt.title('K-Means Clustering on Excel Dataset')
plt.legend()
plt.show()
```

Explanation:

- **import pandas as pd**
  This library is imported for data manipulation.
- **data = pd.read_excel('kmeans_dataset.xlsx')**
  This line of code reads data from excel file *'kmeans_dataset.xlsx'*.
- **X = data[['Feature1', 'Feature2']]**
  This line of code extracts *'Feature1'* and *'Feature2'* into X for clustering.
- **kmeans = KMeans(n_clusters=3, random_state=42)**
  This line of code asks K-Means to create 3 clusters. K-Means initializes cluster centroids randomly during the start. The K-means initializes cluster centroids randomly (reproducibility code 42) during the start.
- **data['Cluster'] = kmeans.fit_predict(X)**
  The predicted cluster for each data point is stored in the '*Cluster*' column of the original DataFrame.
- **new_data = pd.DataFrame('Feature1': [5.1,6.7], 'Feature2': [3.2,2.9])**
  Two new data points created for testing purpose.
- **new_data['Cluster'] = kmeans.predict(new_data)**
  The K-Means model predicts the cluster for two newly created data points.

Output:
The K-means clustering will be performed on a dataset from Excel file and predicts the clusters for two new data points. It visualizes the original clusters, centroids, and new data points on a graph (Figure 14.2). The new data points are colored based on the predicted clusters, helping to visually confirm their placement within the clusters.

iris dataset to divide it into three clusters. After clustering, it creates a scatter plot using two features (sepal length and petal length) to visually display the clusters with different colors (Figure 14.2). The centroids of the clusters are marked as large black crosses. The test dataset is represented by star (*).

14.2 Principal Component Analysis (PCA)

Principal Component Analysis (PCA) is an unsupervised machine learning algorithm used primarily for dimensionality reduction. It helps us simplify datasets with many features by reducing them to a smaller number of components while retaining as much of the original information as possible. PCA is especially useful in fields such as image compression, data

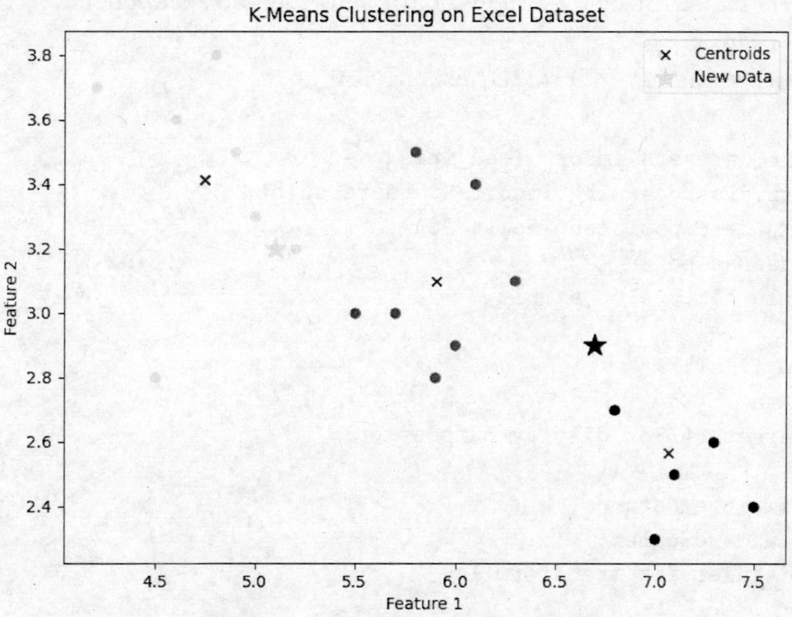

Figure 14.4: K-means classification on data from excel file and prediction for new data.

visualization, and noise reduction. Modern datasets often contain many features (or dimensions), making them challenging to visualize and analyze. High-dimensional data can cause:

- **Redundant features:** Some features may contain similar information.
- **Noise:** Irrelevant information that complicates model training.
- **Difficulty in visualization:** Data with more than 3 dimensions cannot be visualized directly.

PCA helps solve these problems by transforming the data to a lower-dimensional space, focusing on the most important patterns.

14.2.1 Working of PCA

The key idea behind PCA is to find new axes (called *principal components*) along which the variance (spread) of the data is maximized. These new components are linear combinations of the original features.

The following are the steps involved in PCA:

1. **Standardization:** Ensure all features have the same scale by standardizing the data.
2. **Covariance Matrix:** Compute the covariance matrix to find relationships between features.
3. **Eigenvalues and Eigenvectors:** Extract eigenvalues and eigenvectors from the covariance matrix.

4. **Select Principal Components:** Keep the components that explain the most variance.
5. **Transform Data:** Project the original data onto the new components.

Ex.3 Dimensionality reduction (4D to 2D) using PCA

```
from sklearn.datasets import load_iris
from sklearn.preprocessing import StandardScaler
from sklearn.decomposition import PCA
import pandas as pd
import matplotlib.pyplot as plt

iris = load_iris()
X = iris.data
y = iris.target  # For display purpose only

# Standardize the data
scaler = StandardScaler()
X_scaled = scaler.fit_transform(X)

# Apply PCA to reduce dimensions to 2 components
pca = PCA(n_components=2)
X_pca = pca.fit_transform(X_scaled)

# Create a DataFrame with the transformed data
pca_df = pd.DataFrame(data=X_pca, columns=['PC1', 'PC2'])

# Plot the transformed data
plt.figure(figsize=(8, 6))
plt.scatter(pca_df['PC1'], pca_df['PC2'],c=y)
plt.xlabel('Principal Component 1')
plt.ylabel('Principal Component 2')
plt.title('PCA on Iris Dataset')
plt.legend()
plt.show()
```

Explanation:

- **from sklearn.datasets import load_iris**
  Used to load the built-in Iris dataset.
- **from sklearn.preprocessing import StandardScaler**
  StandardScaler standardizes the data so that each feature has a mean of 0 and standard deviation of 1. Many machine learning algorithms (including PCA) are sensitive to

the scale of the input data. Standardization ensures all features contribute equally to the analysis. The Iris dataset has features with different ranges (e.g., sepal length vs. petal width), so scaling is needed before applying PCA.

- **from sklearn.decomposition import PCA**
  It is required to use PCA model in our code.
- **import pandas as pd**:
  Panda provides structures like *DataFrames*, which allow easy manipulation of datasets and plotting.
- **import matplotlib.pyplot as plt**
  This library is required here for creating visualizations in Python.
- **iris = load_iris()**
  It loads the Iris data.
- **X = iris.data**
  iris.data contains the four features (4-dimensional): sepal length, sepal width, petal length, petal width. This line of code extracts the feature data from the dataset.
- **y = iris.target**
  iris.target contains the labels representing the three Iris species (0, 1, 2), which will be used for coloring the plot.
- **scaler = StandardScaler()**
  It initialize the *StandardScaler*, to be used latter for standardizing the features.
- **X_scaled = scaler.fit_transform(X)**
  It standardize the feature data to ensures that all features have a mean of 0 and a standard deviation of 1. It is crucial for PCA to work effectively.
- **pca = PCA(n_components=2)**
  This code initializes PCA with the number of components to be reduced to 2.
- **X_pca = pca.fit_transform(X_scaled)**
  It reduces 4-dimensional data to 2 components while retaining as much variance as possible.
- **pca_df = pd.DataFrame(data=X_pca, columns=['PC1', 'PC2'])**
  A *DataFrame* is created for easy handling of the two principal components (PC1 and PC2). PC1 and PC2 refer to the first and second principal components, respectively, which represent the transformed features after applying PCA on the standardized dataset.
- **plt.scatter(pca_df['PC1'], pca_df['PC2'], c=y)**
  plt.scatter() is used to create a scatter plot. The scatter plot will plot the *PC1* values on the x-axis and the *PC2* values on the y-axis. The *c* parameter determines the color of the points. Here, *y* contains the target labels from the Iris dataset (e.g., 0, 1, 2 representing the three species of flowers). By passing *y* to *c*, each cluster of points corresponding to a particular species will be colored differently. This helps visualize how well the PCA-transformed data is separated based on the original class labels.

Output:
The complete code will reduce the dimensionality of high-dimensional data (*iris*) from 4-D to 2-D, making it easier to visualize clusters. A graph will be plotted at the end (Fig 14.5), showing two new features by reducing 4-D into two features. The points will be plotted along the two new axes (PC1 and PC2), representing the two principal components. Each Iris species (setosa, versicolor, and virginica) will appear in different colors based on their label (0, 1, 2).

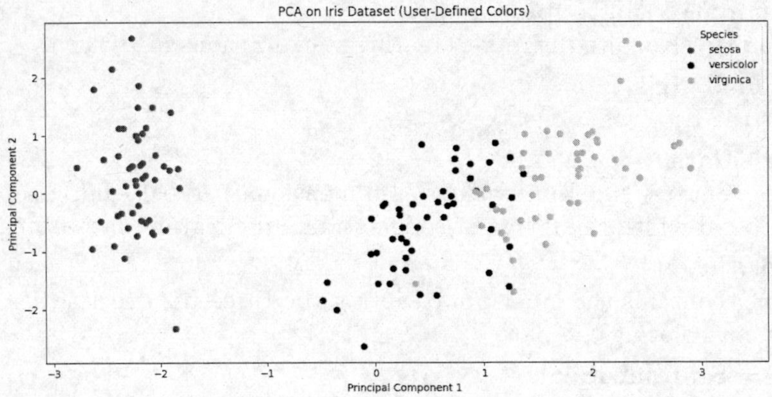

Figure 14.5: Plotted of *iris* data along the two new axes (PC1 and PC2), representing the two principal components

14.3 Syntax of Unsupervised Learning Code

Generalized code for Unsupervised learning algorithm implementation can be summarized as in 5 following steps:

Step 1: Load required library for: (1) excel/csv data loading, (2) data manupulation, (3) graph plotting, (4) Learning Model, etc.

Step 2: Load excel file and extract Features in variable X .

Step 3: Initialize unsupervised learning model of choice.

Step 4: Allow model to learn on respective features through `.fit(X)` or directly assign the cluster labels after learning through `.fit_predict(X)`.

Step 5: Perform prediction for evaluation of trained algorithm using test `.predict(newData)`.

There are two different approach of code writing is available: (1) `.fit(X)` (2) `.fit_predict(X)`. The purpose of first approach is to train the model on the input data X. The algorithm clusters the data and finds the optimal centroids. There is no direct output, and for getting the cluster assignments you have to use `model.labels_`. The purpose of second approach is to train the model and return the cluster labels in a single step. Internally, it performs the same steps as `fit()`, but immediately gives the predicted cluster assignments. Its output is a NumPy array containing the cluster labels for each data point. The difference between these two approach is summarized in Table 14.1. Clustering algorithms (like K-Means, DBSCAN, GMM) often have both `.fit(X)` and `.fit_predict(X)` because they need to assign cluster labels. Dimensionality reduction algorithms (like PCA, Isomap, t-SNE) generally only use `.fit(X)` , with the transformed data obtained using `transform()`.

Table 14.1: Key differences between `.fit(X)` and `.fit_predict(X)`

Aspect	.fit()	.fit_predict(X)
Training	Only trains the model.	Trains the model and assigns clusters.
Cluster Labels	Retrieved later via `model.labels_`	Directly returns the labels.
Convenience	Requires two steps (fit + labels).	One-step process (fit + predict).

14.3.1 .fit(X)

```
model = KMeans(n_clusters=3)
model.fit(X)
print(model.labels_)  # Retrieve the assigned cluster labels
```

14.3.2 .fit_predict(X)

```
model = KMeans(n_clusters=3)
labels = model.fit_predict(X)
print(labels)  # Cluster labels returned directly
```

Some of the model has both (`.fit(X)` and `.fit_predict(X)`) the function available while some model has only one of them is available (see Table 14.2). Required library and model initialization code is summarized in Table 14.3 for different unsupervised machine learning algorithm.

Table 14.2: Comparison of fit() and fit_predict() Availability across Algorithms

Algorithm	fit()	fit_predict()	Explanation
K-Means	✓	✓	`fit()` trains the model, `fit_predict()` returns cluster labels in one step.
DBSCAN	✓	✓	`fit()` fits the data, `fit_predict()` assigns cluster labels directly.
PCA (Principal Component Analysis)	✓	✗	Only `fit()` is available to learn components; predictions are done with `transform()`.
Agglomerative Clustering	✓	✗	Only `fit()` is available, as clustering is hierarchical and labels are obtained through `labels_`.
Gaussian Mixture Models (GMM)	✓	✓	`fit()` trains the model, and `fit_predict()` gives the cluster assignments directly.
Isomap (Dimensionality Reduction)	✓	✗	Only `fit()` is used to learn the embedding; the result is obtained with `transform()`.
Spectral Clustering	✗	✓	Only `fit_predict()` is available because it performs clustering and returns labels in one step.
t-SNE (Dimensionality Reduction)	✓	✗	Only `fit()` is available, used to learn low-dimensional embedding.
K-Nearest Neighbors (KNN) for Unsupervised Learning	✓	✗	Used with `fit()` to train, followed by `kneighbors()` for nearest neighbor lookup.

Table 14.3: Code snippets for implementing Unsupervised Machine Learning algorithms

Algorithm Name	Library to Import	Initialize Model & Training
K-Means Clustering	`from sklearn.cluster import KMeans`	`model = KMeans(n_clusters=3)` `model.fit(X)`
DBSCAN (Density-Based Spatial Clustering)	`from sklearn.cluster import DBSCAN`	`model = DBSCAN(eps=0.5, min_samples=5)` `model.fit(X)`
Agglomerative Clustering	`from sklearn.cluster import AgglomerativeClustering`	`model = AgglomerativeClustering (n_clusters=3) model.fit(X)`
Gaussian Mixture Model (GMM)	`from sklearn.mixture import GaussianMixture`	`model = GaussianMixture(n_components=3)` `model.fit(X)`
Principal Component Analysis (PCA)	`from sklearn.decomposition import PCA`	`model = PCA(n_components=2)` `X_reduced = model.fit_transform(X)`
t-SNE (t-Distributed Stochastic Neighbor Embedding)	`from sklearn.manifold import TSNE`	`model = TSNE(n_components=2)` `X_embedded = model.fit_transform(X)`
Isolation Forest (Anomaly Detection)	`from sklearn.ensemble import IsolationForest`	`model = IsolationForest(random_state=42)` `model.fit(X)`

Index

abc, 130
Abstract Base Classes, 130
abstract class, 130
abstract method, 130
abstraction, 129
Action, 186
Addition, 24
Agent, 186
Anchors, 38
Anomaly Detection, 184
argv, 45
Arithmetic Operator, 24
Assignment Operator, 29

Basic Assignment Operator, 30
Bayesian optimization, 187
bias, 205
Bitwise Operator, 31
Building Blocks of ML, 187

Camel case, 23, 115
Character Classes, 38
class, 113
class attributes, 117
classification, 181
Clustering, 183
Code Blocks, 55
Comma-Separated Assignment Operator, 30
Command-line Argument, 45
command-line input, 43
Comparison Operator, 29
Complex Assignment Operator, 30
Compound Data Type, 18
concrete class, 131
concrete method, 130
Cross-Validation, 210

data, 179
data cleaning, 194
data deletion, 195
data imputation, 194
Data Splitting, 207
Data type, 10
Decision tree, 219

Deep Learning, 188
Dictionary, 19
Dimensionality Reduction, 184
Division, 27
Double quote string, 16
dunder methods, 115

Edge Computing, 188
elif syntax, 59
encapsulation, 124
Entropy, 221
Environment, 186
epsilon-greedy, 185
Escape Character, 38
Exploitation, 186
Exploration, 186
Exponent Operator, 28

facet, 164
Feature Engineering, 204
Features, 179
Federated Learning, 189
File Handling, 91
filter(), 86
fit(), 245
fit_predict(X), 245
Floor Division, 27
For loop, 60
FOR...ELSE Loop, 66
Froze Set, 19
Function Definition, 74

GAN, 188
generative adversarial networks, 188
Generative Models, 188
Gini Impurity, 223
Global Variable, 22
Gradient Descent, 187
grid search, 187
Grouping, 38

History of Python, 5
How useful is the Python, 6
Hyperparameter Tuning, 187

if, 56
if .... elif ... , 59
if .... else , 58
if statement, 56
imputation techniques, 194
Indentation, 55
Indentation Error, 56
independent variables, 179
Information Gain, 221
inheritance, 126
instance attributes, 119
Integer Division, 27
Iteration, 60
Iteration over a Sequence, 60

K-means clustering, 233
KNN, 211

label, 179
Lambda, 83
lazy learner algorithm, 212
LGEB rule, 21
Linux Environment, 6
Literal vs Data type, 8
Literals, 37
Local Variable, 22
Logical Operator, 31

Machine learning, 177
map(), 87
matplotlib, 147
Metacharacters, 37
model, 179
Model-based algorithms, 186
Model-free algorithms, 186
Modifiers, 39
Module, 135
Modulus Operator, 28
MS Window Environment, 6
multiple inheritance, 126
Multiplication, 26

name mangling, 122
Namespace, 145

non-parametric algorithm, 212
None, 9

object, 114
object-oriented programming, 113
OOP, 112
Operator, 24

pairplot, 166
pass, 70
PCA, 240
PEP 8, 23
pip, 144
Plotly, 159
Policy, 186
Polymorphism, 133
predictors, 179
Principal Component Analysis, 240
private variables, 121
procedural programming, 113
programming paradigms, 112
pyplot, 148
Python Enhancement Proposal, 23
Python IDEs, 7
Python Programming Language Features, 5

Q-Learning, 187
Quantifiers, 38

random search, 187
random_state, 237, 240
random_state, 209, 228
Range Function in for loop, 61
Raw data, 191
Regex Function, 41
regression, 182
Regular Expression, 37
Reinforcement learning, 184
Reward, 186

Scope, 145
Scope of Variables, 21
self parameter, 116
sequence filtering, 86
Set, 18
SGD, 187
Single quote string, 16
softmax, 185
sorted(), 88
Special Literal - None, 9
Splitting Data, 207
Starting a Python Session, 6
State, 186
Stochastic Gradient Descent, 187
str() constructor, 16
Stratified Splitting, 209
String Declaration, 16
String Operator, 34
Subtraction, 25
Supervised learning, 180
swarm, 169
sys.argv, 45

Terminating a Python Session, 6
test data, 180
Time-series forecasting, 182
Train-Test Split, 207
training data, 179
Triple double quote string, 16
Triple single quote string, 16
Tuple, 18

Unsupervised learning, 182
user defined data type, 18

VAE, 188
validation data, 180
Value Functions, 187
Variable, 21
variational autoencoders, 188

Where Python, 4
Why Python, 3
Wildcard, 38